SAS® Viya™
The Python Perspective

Kevin D. Smith
Xiangxiang Meng

   sas.com/books

The correct bibliographic citation for this manual is as follows: Smith, Kevin D., Xiangxiang Meng. 2017. *SAS® Viya™: The Python Perspective*. Cary, NC: SAS Institute Inc.

SAS® Viya™: The Python Perspective

Contents

Foreword

SAS® Viya™ marks a new and important chapter in our ever-evolving SAS software. A unified, open, powerful, and cloud-ready platform built on excellence in data management, advanced analytics, and high-performance computing.

These pillars of SAS Viya are important individually, but it is through their combination that the platform comes to life. The ability to access a central data management and computing environment through public APIs and from multiple programming languages, with consistent security and data models is a core competency of the modern analytic platform.

The Python language has quickly grown into one of the important programming languages for data science and analytics. As the SAS R&D team embarked on building SAS Cloud Analytic Services (CAS), the engine of the SAS Viya platform, it was obvious that access from Python would be important.

The Python client for SAS Viya was developed by Kevin Smith as a member of the core team that designed and developed SAS Cloud Analytic Services. This book by Kevin and Xiangxiang Meng takes you on a journey to learn and apply Python programming in the context of the SAS Viya platform. Their deep understanding of the SAS Viya server architecture, the client architecture, and the Python language implementation shines through in every chapter.

As a lifelong learner, I greatly enjoyed the journey and am sure that you will, too.

Oliver Schabenberger, PhD
Executive Vice President and Chief Technology Officer
SAS

x

About This Book

What Does This Book Cover?

This book is an introduction to using the Python client on the SAS Viya platform. SAS Viya is a high-performance, fault-tolerant analytics architecture that can be deployed on both public and private cloud infrastructures. Although SAS Viya can be used by various SAS applications, it also enables you to access analytic methods from SAS, Python, Lua, and Java, as well as through a REST interface using HTTP or HTTPS. Of course, in this book we focus on the perspective of SAS Viya from Python.

SAS Viya consists of multiple components. The central piece of this ecosystem is SAS Cloud Analytic Services (CAS). CAS is the cloud-based server that all clients communicate with to run analytical methods. The Python client is used to drive the CAS component directly using objects and constructs that are familiar to Python programmers.

We assume that you have some knowledge about Python before you approach the topics in this book. However, the book includes an appendix that covers the features of Python that are used in the CAS Python client. We do not assume any knowledge of CAS itself. However, you must have a CAS server that is set up and is running in order to execute the examples in this book.

The chapters in the first part of the book cover topics from installation of Python to the basics of connecting, loading data, and getting simple analyses from CAS. Depending on your familiarity with Python, after reading the "Ten-Minute Guide to Using CAS from Python," you might feel comfortable enough to jump to the chapters later in the book that are dedicated to statistical methods. However, the chapters in the middle of the book cover more detailed information about working with CAS such as constructing action calls to CAS and processing the results, error handling, managing your data in CAS, and using object interfaces to CAS actions and CAS data tables. Finally, the last chapter about advanced topics covers features and workflows that you might want to take advantage of when you are more experienced with the Python client.

This book covers topics that are useful to complete beginners as well as to experienced CAS users. Its examples extend from creating connections to CAS to simple statistics and machine learning. The book is also useful as a desktop reference.

Is This Book for You?

If you are using the SAS Viya platform in your work and you want to access analytics from SAS Cloud Analytic Services (CAS) using Python, then this book is a great starting point. You'll learn about general CAS workflows, as well as the Python client that is used to communicate with CAS.

What Are the Prerequisites for This Book?

Some Python experience is definitely helpful while reading this book. If you do not know Python, there is an appendix that gives a crash course in learning Python. There are also a multitude of resources on the Internet for learning Python. The later chapters in the book cover data analysis and modeling topics. Although the examples provide step-by-step code walk-throughs, some training about these topics beforehand is helpful.

Scope of This Book

This book covers the installation and usage of the Python client for use with CAS. It does not cover the installation, configuration, and maintenance of CAS itself.

What Should You Know about the Examples?

This book includes tutorials for you to follow to gain "hands-on" experience with SAS.

Software Used to Develop the Book's Content

This book was written using version 1.0.0 of the SAS Scripting Wrapper for Analytics Transfer (SWAT) package for Python. SAS Viya 3.1 was used. Various Python resources and packages were used as well. SWAT works with many versions of these packages. The URLs of SWAT and other resources are shown as follows:

SAS Viya
`www.sas.com/en_us/software/viya.html`

SAS Scripting Wrapper for Analytics Transfer (SWAT) – Python client to CAS
`github.com/sassoftware/python-swat` (GitHub repository)
`sassoftware.github.io/python-swat/` (documentation)

Python
`www.python.org/`

Anaconda – Data Science Python Distribution by Continuum Analytics
`www.continuum.io/`

Pandas – Python Data Analysis Library
`pandas.pydata.org/`

Jupyter – Scientific notebook application
`jupyter.org/`

Example Code and Data

You can access the example code and data for this book by linking to its author page at https://support.sas.com/authors or on GitHub at: https://github.com/sassoftware/sas-viya-the-python-perspective.

We Want to Hear from You

SAS Press books are written *by* SAS Users *for* SAS Users. We welcome your participation in their development and your feedback on SAS Press books that you are using. Please visit https://support.sas.com/publishing to do the following:

- Sign up to review a book
- Recommend a topic
- Request information about how to become a SAS Press author
- Provide feedback on a book

Do you have questions about a SAS Press book that you are reading? Contact the author through saspress@sas.com or https://support.sas.com/author_feedback.

SAS has many resources to help you find answers and expand your knowledge. If you need additional help, see our list of resources: https://support.sas.com/publishing.

About These Authors

 Kevin D. Smith has been a software developer at SAS since 1997. He has been involved in the development of PROC TEMPLATE and other underlying ODS technologies for most of his tenure. He has spoken at numerous SAS Global Forum conferences, as well as at regional and local SAS users groups with the "From Scratch" series of presentations that were created to help users of any level master various ODS technologies. More recently, he has been involved in the creation of the scripting language interfaces to SAS Cloud Analytic Services on the SAS Viya platform.

 Xiangxiang Meng, PhD, is a Senior Product Manager at SAS. The current focus of his work is on SAS Visual Statistics, cognitive computing, the Python interface to SAS Cloud Analytic Services, and other new product initiatives. Previously, Xiangxiang worked on SAS LASR Analytic Server, SAS In-Memory Statistics for Hadoop, SAS Recommendation Systems, and SAS Enterpriser Miner. His research interests include decision trees and tree ensemble models, automated and cognitive pipelines for business intelligence and machine learning, and parallelization of machine learning algorithms on distributed data. Xiangxiang received his PhD and MS from the University of Cincinnati.

Learn more about these authors by visiting their author pages, where you can download free book excerpts, access example code and data, read the latest reviews, get updates, and more:

http://support.sas.com/smithk

http://support.sas.com/meng

Chapter 1: Installing Python, SAS SWAT, and CAS

There are three primary pieces of software that must be installed in order to use SAS Cloud Analytic Services (CAS) from Python:

- Python 2.7 if you use Python 2, or a minimum of Python 3.4 if you use Python 3
- the SAS SWAT Python package
- the CAS server

We cover the recommended ways to install each piece of software in this chapter.

Installing Python

The Python packages that are used to connect to CAS have a minimum requirement of Python 2.7. If you are using version 3 of Python, you need a minimum of Python 3.4. There are some significant differences between Python 2 and Python 3, which are only touched on in this book. We recommend that you conduct your own research about the two primary versions of Python and choose the version that is appropriate for your needs. If you are not familiar with Python or if you don't have a version preference, we recommend that you use the most recent release of Python 3. If you have an installation of Python 2 that you are using for existing work, then you can continue to use it. The Python package that is used to connect to CAS is compatible with both Python 2 and Python 3.

If you plan to use Microsoft Windows as your client operating system, you might not have an existing Python installation. If you use the Linux operating system or the Macintosh operating system, you probably have a Python installation already. In either case, you might need to install some prerequisite packages. We recommend that you start with a Python distribution such as Anaconda from Continuum Analytics at www.continuum.io which contains all of the prerequisites.

The Anaconda Python distribution includes dozens of the most popular Python packages, which can be installed easily on Windows, Linux, and Macintosh platforms. It also enables you to install a complete Python installation at any location on your system, including your home directory, so that you don't need administrator privileges. Even if you do have administrator privileges and you have an existing Python installation on the Linux or Macintosh platforms, installing Anaconda as a separate Python is a good idea in order to prevent any mishaps that might occur while installing packages in the existing Python installation.

After you have installed Python, the next step is to install the SWAT package.

Installing SAS SWAT

The SAS SWAT package is the Python package created by SAS which is used to connect to CAS. SWAT stands for SAS Scripting Wrapper for Analytics Transfer. It includes two interfaces to CAS: 1) natively compiled client for binary communication, and 2) a pure Python REST client for HTTP-based connections. Support for the different protocols varies based on the platform that is used. So, you'll have to check the downloads on the GitHub project to find out what is available for your platform.

To install SWAT, you use the standard Python installation tool pip. On Linux and Macintosh, the pip command is in the bin directory of your Anaconda installation. On Windows, it is in the Scripts directory of the Anaconda distribution. The SWAT installers are located at GitHub in the python-swat project of the sassoftware account. The available releases are listed at the following link:

```
https://github.com/sassoftware/python-swat/releases
```

You can install SWAT directly from the download link using pip as follows.

```
pip install https://github.com/sassoftware/python-
    swat/releases/download/vX.X.X/python-swat-X.X.X-platform.tar.gz
```

Where *X.X.X* is the version number, and *platform* is the platform that you are installing on. If your platform isn't available, you can install using the source code URL on the releases page instead, but you are restricted to using the REST interface over HTTP or HTTPS. The source code release is pure Python, so it will run wherever Python and the prerequisite packages are supported.

Note that if you have both Python 2 and Python 3 installed on your system (or even multiple installations of a particular Python version), you need to be careful to run the pip command from the installation where SWAT is installed. In any case, the same SWAT package works for both Python 2 and Python 3.

After SWAT is installed, you should be able to run the following command in Python in order to load the SWAT package:

```
>>> import swat
```

With Anaconda, you can submit the preceding code in several ways. You can use the python command at the command line. However, if you are going to use the command line, we'd recommend that you at least use the ipython command, which is preferred for interactive use. You also have the option of using the Spyder IDE that comes bundled with Anaconda. The Spyder IDE is useful for debugging as well as for development and interactive use. You can also use the popular Jupyter notebook, which was previously known as the IPython notebook. Jupyter is most commonly used within a web browser. It can be launched with the jupyter notebook command at the command line, or you can launch it from the Anaconda Launcher application.

In this book, we primarily show plain text output using the IPython interpreter. However, all of the code from this book is also available in the form of Jupyter notebooks here,

https://github.com/sassoftware/sas-viya-the-python-perspective

Now that we have installed Python and SWAT, the last thing we need is a CAS server.

Installing CAS

The installation of CAS is beyond the scope of this book. Installation on your own server requires a CAS software license and system administrator privileges. You need to contact your system administrator about installing, configuring, and running CAS.

Making Your First Connection

With all of the pieces in place, we can make a test connection just to verify that everything is working. From Python, you should be able to run the following commands:

```
>>> import swat
>>> conn = swat.CAS('server-name.mycompany.com', port-number,
                    'userid', 'password')
>>> conn.serverstatus()
>>> conn.close()
```

Where *server-name.mycompany.com* is the name or IP address of your CAS server, *port-number* is the port number that CAS is listening to, *userid* is your CAS user ID, and *password* is your CAS password. The serverstatus method should return information about the CAS grid that you are connected to, and the close method closes the connection. If the commands run successfully, then you are ready to move on. If not, you'll have to do some troubleshooting before you continue.

Conclusion

At this point, you should have Python and the SWAT package installed, and you should have a running CAS server. In the next chapter, we'll give a brief summary of what it's like to use CAS from Python. Then, we'll dig into the chapters that go into the details of each aspect of SWAT.

Chapter 2: The Ten-Minute Guide to Using CAS from Python

If you are already familiar with Python, have a running CAS server, and just can't wait to get started, we've written this chapter just for you. This chapter is a very quick summary of what you can do with CAS from Python. We don't provide a lot of explanation of the examples; that comes in the later chapters. This chapter is here for those who want to dive in and work through the details in the rest of the book as needed.

In all of the sample code in this chapter, we are using the IPython interface to Python.

Importing SWAT and Getting Connected

The only thing you need to know about the CAS server in order to get connected is the host name, the port number, your user name, and your password. The SWAT package contains the CAS class that is used to communicate with the server. The arguments to the CAS class are hostname, port, username, and password[1], in that order. Note that you can use the REST interface by specifying the HTTP port that is used by the CAS server. The CAS class can autodetect the port type for the standard CAS port and HTTP. However, if you use HTTPS, you must specify protocol='https' as a keyword argument to the CAS constructor. You can also specify 'cas' or 'http' to explicitly override autodetection.

```
In [1]: import swat

In [2]: conn = swat.CAS('server-name.mycompany.com', 5570,
   ...:                  'username', 'password')
```

When you connect to CAS, it creates a session on the server. By default, all resources (CAS actions, data tables, options, and so on) are available only to that session. Some resources can be promoted to a global scope, which we discuss later in the book.

To see what CAS actions are available, use the help method on the CAS connection object, which calls the help action on the CAS server.

```
In [3]: out = conn.help()
NOTE: Available Action Sets and Actions:
NOTE:    accessControl
NOTE:       assumeRole - Assumes a role
NOTE:       dropRole - Relinquishes a role
NOTE:       showRolesIn - Shows the currently active role
NOTE:       showRolesAllowed - Shows the roles that a user
                               is a member of
NOTE:       isInRole - Shows whether a role is assumed
NOTE:       isAuthorized - Shows whether access is authorized
NOTE:       isAuthorizedActions - Shows whether access is
                                  authorized to actions
NOTE:       isAuthorizedTables - Shows whether access is authorized
                                 to tables
NOTE:       isAuthorizedColumns - Shows whether access is authorized
                                  to columns
NOTE:       listAllPrincipals - Lists all principals that have
                                explicit access controls
NOTE:       whatIsEffective - Lists effective access and
                              explanations (Origins)


NOTE:       partition - Partitions a table
NOTE:       recordCount - Shows the number of rows in a Cloud
                          Analytic Services table
NOTE:       loadDataSource - Loads one or more data source interfaces
NOTE:       update - Updates rows in a table
```

The printed notes describe all of the CAS action sets and the actions in those action sets. The help action also returns the action set and action information as a return value. The return values from all actions are in the form of CASResults objects, which are a subclass of the Python collections.OrderedDict class. To see a list of all of the keys, use the keys method just as you would with any Python dictionary. In this case, the keys correspond to the names of the CAS action sets.

```
In [4]: list(out.keys())
Out[4]:
['accessControl',
 'builtins',
 'configuration',
 'dataPreprocess',
 'dataStep',
 'percentile',
 'search',
 'session',
 'sessionProp',
 'simple',
 'table']
```

Printing the contents of the return value shows all of the top-level keys as sections. In the case of the help action, the information about each action set is returned in a table in each section. These tables are stored in the dictionary as Pandas DataFrames.

```
In [5]: out
Out[5]:
[accessControl]
```

```
                 name                                      description
0          assumeRole                                  Assumes a role
1            dropRole                             Relinquishes a role
2         showRolesIn                   Shows the currently active role
3    showRolesAllowed      Shows the roles that a user is a mem...
4            isInRole                   Shows whether a role is assumed
5        isAuthorized               Shows whether access is authorized
6   isAuthorizedActions    Shows whether access is authorized t...
7    isAuthorizedTables    Shows whether access is authorized t...
8   isAuthorizedColumns    Shows whether access is authorized t...
9      listAllPrincipals    Lists all principals that have expli...
10     whatIsEffective    Lists effective access and explanati...
11        listAcsData    Lists access controls for caslibs, t...
12     listAcsActionSet    Lists access controls for an action ...
13     repAllAcsCaslib    Replaces all access controls for a c...
14      repAllAcsTable    Replaces all access controls for a t...
15     repAllAcsColumn    Replaces all access controls for a c...
16   repAllAcsActionSet    Replaces all access controls for an ...
17      repAllAcsAction    Replaces all access controls for an ...
18    updSomeAcsCaslib    Adds, deletes, and modifies some acc...
19     updSomeAcsTable    Adds, deletes, and modifies some acc...

... truncated ...

+ Elapsed: 0.0034s, user: 0.003s, mem: 0.164mb
```

Since the output is based on the dictionary object, you can access each key individually as well.

```
In [6]: out['builtins']
Out[6]:
                 name                                      description
0            addNode                      Adds a machine to the server
1         removeNode      Remove one or more machines from the...
2               help      Shows the parameters for an action o...
3          listNodes      Shows the host names used by the server
4      loadActionSet      Loads an action set for use in this ...
5   installActionSet      Loads an action set in new sessions ...
6                log            Shows and modifies logging levels
7      queryActionSet        Shows whether an action set is loaded
8          queryName      Checks whether a name is an action o...
9            reflect      Shows detailed parameter information...
10      serverStatus              Shows the status of the server
11             about              Shows the status of the server
12          shutdown                    Shuts down the server
13          userInfo      Shows the user information for your ...
14     actionSetInfo      Shows the build information from loa...
15           history      Shows the actions that were run in t...
16         casCommon      Provides parameters that are common ...
17              ping      Sends a single request to the server...
18              echo      Prints the supplied parameters to th...
19       modifyQueue      Modifies the action response queue s...
20     getLicenseInfo      Shows the license information for a ...
21     refreshLicense      Refresh SAS license information from...
22       httpAddress      Shows the HTTP address for the serve...
```

The keys are commonly alphanumeric, so the CASResults object was extended to enable you to access keys as attributes as well. This just keeps your code a bit cleaner. However, you should be aware that if a result key has the same name as a Python dictionary method, the dictionary method takes precedence. In the following code, we access the builtins key again, but this time we access it as if it were an attribute.

```
In [7]: out.builtins
Out[7]:
                    name                                    description
0                addNode                  Adds a machine to the server
1             removeNode        Remove one or more machines from the...
2                   help        Shows the parameters for an action o...
3              listNodes        Shows the host names used by the server
4          loadActionSet        Loads an action set for use in this ...
5       installActionSet        Loads an action set in new sessions ...
6                    log                  Shows and modifies logging levels
7          queryActionSet          Shows whether an action set is loaded
8              queryName        Checks whether a name is an action o...
9                reflect        Shows detailed parameter information...
10          serverStatus                 Shows the status of the server
11                 about                 Shows the status of the server
12              shutdown                      Shuts down the server
13              userInfo        Shows the user information for your ...
14         actionSetInfo        Shows the build information from loa...
15               history        Shows the actions that were run in t...
16             casCommon        Provides parameters that are common ...
17                  ping        Sends a single request to the server...
18                  echo        Prints the supplied parameters to th...
19           modifyQueue        Modifies the action response queue s...
20        getLicenseInfo        Shows the license information for a ...
21        refreshLicense        Refresh SAS license information from...
22           httpAddress        Shows the HTTP address for the serve...
```

Running CAS Actions

Just like the help action, all of the action sets and actions are available as attributes and methods on the CAS connection object. For example, the userinfo action is called as follows.

```
In [8]: conn.userinfo()
Out[8]:
[userInfo]

 {'anonymous': False,
  'groups': ['users'],
  'hostAccount': True,
  'providedName': 'username',
  'providerName': 'Active Directory',
  'uniqueId': 'username',
  'userId': 'username'}

+ Elapsed: 0.000291s, mem: 0.0826mb
```

The result this time is a CASResults object, the contents of which is a dictionary under a single key (userInfo) that contains information about your user account. Although all actions return a CASResults object, there are no strict rules about what keys and values are in that object. The returned values are determined by the action and vary depending on the type of information returned. Analytic actions typically return one or more DataFrames. If you aren't using IPython to format your results automatically, you can cast the result to a dictionary and then print it using pprint for a nicer representation.

```
In [9]: from pprint import pprint
In [10]: pprint(dict(conn.userinfo()))
{'userInfo': {'anonymous': False,
              'groups': ['users'],
              'hostAccount': True,
              'providedName': 'username',
              'providerName': 'Active Directory',
              'uniqueId': 'username',
              'userId': 'username'}}
```

When calling the help and userinfo actions, we actually used a shortcut. In some cases, you might need to specify the fully qualified name of the action, which includes the action set name. This can happen if two action sets have an action of the same name, or an action name collides with an existing method or attribute name on the CAS object. The userinfo action is contained in the builtins action set. To call it using the fully qualified name, you use builtins.userinfo rather than userinfo on the CAS object. The builtins level in this call corresponds to a CASActionSet object that contains all of the actions in the builtins action set.

```
In [11]: conn.builtins.userinfo()
```

The preceding code provides you with the same result as the previous example does.

Loading Data

The easiest way to load data into a CAS server is by using the upload method on the CAS connection object. This method uses a file path or URL that points to a file in various possible formats including CSV, Excel, and SAS data sets. You can also pass a Pandas DataFrame object to the upload method in order to upload the data from that DataFrame to a CAS table. We use the classic Iris data set in the following data loading example.

```
In [12]: out = conn.upload('https://raw.githubusercontent.com/' +
    ....:                   'pydata/pandas/master/pandas/tests/' +
    ....:                   'data/iris.csv')

In [13]: out
Out[13]:
[caslib]

 'CASUSER(username)'

[tableName]

 'IRIS'

[casTable]

 CASTable('IRIS', caslib='CASUSER(username)')

+ Elapsed: 0.0629s, user: 0.037s, sys: 0.021s, mem: 48.4mb
```

The output from the upload method is, again, a CASResults object. The output contains the name of the created table, the CASLib that the table was created in, and a CASTable object that can be used to interact with the table on the server. CASTable objects have all of the same CAS action set and action methods of the connection that created it. They also include many of the methods that are defined by Pandas DataFrames so that you can operate on them as if they were local DataFrames. However, until you explicitly fetch the data or call a method that returns data from the table (such as head or tail), all operations are simply combined on the client side (essentially creating a client-side view) until data is actually retrieved from the server.

We can use actions such as tableinfo and columninfo to access general information about the table itself and its columns.

```
# Store CASTable object in its own variable.
In [14]: iris = out.casTable

# Call the tableinfo action on the CASTable object.
In [15]: iris.tableinfo()
Out[15]:
[TableInfo]

     Name   Rows  Columns  Encoding  CreateTimeFormatted   \
  0  IRIS    150        5     utf-8  01Nov2016:16:38:59

       ModTimeFormatted  JavaCharSet    CreateTime       ModTime   \
  0   01Nov2016:16:38:59         UTF8  1.793638e+09  1.793638e+09

     Global  Repeated  View  SourceName  SourceCaslib  Compressed   \
  0        0         0     0                                      0

     Creator  Modifier
  0  username

+ Elapsed: 0.000856s, mem: 0.104mb

# Call the columninfo action on the CASTable.
In [16]: iris.columninfo()
Out[16]:
[ColumnInfo]

            Column  ID      Type  RawLength  FormattedLength  NFL  NFD
  0    SepalLength   1    double          8               12    0    0
  1     SepalWidth   2    double          8               12    0    0
  2    PetalLength   3    double          8               12    0    0
  3     PetalWidth   4    double          8               12    0    0
  4           Name   5   varchar         15               15    0    0

+ Elapsed: 0.000727s, mem: 0.175mb
```

Now that we have some data, let's run some more interesting CAS actions on it.

Executing Actions on CAS Tables

The simple action set that comes with CAS contains some basic analytic actions. You can use either the help action or the IPython ? operator to view the available actions.

```
In [17]: conn.simple?
Type:        Simple
String form: <swat.cas.actions.Simple object at 0x4582b10>
File: swat/cas/actions.py
Definition:  conn.simple(self, *args, **kwargs)
Docstring:
Analytics

Actions
-------
simple.correlation : Generates a matrix of Pearson product-moment
                     correlation coefficients
simple.crosstab    : Performs one-way or two-way tabulations
simple.distinct    : Computes the distinct number of values of the
                     variables in the variable list
simple.freq        : Generates a frequency distribution for one or
                     more variables
simple.groupby     : Builds BY groups in terms of the variable value
                     combinations given the variables in the variable
                     list
simple.mdsummary   : Calculates multidimensional summaries of numeric
                     variables
simple.numrows     : Shows the number of rows in a Cloud Analytic
                     Services table
simple.paracoord   : Generates a parallel coordinates plot of the
                     variables in the variable list
simple.regression  : Performs a linear regression up to 3rd-order
                     polynomials
simple.summary     : Generates descriptive statistics of numeric
                     variables such as the sample mean, sample
                     variance, sample size, sum of squares, and so on
simple.topk        : Returns the top-K and bottom-K distinct values of
                     each variable included in the variable list based
                     on a user-specified ranking order
```

Let's run the summary action on our CAS table.

```
In [18]: summ = iris.summary()

In [19]: summ
Out[19]:
[Summary]

 Descriptive Statistics for IRIS

          Column  Min  Max      N  NMiss      Mean     Sum       Std  \
0    SepalLength  4.3  7.9  150.0    0.0  5.843333   876.5  0.828066
1     SepalWidth  2.0  4.4  150.0    0.0  3.054000   458.1  0.433594
2    PetalLength  1.0  6.9  150.0    0.0  3.758667   563.8  1.764420
3     PetalWidth  0.1  2.5  150.0    0.0  1.198667   179.8  0.763161
```

```
         StdErr        Var       USS        CSS         CV     TValue   \
0     0.067611   0.685694   5223.85   102.168333   14.171126   86.425375
1     0.035403   0.188004   1427.05    28.012600   14.197587   86.264297
2     0.144064   3.113179   2583.00   463.863733   46.942721   26.090198
3     0.062312   0.582414    302.30    86.779733   63.667470   19.236588

            ProbT
0   3.331256e-129
1   4.374977e-129
2    1.994305e-57
3    3.209704e-42

+ Elapsed: 0.0256s, user: 0.019s, sys: 0.009s, mem: 1.74mb
```

The summary action displays summary statistics in a form that is familiar to SAS users. If you want them in a form similar to what Pandas users are used to, you can use the describe method (just like on DataFrames).

```
In [20]: iris.describe()
Out[20]:
        SepalLength  SepalWidth  PetalLength  PetalWidth
count   150.000000   150.000000   150.000000   150.000000
mean      5.843333     3.054000     3.758667     1.198667
std       0.828066     0.433594     1.764420     0.763161
min       4.300000     2.000000     1.000000     0.100000
25%       5.100000     2.800000     1.600000     0.300000
50%       5.800000     3.000000     4.350000     1.300000
75%       6.400000     3.300000     5.100000     1.800000
max       7.900000     4.400000     6.900000     2.500000
```

Note that when you call the describe method on a CASTable object, it calls various CAS actions in the background to do the calculations. This includes the summary, percentile, and topk actions. The output of those actions is combined into a DataFrame in the same form that the real Pandas DataFrame describe method returns. This enables you to use CASTable objects and DataFrame objects interchangeably in your workflow for this method and many other methods.

Data Visualization

Since the tables that come back from the CAS server are subclasses of Pandas DataFrames, you can do anything to them that works on DataFrames. You can plot the results of your actions using the plot method or use them as input to more advanced packages such as Matplotlib and Bokeh, which are covered in more detail in a later section.

The following example uses the plot method to download the entire data set and plot it using the default options.

```
In [21]: iris.plot()
Out[21]: <matplotlib.axes.AxesSubplot at 0x5339050>
```

If the plot doesn't show up automatically, you might have to tell Matplotlib to display it.

```
In [22]: import matplotlib.pyplot as plt
```

```
In [23]: plt.show()
```

The output that is created by the plot method follows.

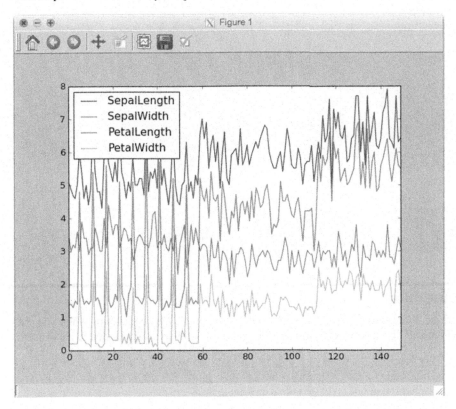

Even if you loaded the same data set that we have used in this example, your plot might look different since CAS stores data in a distributed manner. Because of this, the ordering of data from the server is not deterministic unless you sort it when it is fetched. If you run the following commands, you plot the data sorted by SepalLength and SepalWidth.

```
In [24]: iris.sort_values(['SepalLength', 'SepalWidth']).plot()
```

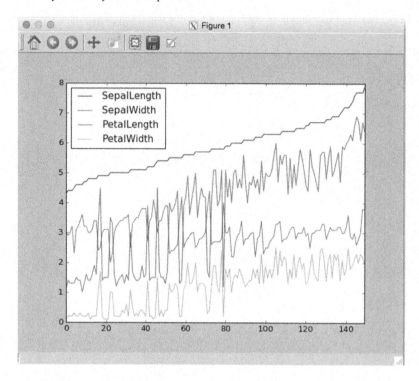

Closing the Connection

As with any network or file resource in Python, you should close your CAS connections when you are finished. They time out and disappear eventually if left open, but it's always a good idea to clean them up explicitly.

```
In [25]: conn.close()
```

Conclusion

Hopefully this 10-minute guide was enough to give you an idea of the basic workflow and capabilities of the Python CAS client. In the following chapters, we dig deeper into the details of the Python CAS client and how to blend the power of SAS analytics with the tools that are available in the Python environment.

---

[1] Later in the book, we show you how to store your password so that you do not need to specify it in your programs.

Chapter 3: The Fundamentals of Using Python with CAS

The SAS SWAT package includes an object-oriented interface to CAS as well as utilities to handle results, format data values, and upload data to CAS. We have already covered the installation of SWAT in an earlier chapter, so let's jump right into connecting to CAS.

There is a lot of detailed information about parameter structures, error handling, and authentication in this chapter. If you feel like you are getting bogged down, you can always skim over this chapter and come back to it later when you need more formal information about programming using the CAS interface.

Connecting to CAS

In order to connect to a CAS host, you need some form of authentication. There are various authentication mechanisms that you can use with CAS. The different forms of authentication are beyond the scope of this book, so we use user name and password authentication in all of our examples. This form of authentication assumes that you have a login account on the CAS server that you are connecting to. The disadvantage of using a user name and password is that you typically include your password in the source code. However, Authinfo is a solution to this problem, so we'll show you how to store authentication information using Authinfo as well.

Let's make a connection to CAS using an explicit user name and a password. For this example, we use an IPython shell. As described previously, to run IPython, you use the ipython command from a command shell or the Anaconda menu in Windows.

The first thing you need to do after starting IPython is to import the SWAT package. This package contains a class called CAS that is the primary interface to your CAS server. It requires at least two arguments: CAS host name or IP address, and the port number that CAS is running on[1]. Since we use user name and password authentication, we must specify them as the next two arguments. If there are no connection errors, you should now have an open CAS session that is referred to by the conn variable.

```
In [1]: import swat

In [2]: conn = swat.CAS('server-name.mycompany.com', 5570,
                        'username', 'password')

In [3]: conn
Out[3]: CAS('server-name.mycompany.com', 5570, 'username',
            protocol='cas', name='py-session-1',
            session='ffee6422-96b9-484f-a868-03505b320987')
```

As you can see in Out[3], we display the string representation of the CAS object. You see that it echoes the host name, the port, the user name, and several fields that were not specified. The name and session fields are created once the session is created. The session value contains a unique ID that can be used to make other connections to that same session. The name field is a user-friendly name that is used to tag the session on the server to make it easier to distinguish when querying information about current sessions. This is discussed in more depth later in the chapter.

We mentioned using Authinfo rather than specifying your user name and password explicitly in your programs. The Authinfo specification is based on an older file format called Netrc. Netrc was used by FTP programs to store user names and passwords so that you don't have to enter authentication information manually. Authinfo works the same way, but adds a few extensions.

The basic format of an Authinfo file follows: (The format occupies two lines to enhance readability.)

```
host server-name.mycompany.com port 5570
     user username password password
```

Where *server-name.mycompany.com* is the host name of your CAS server (an IP address can also be used), *5570* is the port number of the CAS server, *username* is your user ID on that machine, and *password* is your password on that machine. If you don't specify a port number, the same user name and password are used on any port on that machine. Each CAS host requires a separate host definition line. In addition, the host name must match exactly what is specified in the CAS constructor. There is no DNS name expansion if you use a shortened name such as *server-name*.

By default, the Authinfo file is accessed from your home directory under the name .authinfo (on Windows, the name _authinfo is used). It also must have permissions that are set up so that only the owner can read it. This is done using the following command on Linux.

```
chmod 0600 ~/.authinfo
```

On Windows, the file permissions should be set so that the file isn't readable by the Everyone group. Once that file is in place and has the correct permissions, you should be able to make a connection to CAS without specifying your user name and password explicitly.

```
In [1]: import swat

In [2]: conn = swat.CAS('server-name.mycompany.com', 5570)
```

```
In [3]: conn
Out[3]: CAS('server-name.mycompany.com', 5570, 'username',
            protocol='cas', name='py-session-1',
            session='ffee6422-96b9-484f-a868-03505b320987')
```

After connecting to CAS, we can continue to a more interesting topic: running CAS actions.

Running CAS Actions

In the previous section, we made a connection to CAS, but didn't explicitly perform any actions. However, after the connection was made, many actions were performed to obtain information about the server and what resources are available to the CAS installation. One of the things queried for is information about the currently loaded *action sets*. An action set is a collection of actions that can be executed. Actions can do various things such as return information about the server setup, load data, and perform advanced analytics. To see what action sets and actions are already loaded, you can call the help action on the CAS object that we previously created.

```
In [4]: out = conn.help()
NOTE: Available Action Sets and Actions:
NOTE:    accessControl
NOTE:       assumeRole - Assumes a role
NOTE:       dropRole - Relinquishes a role
NOTE:       showRolesIn - Shows the currently active role
NOTE:       showRolesAllowed - Shows the roles that a user is
                               a member of
NOTE:       isInRole - Shows whether a role is assumed
NOTE:       isAuthorized - Shows whether access is authorized
NOTE:       isAuthorizedActions - Shows whether access is
                  authorized to actions
NOTE:       isAuthorizedTables - Shows whether access is authorized
                                 to tables
NOTE:       isAuthorizedColumns - Shows whether access is authorized
                                  to columns
NOTE:       listAllPrincipals - Lists all principals that have
                                explicit access controls
NOTE:       whatIsEffective - Lists effective access and
                              explanations (Origins)
NOTE:       listAcsData - Lists access controls for caslibs, tables,
                          and columns
NOTE:       listAcsActionSet - Lists access controls for an action
                               or action set
NOTE:       repAllAcsCaslib - Replaces all access controls for
                              a caslib
NOTE:       repAllAcsTable - Replaces all access controls for a table
NOTE:       repAllAcsColumn - Replaces all access controls for
                              a column
NOTE:       repAllAcsActionSet - Replaces all access controls for
                                 an action set
NOTE:       repAllAcsAction - Replaces all access controls for
                              an action
NOTE:       updSomeAcsCaslib - Adds, deletes, and modifies some
                               access controls for a caslib
NOTE:       updSomeAcsTable - Adds, deletes, and modifies some
                              access controls for a table
```

```
NOTE:          updSomeAcsColumn - Adds, deletes, and modifies some
                              access controls for a column
NOTE:          updSomeAcsActionSet - Adds, deletes, and modifies some
                              access controls for an action set
NOTE:          updSomeAcsAction - Adds, deletes, and modifies some
                              access controls for an action
NOTE:          remAllAcsData - Removes all access controls for a
                              caslib, table, or column

... truncated ...
```

This prints out a listing of all of the loaded action sets and the actions within them. It also returns a CASResults structure that contains the action set information in tabular form. The results of CAS actions are discussed later in this chapter.

The help action takes arguments that specify which action sets and actions you want information about. To display help for an action set, use the actionset keyword parameter. The following code displays the help content for the builtins action set.

```
In [5]: out = conn.help(actionset='builtins')
NOTE: Information for action set 'builtins':
NOTE:     builtins
NOTE:        addNode - Adds a machine to the server
NOTE:        removeNode - Remove one or more machines from the server
NOTE:        help - Shows the parameters for an action or lists all
                    available actions
NOTE:        listNodes - Shows the host names used by the server
NOTE:        loadActionSet - Loads an action set for use in this
                    session
NOTE:        installActionSet - Loads an action set in new sessions
                    automatically
NOTE:        log - Shows and modifies logging levels
NOTE:        queryActionSet - Shows whether an action set is loaded
NOTE:        queryName - Checks whether a name is an action or
                    action set name
NOTE:        reflect - Shows detailed parameter information for an
                    action or all actions in an action set
NOTE:        serverStatus - Shows the status of the server
NOTE:        about - Shows the status of the server
NOTE:        shutdown - Shuts down the server
NOTE:        userInfo - Shows the user information for your connection
NOTE:        actionSetInfo - Shows the build information from loaded
                    action sets
NOTE:        history - Shows the actions that were run in this session
NOTE:        casCommon - Provides parameters that are common to many
                    actions
NOTE:        ping - Sends a single request to the server to confirm
                    that the connection is working
NOTE:        echo - Prints the supplied parameters to the client log
NOTE:        modifyQueue - Modifies the action response queue settings
NOTE:        getLicenseInfo - Shows the license information for a
                    SAS product
NOTE:        refreshLicense - Refresh SAS license information from
                    a file
NOTE:        httpAddress - Shows the HTTP address for the server
                    monitor
```

Notice that help is one of the actions in the builtins action set. To display the Help for an action, use the action keyword argument. You can display the Help for the help action as follows:

```
In [6]: out = conn.help(action='help')
NOTE: Information for action 'builtins.help':
NOTE: The following parameters are accepted.
      Default values are shown.
NOTE:    string action=NULL,
NOTE:        specifies the name of the action for which you want help.
             The name can be in the form 'actionSetName.actionName' or
             just 'actionName'.
NOTE:    string actionSet=NULL,
NOTE:        specifies the name of the action set for which you
             want help. This parameter is ignored if the action
             parameter is specified.
NOTE:    boolean verbose=true
NOTE:        when set to True, provides more detail for each parameter.
```

Looking at the printed notes, you can see that the help action takes the parameters actionset, action, and verbose. We have previously seen the actionset and action parameters. The verbose parameter is enabled, which means that you will get a full description of all of the parameters of the action. You can suppress the parameter descriptions by specifying verbose=False as follows:

```
In [7]: out = conn.help(action='help', verbose=False)
NOTE: Information for action 'builtins.help':
NOTE: The following parameters are accepted.
      Default values are shown.
NOTE:    string action=NULL,
NOTE:    string actionSet=NULL,
NOTE:    boolean verbose=true
```

In addition to the Help system that is provided by CAS, the SWAT module also enables you to access the action set and action information using mechanisms supplied by Python and IPython. Python supplies the help function to display information about Python objects. This same function can be used to display information about CAS action sets and actions. We have been using the help action on our CAS object. Let's see what the Python help function displays.

```
In [8]: help(conn.help)
Help on builtins.Help in module swat.cas.actions object:

class builtins.Help(CASAction)
 |   Shows the parameters for an action or lists all available actions
 |
 |   Parameters
 |   ----------
 |   action : string, optional
 |       specifies the name of the action for which you want help.
 |       The name can be in the form 'actionSetName.actionName' or
 |       just 'actionName'.
 |
 |   actionset : string, optional
 |       specifies the name of the action set for which you want help.
 |       This parameter is ignored if the action parameter is
 |       specified.
 |
```

```
|   verbose : boolean, optional
|       when set to True, provides more detail for each parameter.
|       Default: True
|
|   Returns
|   -------
|   Help object

... truncated ...
```

It gets a little confusing in that code snippet because both the name of the function in Python and the name of the action are the same, but you see that the information displayed by Python's Help system is essentially the same as what CAS displayed. You can also use the IPython/Jupyter Help system (our preferred method) by following the action name with a question mark.

```
In [9]: conn.help?
Type:           builtins.Help
String form:    ?.builtins.Help()
File: swat/cas/actions.py
Definition:     ?.help(_self_, action=None,
                                actionset=None,
                                verbose=True, **kwargs)
Docstring:
Shows the parameters for an action or lists all available actions

Parameters
----------
action : string, optional
    specifies the name of the action for which you want help. The name
    can be in the form 'actionSetName.actionName' or just 'actionName.

actionset : string, optional
    specifies the name of the action set for which you want help. This
    parameter is ignored if the action parameter is specified.

verbose : boolean, optional
    when set to True, provides more detail for each parameter.
    Default: True

Returns
-------
Help object

... truncated ...
```

These methods of getting help work both on actions and action sets. For example, we know that there is a builtins action set that the help action belongs to. The CAS object has an attribute that maps to the builtins action set just like the help action. We can display the help for the builtins action set as follows:

```
In [10]: conn.builtins?
Type:           Builtins
String form: <swat.cas.actions.Builtins object at 0x7f7ad35b9048>
File: swat/cas/actions.py
Docstring:
System
```

```
Actions
-------
builtins.about           : Shows the status of the server
builtins.actionsetinfo   : Shows the build information from loaded
                           action sets
builtins.addnode         : Adds a machine to the server
builtins.cascommon       : Provides parameters that are common to
                           many actions
builtins.echo            : Prints the supplied parameters to the
                           client log
builtins.getgroups       : Shows the groups from the authentication
                           provider
builtins.getlicenseinfo  : Shows the license information for a SAS
                           product
builtins.getusers        : Shows the users from the authentication
                           provider
builtins.help            : Shows the parameters for an action or
                           lists all available actions
builtins.history         : Shows the actions that were run in this
                           session
builtins.httpaddress     : Shows the HTTP address for the server
                           monitor
builtins.installactionset : Loads an action set in new sessions
                           automatically
builtins.listactions     : Shows the parameters for an action or
                           lists all available actions
builtins.listnodes       : Shows the host names used by the server
builtins.loadactionset   : Loads an action set for use in this
                           session
builtins.log             : Shows and modifies logging levels
builtins.modifyqueue     : Modifies the action response queue
                           settings
builtins.ping            : Sends a single request to the server to
                           confirm that the connection is working
builtins.queryactionset  : Shows whether an action set is loaded
builtins.queryname       : Checks whether a name is an action or
                           action set name
builtins.reflect         : Shows detailed parameter information for
                           an action or all actions in an action set
builtins.refreshlicense  : Refresh SAS license information from a
                           file
builtins.refreshtoken    : Refreshes an authentication token for this
                           session
builtins.removenode      : Remove one or more machines from the
                           server
builtins.serverstatus    : Shows the status of the server
builtins.setlicenseinfo  : Sets the license information for a SAS
                           product
builtins.shutdown        : Shuts down the server
builtins.userinfo        : Shows the user information for your
                           connection
```

Each time that an action set is loaded into the server, the information about the action set and its actions are reflected back to SWAT. SWAT then creates attributes on the CAS object that map to the new action sets and actions, including all of the documentation and Help system hooks. The advantage is that the documentation about actions can never get out of date in the Python client.

In addition to the documentation, since the action sets and actions appear as attributes on the CAS object, you can also use tab completion to display what is in an action set.

```
In [11]: conn.builtins.<tab>
conn.builtins.about               conn.builtins.loadactionset
conn.builtins.actionsetinfo       conn.builtins.log
conn.builtins.addnode             conn.builtins.modifyqueue
conn.builtins.cascommon           conn.builtins.ping
conn.builtins.echo                conn.builtins.queryactionset
conn.builtins.getgroups           conn.builtins.queryname
conn.builtins.getlicenseinfo      conn.builtins.reflect
conn.builtins.getusers            conn.builtins.refreshlicense
conn.builtins.help                conn.builtins.refreshtoken
conn.builtins.history             conn.builtins.removenode
conn.builtins.httpaddress         conn.builtins.serverstatus
conn.builtins.installactionset    conn.builtins.setlicenseinfo
conn.builtins.listactions         conn.builtins.shutdown
conn.builtins.listnodes           conn.builtins.userinfo
```

Now that we have seen how to query the server for available action sets and actions, and we know how to get help for the actions, we can move on to some more advanced action calls.

Specifying Action Parameters

We have already seen a few action parameters being used on the help action (action, actionset, and verbose). When a CAS action is added to the CAS object, all action parameters are mapped to Python keyword parameters. Let's look at the function signature of help to see the supported action parameters.

```
In [12]: conn.help?
Type:           builtins.Help
String form:    ?.builtins.Help()
File: swat/cas/actions.py
Definition:     ?.help(_self_, action=None,
                       actionset=None,
                       verbose=True, **kwargs)
... truncated ...
```

You see that there is one positional argument (_self_[2]). It is simply the Python object that help is being called on. The rest of the arguments are keyword arguments that are converted to action parameters and passed to the action. The **kwargs argument is always specified on actions as well. It enables the use of extra parameters for debugging and system use. Now let's look at the descriptions of the parameters (the following output is continued from the preceding help? invocation).

```
Docstring:
Shows the parameters for an action or lists all available actions

Parameters
----------
action : string, optional
    specifies the name of the action for which you want help. The name
    can be in the form 'actionSetName.actionName' or just
    'actionName'.

actionset : string, optional
    specifies the name of the action set for which you want help. This
    parameter is ignored if the action parameter is specified.
```

```
verbose : boolean, optional
    when set to True, provides more detail for each parameter.
    Default: True
```

You see that action and actionset are declared as strings, and verbose is declared as a Boolean. Action parameters can take many types of values. The following table shows the supported types:

CAS Type	Python Type	Description
Boolean	bool	Value that indicates true or false. This should always be specified using Python's True or False values.
double	float swat.float64	64-bit floating point number
int32	int swat.int32	32-bit integer
int64	long (Python 2) int (Python 3) swat.int64	64-bit integer
string	Unicode (Python 2) str (Python 3)	Character content. Note that if a byte string is passed as an argument, SWAT attempts to convert it to Unicode using the default encoding.
value list	list or dict	Collection of items. Python lists become indexed CAS value lists. Python dicts become keyed CAS value lists.

The easiest way to practice more complex arguments is by using the echo action. This action simply prints the value of all parameters that were specified in the action call. The following code demonstrates the echo action with all of the parameter types in the preceding table.

```
In [13]: out = conn.echo(
    ...:                 boolean_true = True,
    ...:                 boolean_false = False,
    ...:                 double = 3.14159,
    ...:                 int32 = 1776,
    ...:                 int64 = 2**60,
    ...:                 string = u'I like snowmen! \u2603',
    ...:                 list = [u'item1', u'item2', u'item3'],
    ...:                 dict = {'key1': 'value1',
    ...:                         'key2': 'value2',
    ...:                         'key3': 3}
    ...:                     )
NOTE: builtin.echo called with 8 parameters.
NOTE:    parameter 1: int32 = 1776
NOTE:    parameter 2: boolean_false = false
```

```
NOTE:        parameter 3: list = {'item1', 'item2', 'item3'}
NOTE:        parameter 4: boolean_true = true
NOTE:        parameter 5: int64 = 1152921504606846976
NOTE:        parameter 6: double = 3.14159
NOTE:        parameter 7: string = 'I like snowmen! '
NOTE:        parameter 8: dict = {key1 = 'value1', key3 = 3,
                                  key2 = 'value2'}
```

You might notice that the parameters are printed in a different order than what was specified in the echo call. This is simply because keyword parameters in Python are stored in a dictionary, and dictionaries don't keep keys in a specified order.

You might also notice that the printed syntax is not Python syntax. It is a pseudo-code syntax more similar to the Lua programming language. Lua is used in other parts of CAS as well (such as the history action), so most code-like objects that are printed from CAS are in Lua or syntax that is like Lua. However, the syntax of the two languages (as far as parameter data structures goes) are similar enough that it is easy to see the mapping from one to the other. The biggest differences are in the value list parameters. Indexed lists in the printout use braces, whereas Python uses square brackets. Also, in the keyed list, Python's keys must be quoted, and the separator that is used between the key and the value is a colon (:) rather than an equal sign (=).

The complexity of the parameter structures is unlimited. Lists can be nested inside dictionaries, and dictionaries can be nested inside lists. A demonstration of nested structures in echo follows:

```
In [14]: out = conn.echo(
   ...:                     list = ['item1',
   ...:                             'item2',
   ...:                             {
   ...:                                'key1': 'value1',
   ...:                                'key2': {
   ...:                                          'value2': [0, 1, 1, 2, 3]
   ...:                                        }
   ...:                             }
   ...:                     ])
NOTE: builtin.echo called with 1 parameters.
NOTE:      parameter 1: list = {'item1', 'item2',
                                {key1 = 'value1',
                                 key2 = {value2 = {0, 1, 1, 2, 3}}}}
```

Nested dictionary parameters are fairly common in CAS and can create some confusion with the nesting levels and differences between keyword arguments and dictionary literals. Because of this, some utility functions have been added to SWAT to aid in the construction of nested parameters.

Constructing Nested Action Parameters

While specifying dictionary parameters, you can suffer from cognitive dissonance when you switch from keyword arguments to dictionary literals. In keyword arguments, you don't quote the name of the argument, but in dictionary literals, you do quote the key value. Also, in keyword arguments, you use an equal sign between the name and value, whereas in dictionary literals, you use a colon. Because of this potential confusion, we prefer to use the dict constructor with keyword arguments when nesting action parameters. The preceding code is shown as follows, but instead uses the dict object in Python for nested dictionaries.

```
In [15]: out = conn.echo(
    ...:                 list = ['item1',
    ...:                         'item2',
    ...:                         dict(
    ...:                             key1 = 'value1',
    ...:                             key2 = dict(
    ...:                                     value2 = [0, 1, 1, 2, 3]
    ...:                                 )
    ...:                         )
    ...:                 ])
NOTE: builtin.echo called with 1 parameters.
NOTE:    parameter 1: list = {'item1', 'item2',
                            {key1 = 'value1',
                            key2 = {value2 = {0, 1, 1, 2, 3}}}}
```

The SWAT package also includes a utility function called vl (for "value list"). This function returns an enhanced type of dictionary that enables you to build nested structures quickly and easily. It can be used directly in place of the dict call in the preceding code in its simplest form, but it can also be used outside of the action to build up parameter lists before the action call.

The primary feature of the dictionary object that vl returns is that it automatically adds any key to the dictionary when the key is accessed. For example, the following code builds the same nested structure that the previous example does.

```
In [16]: params = swat.vl()

In [17]: params.list[0] = 'item1'

In [18]: params.list[1] = 'item2'

In [19]: params.list[2].key1 = 'value1'

In [20]: params.list[2].key2.value2 = [0, 1, 1, 2, 3]

In [21]: params
Out[21]:
{'list': {0: 'item1',
    1: 'item2',
    2: {'key1': 'value1', 'key2': {'value2': [0, 1, 1, 2, 3]}}}}
```

As you can see in Out[21], just by accessing the key names and index values as if they existed, the nested parameter structure is automatically created behind the scenes. However, note that this does make it fairly easy to introduce errors into the structure with typographical errors. The object will create key values with mistakes in them since it has no way of telling a good key name from a bad one.

Using the special dictionary returned by vl does create some structures that might be surprising. If you look at Out[21], you see that the list parameter, which was a Python list in the previous example, is now a dictionary with integer keys. This discrepancy makes no difference to SWAT. It automatically converts dictionaries with integer keys into Python lists.

Using Python's ** operator for passing a dictionary as keyword arguments, you see, as follows, that we get the same output from the echo action as we did previously while using the contents of our vl object.

```
In [22]: out = conn.echo(**params)
NOTE: builtin.echo called with 1 parameters.
```

```
NOTE:      parameter 1: list = {'item1', 'item2',
                                {key2 = {value2 = {0, 1, 1, 2, 3}},
                                key1 = 'value1'}}
```

In addition to constructing parameters, you can also tear them down using Python syntax. For example, the following code deletes the value2 key of the list[2].key2 parameter.

```
In [23]: del params.list[2].key2.value2

In [24]: params
Out[24]: {'list': {0: 'item1', 1: 'item2',
                   2: {'key1': 'value1', 'key2': {}}}}
```

With the ability to construct CAS action parameters under our belt, there are a couple of features of the CAS parameter processor that can make your life a bit easier. We look at those in the next section.

Automatic Type Casting

So far, we have constructed arguments using either the exact data types expected by the action or the arbitrary parameters in echo. However, the CAS action parameter processor on the server is flexible enough to allow passing in parameters of various types. If possible, those parameters are converted to the proper type before they are used by the action.

The easiest form of type casting to demonstrate is the conversion of strings to numeric values. If an action parameter takes a numeric value, but you pass in a string that contains a numeric representation as its content, the CAS action processor parses out the numeric and sends that value to the action. This behavior can be seen in the following action calls to history, which shows the action call history. The first call uses integers for first and last, but the second call uses strings. In either case, the result is the same due to the automatic conversion on the server side.

```
# Using integers
In [25]: out = conn.history(first=5, last=7)
NOTE: 5: action session.sessionname / name='py-session-1',
            _apptag='UI', _messageLevel='error'; /* (SUCCESS) */
NOTE: 6: action builtins.echo...; /* (SUCCESS) */
NOTE: 7: action builtins.echo...; /* (SUCCESS) */

# Using strings as integer values
In [26]: out = conn.history(first='5', last='7')
NOTE: 5: action session.sessionname / name='py-session-1',
            _apptag='UI', _messageLevel='error'; /* (SUCCESS) */
NOTE: 6: action builtins.echo...; /* (SUCCESS) */
NOTE: 7: action builtins.echo...; /* (SUCCESS) */
```

Although the server can do some conversions between types, it is generally a good idea to use the correct type. There is another type of automatic conversion that adds syntactical enhancement to action calls. This is the conversion of a scalar-valued parameter to a dictionary value. This is described in the next section.

Scalar Parameter to Dictionary Conversion

Many times when using an action parameter that requires a dictionary as an argument, you use only the first key in the dictionary to specify the parameter. For example, the history action takes a parameter called casout. This parameter specifies an output table to put the history information into. The specification for this parameter follows: (You can use conn.history? in IPython to see the parameter definition.)

```
casout : dict or CASTable, optional
    specifies the settings for saving the action history to an
    output table.

    casout.name : string or CASTable, optional
        specifies the name to associate with the table.

    casout.caslib : string, optional
        specifies the name of the caslib to use.

    casout.timestamp : string, optional
        specifies the timestamp to apply to the table. Specify
        the value in the form that is appropriate for your
        session locale.

    casout.compress : boolean, optional
        when set to True, data compression is applied to the table.
        Default: False

    casout.replace : boolean, optional
        specifies whether to overwrite an existing table with the same
        name.
        Default: False

    ... truncated ...
```

The first key in the casout parameter is name and indicates the name of the CAS table to create. The complete way of specifying this parameter with only the name key follows:

```
In [27]: out = conn.history(casout=dict(name='hist'))
```

This is such a common idiom that the server enables you to specify dictionary values with only the first specified key given (for example, name), just using the value of that key. That is a mouthful, but it is easier than it sounds. It just means that rather than having to use the dict to create a nested dictionary, you could simply do the following:

```
In [28]: out = conn.history(casout='hist')
```

Of course, if you need to use any other keys in the casout parameter, you must use the dict form. This conversion of a scalar value to a dictionary value is common when specifying input tables and variable lists of tables, which we see later on.

Now that we have spent some time on the input side of CAS actions, let's look at the output side.

CAS Action Results

Up to now, all of our examples have stored the result of the action calls in a variable, but we have not done anything with the results yet. Let's start by using our example of all of the CAS parameter types.

```
In [29]: out = conn.echo(
    ....:                 boolean_true = True,
    ....:                 boolean_false = False,
    ....:                 double = 3.14159,
    ....:                 int32 = 1776,
    ....:                 int64 = 2**60,
    ....:                 string = u'I like snowmen! \u2603',
    ....:                 list = [u'item1', u'item2', u'item3'],
    ....:                 dict = {'key1': 'value1',
    ....:                         'key2': 'value2',
    ....:                         'key3': 3}
    ....:                 )
```

Displaying the contents of the out variable gives:

```
In [30]: out
Out[30]:
[int32]

 1776

[boolean_false]

 False

[list]

 ['item1', 'item2', 'item3']

[boolean_true]

 True

[int64]

 1152921504606846976

[double]

 3.14159

[string]

 'I like snowmen! ☃'

[dict]

 {'key1': 'value1', 'key2': 'value2', 'key3': 3}

+ Elapsed: 0.000494s, mem: 0.0546mb
```

The object that is held in the out variable is an instance of a Python class called CASResults. The CASResults class is a subclass of collections.OrderedDict. This class is a dictionary-like object that preserves the order of the items in it. If you want only a plain Python dictionary, you can convert it as follows, but you lose the ordering of the items.

```
In [31]: dict(out)
Out[31]:
{'boolean_false': False,
 'boolean_true': True,
 'dict': {'key1': 'value1', 'key2': 'value2', 'key3': 3},
 'double': 3.14159,
 'int32': 1776,
 'int64': 1152921504606846976,
 'list': ['item1', 'item2', 'item3'],
 'string': 'I like snowmen! ☃'}
```

In either case, you can traverse and modify the result just as you could any other Python dictionary. For example, if you wanted to walk through the items and print each key and value explicitly, you could do the following:

```
In [32]: for key, value in out.items():
    ....:     print(key)
    ....:     print(value)
    ....:     print('')
    ....:
int32
1776

boolean_false
False

list
['item1', 'item2', 'item3']

boolean_true
True

int64
1152921504606846976

double
3.14159

string
I like snowmen! ☃

dict
{'key1': 'value1', 'key3': 3, 'key2': 'value2'}
```

Although the object that is returned by an action is always a CASResults object, the contents of that object depend completely on the purpose of that action. It could be as simple as key/value pairs of scalars and as complex as a complex nested structure of dictionaries such as our parameters in the previous section. Actions that perform analytics typically return one or more DataFrames that contain the results.

Since the results objects are simply Python dictionaries, we assume that you are able to handle operations on them. But we will take a closer look at DataFrames in the next section.

Using DataFrames

The DataFrames that are returned by CAS actions are extensions of the DataFrames that are defined by the Pandas package. Largely, both work the same way. The only difference is that the DataFrames returned by CAS contain extra metadata that is found in typical SAS data sets. This metadata includes things such as SAS data format names, the SAS data type, and column and table labels.

One of the builtins actions that returns a DataFrame is help. This action returns a DataFrame that is filled with the names and descriptions of all the actions that are installed on the server. Each action set gets its own key in the result. Let's look at some output from help.

The following code runs the help action, lists the keys in the CASResults object that is returned, verifies that it is a SASDataFrame object using Python's type function, and displays the contents of the DataFrame (some output is reformatted slightly for readability):

```
In [33]: out = conn.help()

In [34]: list(out.keys())
Out[34]:
['accessControl',
 'builtins',
 'loadStreams',
 'search',
 'session',
 'sessionProp',
 'table',
 'tutorial']

In [35]: type(out['builtins'])
Out[35]: swat.dataframe.SASDataFrame

In [36]: out['builtins']
Out[36]:
                   name                           description
0                addNode             Adds a machine to the server
1             removeNode     Remove one or more machines from the...
2                   help     Shows the parameters for an action o...
3              listNodes     Shows the host names used by the server
4           loadActionSet   Loads an action set for use in this ...
5        installActionSet   Loads an action set in new sessions ...
6                    log       Shows and modifies logging levels
7         queryActionSet      Shows whether an action set is loaded
8              queryName     Checks whether a name is an action o...
9                reflect     Shows detailed parameter information...
10          serverStatus           Shows the status of the server
11                 about           Shows the status of the server
12              shutdown               Shuts down the server
13              userInfo     Shows the user information for your ...
14         actionSetInfo     Shows the build information from loa...
15               history     Shows the actions that were run in t...
16             casCommon     Provides parameters that are common ...
17                  ping     Sends a single request to the server...
18                  echo     Prints the supplied parameters to th...
```

```
19      modifyQueue  Modifies the action response queue s...
20    getLicenseInfo  Shows the license information for a ...
21    refreshLicense  Refresh SAS license information from...
22       httpAddress  Shows the HTTP address for the serve...
```

We can store this DataFrame in another variable to make it a bit easier to work with. Much like Pandas DataFrames, CASResults objects enable you to access keys as attributes (as long as the name of the key doesn't collide with an existing attribute or method). This means that we can access the builtins key of the out variable in either of the following ways:

In [37]: blt = out['builtins']

In [38]: blt = out.builtins

Which syntax you use depends on personal preference. The dot syntax is a bit cleaner, but the bracketed syntax works regardless of the key value (including white space, or name collisions with existing attributes). Typically, you might use the attribute-style syntax in interactive programming, but the bracketed syntax is better for production code.

Now that we have a handle on the DataFrame, we can do typical DataFrame operations on it such as sorting and filtering. For example, to sort the builtins actions by the name column, you might do the following.

```
In [39]: blt.sort_values('name')
Out[39]:
                  name                          description
11               about          Shows the status of the server
14       actionSetInfo  Shows the build information from loa...
0                addNode             Adds a machine to the server
16           casCommon  Provides parameters that are common ...
18                echo  Prints the supplied parameters to th...
20      getLicenseInfo  Shows the license information for a ...
2                 help  Shows the parameters for an action o...
15             history  Shows the actions that were run in t...
22         httpAddress  Shows the HTTP address for the serve...
5     installActionSet  Loads an action set in new sessions ...
3            listNodes  Shows the host names used by the server
4        loadActionSet  Loads an action set for use in this ...
6                  log        Shows and modifies logging levels
19         modifyQueue  Modifies the action response queue s...
17                ping  Sends a single request to the server...
7        queryActionSet     Shows whether an action set is loaded
8            queryName  Checks whether a name is an action o...
9              reflect  Shows detailed parameter information...
21      refreshLicense  Refresh SAS license information from...
1           removeNode  Remove one or more machines from the...
10        serverStatus          Shows the status of the server
12            shutdown               Shuts down the server
13            userInfo  Shows the user information for your ...
```

If we wanted to combine all of the output DataFrames into one DataFrame, we can use the concat function in the Pandas package. We use the values method of the CASResults object to get all of the values in the dictionary (which are DataFrames, in this case). Then we concatenate them using concat with the ignore_index=True option so that it creates a new unique index for each row.

```
In [40]: import pandas as pd

In [41]: pd.concat(out.values(), ignore_index=True)
Out[41]:
                       name                         description
0                 assumeRole                   Assumes a role
1                   dropRole               Relinquishes a role
2                showRolesIn       Shows the currently active role
3           showRolesAllowed  Shows the roles that a user is a mem...
4                   isInRole       Shows whether a role is assu...
137               queryCaslib       Checks whether a caslib exists
138                 partition               Partitions a table
139               recordCount  Shows the number of rows in a Cloud ...
140            loadDataSource  Loads one or more data source interf...
141                    update             Updates rows in a table

[142 rows x 2 columns]
```

In addition to result values, the CASResults object also contains information about the return status of the action. We look at that in the next section.

Checking the Return Status of CAS Actions

In a perfect world, we always get the parameters to CAS actions correct and the results that we want are always returned. However, in the real world, errors occur. There are several attributes on the CASResults object that can tell you the return status information of a CAS action. They are described in the following table:

Attribute Name	Description
severity	An integer value that indicates the severity of the return status. A zero status means that the action ran without errors or warnings. A value of 1 means that warnings were generated. A value of 2 means that errors were generated.
reason	A string value that indicates the class of error that occurred. Reason codes are described in the "Details" section later in this chapter.
status	A text message that describes the error that occurred.
status_code	An encoded integer that contains information that can be used by Technical Support to help determine the cause of the error.

In addition to the attributes previously described, the messages attribute contains any messages that were printed during the execution of the action. While you likely saw the messages as they were being printed by the action, it can sometimes be useful to have them accessible on the CASResults object for programmatic inspection. Let's use the help action for help on an action that does exist and also an action that doesn't exist to see the status information attributes in action.

The first example, as follows, asks for help on an existing action. The returned status attributes are all zeros for numeric values and None for reason and status. The messages attribute contains a list of all messages that are printed by the server.

```
In [42]: out = conn.help(action='help')
NOTE: Information for action 'builtins.help':
NOTE: The following parameters are accepted.
      Default values are shown.
NOTE:    string action=NULL,
NOTE:       specifies the name of the action for which you want help.
            The name can be in the form 'actionSetName.actionName'
            or just 'actionName'.
NOTE:    string actionSet=NULL,
NOTE:       specifies the name of the action set for which you
            want help. This parameter is ignored if the action
            parameter is specified.
NOTE:    boolean verbose=true
NOTE:       when set to True, provides more detail for each parameter.

In [43]: print(out.status)
None

In [44]: out.status_code
Out[44]: 0

In [45]: print(out.reason)
None

In [46]: out.severity
Out[46]: 0

In [47]: out.messages
Out[47]:
["NOTE: Information for action 'builtins.help':",
 'NOTE: The following parameters are accepted. Default values are
shown.',
 'NOTE:    string action=NULL,',
 "NOTE:       specifies the name of the action for which you want help.
The name can be in the form 'actionSetName.actionName' or just
'actionName.",
 'NOTE:    string actionSet=NULL,',
 'NOTE:       specifies the name of the action set for which you want
help. This parameter is ignored if the action parameter is specified.',
 'NOTE:    boolean verbose=true',
 'NOTE:       when set to True, provides more detail for each
parameter.']
```

Now let's ask for help on a nonexistent action.

```
In [48]: out = conn.help(action='nonexistent')
ERROR: Action 'nonexistent' was not found.
ERROR: The action stopped due to errors.

In [49]: out.status
Out[49]: 'The specified action was not found.'
```

```
In [50]: out.status_code
Out[50]: 2720406

In [51]: out.reason
Out[51]: 'abort'

In [52]: out.severity
Out[52]: 2

In [53]: out.messages
Out[53]:
["ERROR: Action 'nonexistent' was not found.",
 'ERROR: The action stopped due to errors.']
```

In this case, all of the attributes contain information about the error that was generated. You can use this information about the CASResults object to capture and handle errors more gracefully in your programs.

If you prefer to use exceptions rather than status codes, you can set the cas.exception_on_severity option to 1 to raise exceptions on warnings, or you can set the option to 2 to raise exceptions on errors. The options system is covered in detail later in this chapter.

```
In [54]: swat.set_option('cas.exception_on_severity', 2)

In [55]: try:
   ....:     out = conn.help(action='nonexistent')
   ....: except swat.SWATCASActionError as err:
   ....:     print(err.response)
   ....:     print('')
   ....:     print(err.connection)
   ....:     print('')
   ....:     # Since this action call fails before producing
   ....:     # results, this will be empty. In actions that
   ....:     # fail partway through, this may contain results
   ....:     # up to the point of failure.
   ....:     print(err.results)
   ....:
ERROR: Action 'nonexistent' was not found.
ERROR: The action stopped due to errors.
CASResponse(messages=[],
disposition=CASDisposition(
    debug=0x88bfc196:TKCASA_GEN_ACTION_NOT_FOUND, reason=abort,
    severity=2, status=The specified action was not found.,
    status_code=2720406), performance=CASPerformance(cpu_system_time=0.0,
cpu_user_time=0.0,
    data_movement_bytes=0, data_movement_time=0.0,
    elapsed_time=0.000279, memory=50080, memory_os=8441856,
    memory_quota=12111872, system_cores=32, system_nodes=1,
    system_total_memory=202931654656))

CAS('server-name.mycompany.com', 5570, 'username',
    protocol='cas', name='py-session-1',
    session='292319d5-151f-f241-b27c-c3b6a93c1814')
```

As you can see, working with results from CAS actions is the same as the workflow with any other Python framework. You connect to a CAS host, run a CAS action (either using keyword arguments, building the

parameters ahead of time, or using a mixture of methods), check the return status, and process the dict-like
CASResults object that is returned.

Now that we understand the basics of the workflow, let's look at how to add additional action sets and
actions to your CAS session.

Working with CAS Action Sets

In the previous sections, we have already seen that a CAS session has access to multiple action sets that
each contain multiple actions. However, all of the action sets we have seen so far have been installed
automatically when we connect to CAS. We haven't shown how to load additional action sets in order to do
additional operations such as advanced analytics, machine learning, streaming data analysis, and so on.

In order to load new action sets, we must first see what action sets are available on our server. We can use
the actionsetinfo action to do that. We are going to use the all=True option to see all of the action sets that
are installed on the server rather than only the ones that are currently loaded.

```
# Run the actionsetinfo action.
In [56]: asinfo = conn.actionsetinfo(all=True)

# Filter the DataFrame to contain only action sets that
# have not been loaded yet.
In [57]: asinfo = asinfo.setinfo[asinfo.setinfo.loaded == 0]

# Create a new DataFrame with only columns between
# actionset and label.
In [58]: asinfo = asinfo.ix[:, 'actionset':'label']

In [59]: asinfo
Out[59]:
Action set information
```

	actionset	label
0	access	
1	aggregation	
2	astore	
3	autotune	
4	boolRule	
5	cardinality	
6	clustering	
7	decisionTree	
...	...	...
41	svm	
42	textMining	
43	textParse	
44	transpose	
45	varReduce	
46	casfors	Simple forecast service
47	tkcsestst	Session Tests
48	cmpcas	
59	tkovrd	Forecast override
50	qlimreg	QLIMREG CAS Action Library
51	panel	Panel Data

```
52              mdchoice          MDCHOICE CAS Action Library
53                copula  CAS Copula Simulation Action Library
54          optimization                         Optimization
55           localsearch          Local Search Optimization

[56 rows x 2 columns]
```

Depending on your installation and licensing, the list varies from system to system. One very useful action set that should be automatically available on all systems is the simple action set. This action set contains actions for simple statistics such as summary statistics (max, min, mean, and so on), histograms, correlations, and frequencies. To load an action set, use the loadactionset action:

```
In [60]: conn.loadactionset('simple')
NOTE: Added action set 'simple'.
Out[60]:
[actionset]

 'simple

+ Elapsed: 0.0175s, user: 0.017s, mem: 0.255mb
```

As you can see, this action returns a CASResults object as described in the previous section. It contains a single key called actionset that contains the name of the action set that was loaded. Typically, you do not need this return value, but it can be used to verify that the action set has been loaded. If you attempt to load an action set that cannot be loaded for some reason (such as incorrect name, no license, or no authorization), the CASResults object is empty.

Now that we have loaded the simple action set, we can get help on it using the usual Python methods.

```
In [61]: conn.simple?
Type:        Simple
String form: <swat.cas.actions.Simple object at 0x7f3cdf7c07f0>
File: swat/cas/actions.py
Docstring:
Analytics

Actions
-------
simple.correlation : Generates a matrix of Pearson product-moment
                     correlation coefficients
simple.crosstab    : Performs one-way or two-way tabulations
simple.distinct    : Computes the distinct number of values of the
                     variables in the variable list
simple.freq        : Generates a frequency distribution for one or
                     more variables
simple.groupby     : Builds BY groups in terms of the variable value
                     combinations given the variables in the variable
                     list
simple.mdsummary   : Calculates multidimensional summaries of numeric
                     variables
simple.numrows     : Shows the number of rows in a Cloud Analytic
                     Services table
simple.paracoord   : Generates a parallel coordinates plot of the
                     variables in the variable list
simple.regression  : Performs a linear regression up to 3rd-order
                     polynomials
```

```
simple.summary      : Generates descriptive statistics of numeric
                      variables such as the sample mean, sample
                      variance, sample size, sum of squares, and so on
simple.topk         : Returns the top-K and bottom-K distinct values of
                      each variable included in the variable list based
                      on a user-specified ranking order
```

Once an action set has been loaded, it cannot be unloaded. The overhead for keeping an action set loaded is minimal, so this issue doesn't make a significant difference.

That is really all there is to loading action sets. We still do not have data in our system, so we cannot use any of the simple statistics actions yet. Let's review some final details about options and dealing with errors in the next section, then the following chapter gets into the ways of loading data and using the analytical actions on those data sets.

Details

We have covered the overall workings of connecting to a CAS host, running CAS actions, working with the results of CAS actions, and loading CAS action sets. However, there are some details that we haven't covered. Although these items aren't necessary for using SWAT and CAS, they can be quite useful to have in your tool belt.

Getting Help

Even though we have already covered the methods for getting help from CAS, it is an important topic to recap. Every object in the SWAT package uses the standard Python method of surfacing documentation. This includes the help function in Python (for example, help(swat.CAS)), the ? suffix operator in IPython and Jupyter (for example, swat.CAS?), and any other tool that uses Python's docstrings.

In addition, action sets and actions that are loaded dynamically also support the same Python, IPython, and Jupyter Help system hooks (for example, conn.summary?).

Keep in mind that tab completion on the CAS objects and other objects in the SWAT package can be a quick reminder of the attributes and methods of that object.

These Help system hooks should be sufficient to help you get information about any objects in the SWAT package, CAS action sets, and CAS actions and their parameters. If more detailed information is needed, it is available in the official SAS Viya documentation on the SAS website.

Dealing with Errors

The issue of CAS action errors was discussed to some extent previously in the chapter. There are two methods for dealing with CAS action errors: return codes and exceptions. The default behavior is to surface return codes, but SWAT can be configured to raise exceptions. In the case of return codes, they are available in the severity attribute of the CASResults object that is returned by CAS action methods. The possible values are shown in the following table:

Severity	Description
0	An action was executed with no warnings or errors.
1	Warnings were generated.
2	An error occurred.

In addition to the severity attribute, the CASResults object has an attribute named reason, which is a string that contains the general reason for the warning or error. The possible reasons are shown in the following table:

Reason	Description
ok	The action was executed with no warnings or errors.
abort	The action was aborted.
authentication	The action could not authenticate user credentials.
authorization	The action was unable to access a resource due to permissions settings.
exception	An exception occurred during the execution of an action.
expired-token	An authentication token expired.
io	An input/output error occurred.
memory	Out of memory.
network	Networking failure.
session-retry	An action restarted and results already returned should be ignored.
unknown	The reason is unknown.

The last two attributes to note are status and status_code. The status attribute of CASResults contains a human-readable formatted message that describes the action result. The status_code is a numeric code that can be supplied to Technical Support if further assistance is required. The code contains information that might be useful to Technical Support for determining the source of the problem.

Using CAS Action Exceptions

As mentioned previously, it is possible for SWAT to raise an exception when an error or warning occurs in a CAS action. This is enabled by setting an option in the SWAT package. We haven't covered SWAT options yet. It is covered in the next section in this chapter. However, the simplest way to enable exceptions is to submit the following code:

```
In [62]: swat.options.cas.exception_on_severity = 2
```

This causes SWAT to throw a swat.SWATCASActionError exception when the severity of the response is 2. For exceptions to be raised on warnings and errors, you set the value of the option to 1. Setting it to None disables this feature.

The swat.SWATCASActionError exception contains several attributes that contain information about the context of the exception when it was raised. The attributes are described in the following table:

Attribute Name	Description
message	The formatted status message from the CAS action.
response	The CASResponse object that contains the final response from the CAS host.
connection	The CAS connection object that the action was running in.
results	The compiled result up to the point of the exception.

The message attribute is simply the same value as the status attribute of the response. The response attribute is an object that we haven't discussed yet: CASResponse. This object isn't seen when using the CAS action methods on a CAS object. It is used behind the scenes when compiling the results of a CAS action. Then it discarded. It is possible to use more advanced methods of traversing the responses from CAS where you deal with CASResponse objects directly, but that is not discussed until much later in this book. For now, it is sufficient to know that the CASResponse object has several attributes, including one named disposition, which contains the same result code fields that the CASResults object also contains.

The connection attribute of swat.SWATCASActionError contains the CAS connection object that executed the action. And finally, the results attribute contains the results that have been compiled up to that point. Normally, this is a CASResults object, but there are options on the CAS action methods that we haven't yet discussed that cause other data values to be inserted into that attribute.

Catching a swat.SWATCASActionError is just like catching any other Python exception. You use a try/except block, where the except statement specifies swat.SWATCASActionError (or any of its parent classes). In the following code, we try to get help on a nonexistent action. The action call is wrapped in a try/except block in which the except statement captures the exception as the variable err. In the except section, the message attribute of the exception is printed. Of course, you can use any of the other fields to handle the exception in any way you prefer.

```
In [63]: try:
    ...:         out = conn.help(action='nonexistent')
    ...: except swat.SWATCASActionError as err:
    ...:         print(err.message)
    ...:
ERROR: Action 'nonexistent' was not found.
ERROR: The action stopped due to errors.
The specified action was not found.
```

In addition to CAS action errors, there are other types of errors that you might run into while working with CAS. Let's look at how to resolve CAS action parameter problems in the next section. But first, let's reset the exception option back to the default value.

```
In [64]: swat.options.reset_option('cas.exception_on_severity')
```

Resolving CAS Action Parameter Problems

CAS action parameter problems can come in many forms: invalid parameter names, invalid parameter values, incorrect nesting of parameter lists, and so on. It can sometimes be difficult to immediately identify the problem. We provide you with some tips in this section that hopefully simplify your correction of CAS action parameter errors.

Let's start with an action call that creates a parameter error. We haven't covered the actions being used in this example, but you don't need to know what they do in order to see what the error is and how to fix it.

```
In [65]: out = conn.summary(table=dict(name='test',
    ....:                                groupby=['var1', 'var2', 3]))
ERROR: An attempt was made to convert parameter 'table.groupby[2]' from
int64 to parameter list, but the conversion failed.
ERROR: The action stopped due to errors.
```

In the preceding action call, we see that we get an error concerning table.groupby[2]. When you start building parameter structures that are deeply nested, it can be difficult to see exactly what element the message refers to. One of the best tools to track down the error is the cas.trace_actions option. We haven't reached the section on setting SWAT options, but you can simply submit the following code in order to enable this option:

```
In [66]: swat.set_option('cas.trace_actions', True)
```

With this option enabled, we see all of the actions and action parameters printed out in a form that matches the error message from the server. Let's run the summary action from In[65] again.

```
In [67]: out = conn.summary(table=dict(name='test',
    ....:                                groupby=['var1', 'var2', 3]))
[simple.summary]
    table.groupby[0] = "var1" (string)
    table.groupby[1] = "var2" (string)
    table.groupby[2] = 3 (int64)
    table.name      = "test" (string)

ERROR: An attempt was made to convert parameter 'table.groupby[2]' from
int64 to parameter list, but the conversion failed.
ERROR: The action stopped due to errors.
```

This time we can see from the printed output that table.groupby[2] is the value 3. According to the definition of the summary action, those values must be strings, so that is the source of the error. We can now go into our action call and change the 3 to the proper value.

If you still do not see the problem, it might be a good idea to separate the parameter construction from the action call as we saw in the section on specifying action parameters. Let's build the action parameters, one at a time, including the erroneous value.

```
In [68]: params = swat.vl()

In [69]: params.table.name = 'test'

In [70]: params.table.groupby[0] = 'var1'

In [71]: params.table.groupby[1] = 'var2'

In [72]: params.table.groupby[2] = 3

In [73]: out = conn.summary(**params)
[simple.summary]
    table.groupby[0] = "var1" (string)
    table.groupby[1] = "var2" (string)
    table.groupby[2] = 3 (int64)
```

```
    table.name    = "test" (string)

ERROR: An attempt was made to convert parameter 'table.groupby[2]' from
int64 to parameter list, but the conversion failed.
ERROR: The action stopped due to errors.
```

Of course, in this case the error is pretty obvious since we entered it in a line by itself. But you have parameters that are built in programmatic ways that might not be so obvious. Now our parameters are held in an object that has a syntax that maps perfectly to the output that is created by the cas.trace_actions option as well as the error message from the server. When we see this error message, we can simply display it directly from the params variable to see what the problem is and correct it.

```
In [74]: params.table.groupby[2]
Out[74]: 3

In [75]: params.table.groupby[2] = 'var3'
```

Now let's move on to the remaining class of errors.

Handling Other Errors

All of the other errors that you encounter in SWAT are raised as swat.SWATErrors. Reasons for these errors include the inability to connect to the CAS host, out-of-memory errors, and any other errors that can occur in a networking environment. These can all be handled in the standard Python way of using try/except blocks in your code to capture them.

SWAT Options

As we have seen more than once in this chapter, the cas.exception_on_severity option is one way of changing the behavior of the SWAT package. But there are many others. The options system in SWAT is modeled after the options system in the Pandas package. Most of the function names and behaviors are the same between the two. The primary functions that are used to get, to set, and to query options are shown in the following table.

Function Name	Description
describe_option	Prints the description of one or more options.
get_option	Gets the current value of an option.
set_option	Sets the value of one or more options.
reset_option	Resets the value of one or more options back to the default.
option_context	Creates a context_manager that enables you to set options temporarily in a particular context.

The first thing you might want to do is run the swat.describe_option with no arguments. This prints out a description of all of the available options. Printing the description of all options can be rather lengthy. Only a portion is displayed here:

```
In [76]: swat.describe_option()
cas.dataset.auto_castable : boolean
    Should a column of CASTable objects be automatically
    created if a CASLib and CAS table name are columns in the data?
    NOTE: This applies to all except the 'tuples' format.
    [default: True] [currently: True]
```

```
cas.dataset.bygroup_as_index : boolean
    If True, any by group columns are set as the DataFrame index.
    [default: True] [currently: True]


cas.dataset.bygroup_collision_suffix : string
    Suffix to use on the By group column name when a By group column
    is also included as a data column.
    [default: _by] [currently: _by]

    ... truncated ...
```

As you can see, the option information is formatted very much like options in Pandas. The description includes the full name of the option, the expected values or data type, a short description of the option, the default value, and the current value.

Since we have already used the cas.exception_on_severity option, let's look at its description using describe_option, as follows:

```
In [77]: swat.describe_option('cas.exception_on_severity')
cas.exception_on_severity : int or None
    Indicates the CAS action severity level at which an exception
    should be raised. None means that no exception should be raised.
    1 would raise exceptions on warnings. 2 would raise exceptions
    on errors.
    [default: None] [currently: None]
```

As you can see from the description, by default, this option is set to None, which means that exceptions are never thrown. The current value is 2, for exceptions on errors. We can also get the current value of the option by using swat.get_option as follows:

```
In [78]: print(swat.get_option('cas.exception_on_severity'))
Out[78]: None
```

Setting options is done using the swat.set_option function. This function accepts parameters in multiple forms. The most explicit way to set an option is to pass in the name of the option as a string followed by the value of the option in the next argument. We have seen this already when we set the cas.exception_on_severity option.

```
In [79]: swat.set_option('cas.exception_on_severity', 2)
```

Another form of setting options works only if the last segment of the option name (for example, exception_on_severity for cas.exception_on_severity) is unique among all of the options. If so, then you can use that name as a keyword argument to swat.set_option. The following code is equivalent to the last example:

```
In [80]: swat.set_option(exception_on_severity=2)
```

In either of the forms, it is possible to set multiple options with one call to swat.set_option. In the first form, you simply continue to add option names and values as consecutive arguments. In the second form, you add additional keyword arguments. Also, you can mix both. The only caveat is that if you mix them, you must put the positional arguments first just like with any Python function.

```
In [81]: swat.set_option('cas.dataset.index_name', 'Variable',
    ....:                 'cas.dataset.format', 'dataframe',
    ....:                 exception_on_severity=2,
    ....:                 print_messages=False)
```

The next function, swat.reset_option, resets options back to their default value:

```
In [82]: swat.reset_option('cas.exception_on_severity')
```

```
In [83]: print(swat.get_option('cas.exception_on_severity'))
None
```

Note that we used the print function in the preceding code since IPython does not display a None value as a result. Nonetheless, you can see that the value of cas.exception_on_severity was set back to the default of None.

Just as with swat.describe_option, you can specify multiple names of options to reset. In addition, executing swat.reset_option with no arguments resets all of the option values back to their default values.

The final option function is swat.option_context. Again, this works just like its counterpart in Pandas. It enables you to specify option settings for a particular context in Python using the with statement. For example, if we wanted to turn on CAS action tracing for a block of code, the swat.option_context in conjunction with the Python with statement sets up an environment where the options are set at the beginning of the context and are reset back to their previous values at the end of the context. Let's see this in action using the cas.trace_actions option:

```
In [84]: swat.reset_option('trace_actions')
```

```
In [85]: swat.get_option('trace_actions')
Out[85]: False
```

```
In [86]: with swat.option_context('cas.trace_actions', True):
    ....:     print(swat.get_option('cas.trace_actions'))
    ....:
True
```

```
In [87]: swat.get_option('cas.trace_actions')
Out[87]: False
```

As you can see in the preceding example, cas.trace_actions was False before the with context was run. The cas.trace_actions was True when it was inside the with context, and afterward, it went back to False. The swat.option_context arguments work the same way as swat.set_option. So you can specify as many options for the context as you prefer, and they can even be nested in multiple with contexts.

Partial Option Name Matches

As we have seen with swat.set_option and swat.option_context, you can use keyword arguments if the last segment of the option name is unique among all the options. You can also use the same technique with the option names using positional string arguments. In addition, in all of the functions, you can specify any number of the trailing segments as long as they match only one option name. For example, all of the following lines of code are equivalent:

```
In [88]: swat.set_option('cas.dataset.max_rows_fetched', 500)
```

```
In [89]: swat.set_option('dataset.max_rows_fetched', 500)
```

```
In [90]: swat.set_option('max_rows_fetched', 500)
```

The swat.describe_option also works with patterns that match the beginning of multiple option names. This means that you can display all cas.dataset options by just giving the cas.dataset prefix as an argument to swat.describe_option.

```
In [91]: swat.describe_option('cas.dataset')
cas.dataset.max_rows_fetched : int
    The maximum number of rows to fetch with methods that use
    the table.fetch action in the background (i.e. the head, tail,
    values, etc. of CASTable).
    [default: 3000] [currently: 500]



cas.dataset.auto_castable : boolean
    Should a column of CASTable objects be automatically
    created if a CASLib and CAS table name are columns in the data?
    NOTE: This applies to all except the 'tuples' format.
    [default: True] [currently: True]
```

This same technique also works to reset a group of options using swat.reset_option. In either case, you must specify full segment names (for example, cas.dataset), and not just any substring (for example, cas.data).

The swat.options Object

In addition to the option functions in the SWAT package, there is an object-based interface as well: swat.options. This method of settings options is just like using the Pandas options object.

Much like using describe_option without any arguments, using Python's Help system, you can also display all of the option descriptions with swat.options?.

```
In [92]: swat.options?
Type:           AttrOption
String form:    <swat.utils.config.AttrOption object at 0x269a0d0>
File: swat/utils/config.py
Definition:     swat.options(self, *args, **kwargs)
Docstring
cas.dataset.auto_castable : boolean
    Should a column of CASTable objects be automatically
    created if a CASLib and CAS table name are columns in the data?
    NOTE: This applies to all except the 'tuples' format.
    [default: True] [currently: True]

cas.dataset.bygroup_as_index : boolean
    If True, any by group columns are set as the DataFrame index.
    [default: True] [currently: True]

cas.dataset.bygroup_collision_suffix : string
    Suffix to use on the By group column name when a By group column
    is also included as a data column.
    [default: _by] [currently: _by]

... truncated ...
```

Tab completion can also be used to see what options are available.

```
In [93]: swat.options.<tab>
swat.options.cas.dataset.auto_castable
swat.options.cas.dataset.bygroup_as_index
swat.options.cas.dataset.bygroup_collision_suffix
swat.options.cas.dataset.bygroup_columns
swat.options.cas.dataset.bygroup_formatted_suffix
swat.options.cas.dataset.drop_index_name
swat.options.cas.dataset.format
swat.options.cas.dataset.index_adjustment
swat.options.cas.dataset.index_name
swat.options.cas.dataset.max_rows_fetched
swat.options.cas.exception_on_severity
swat.options.cas.hostname
swat.options.cas.port
swat.options.cas.print_messages
swat.options.cas.protocol
swat.options.cas.trace_actions
swat.options.cas.trace_ui_actions
swat.options.encoding_errors
swat.options.interactive_mode
swat.options.tkpath
```

Getting the value of an option is as simple as entering the full name of an option as displayed in the tab-completed output.

```
In [94]: swat.options.cas.trace_actions
Out[94]: False
```

You set options as you would set any other Python variable.

```
In [95]: swat.options.cas.trace_actions = True
```

Just as with set_option and get_option, if the final segment of the option name is unique among all options, you can shorten your swat.options call to include only that segment. This is shown below by eliminating the cas portion of the option name.

```
In [96]: swat.options.trace_actions = False
```

The swat.options object also defines a callable interface that returns a context manager like option_context. The following is equivalent to using with swat.option_context(…).

```
In [97]: with swat.options(trace_actions=True):
    ....:     out = conn.help(action='loadactionset')
    ....:
[builtins.help]
    action = "loadactionset" (string)
```

The interface that you use is purely a personal preference. The only thing that the swat.options interface is missing is a way to reset options. You must fall back to reset_option to do that.

In addition to the SWAT options, CAS server sessions also have options. Let's look at those in the next section.

CAS Session Options

The session on the CAS host has options that can be set to change certain behaviors for the current session. These options are set using the setsessopt action. You can view them and get current values using listsessopt and getsessopt. The best way to see all of the options that are available is to use Python's Help system on the setsessopt action.

```
In [98]: conn.setsessopt?

...

Docstring
Sets a session option

Parameters
----------
actionmaxtime : int64, optional
    specifies the maximum action time.
    Default: -1
    Note: Value range is -1 <= n <= 86400

apptag : string, optional
    specifies the string to prefix to log messages.
    Default:

caslib : string, optional
    specifies the caslib name to set as the active caslib.
    Default:

collate : string, optional
    specifies the collating sequence for sorting.
    Default: UCA
    Values: MVA, UCA

fmtcaslib : string, optional
    specifies the caslib where persisted format libraries are retained.
    Default: FORMATS

fmtsearch : string, optional
    specifies the format library search order.
    Default:

fmtsearchposition : string, optional
    specifies the position in the format library list where additions
    are made.
    Default: APPEND
    Values: APPEND, CLEAR, INSERT, REPLACE

locale : string, optional
    specifies the locale to use for sorting and formatting.
    Default: en_US

logflushtime : int64, optional
    specifies the log flush time, in milliseconds. A value of -1
    indicates to flush logs after each action completes. A value of 0
    indicates to flush logs as they are produced.
    Default: 100
```

```
        Note: Value range is -1 <= n <= 86400

maxtablemem : int64, optional
        specifies the maximum amount of physical memory, in bytes, to
        allocate for a table. After this threshold is reached, the server
        uses temporary files and operating system facilities for memory
        management.
        Default: 16777216

metrics : boolean, optional
        when set to True, action metrics are displayed.
        Default: False

... truncated ...
```

There are options for setting the session locale, collation order, time-outs, memory limits, and so on. The metrics option is simple to demonstrate. Let's get its current value using getsessopt:

```
In [99]: out = conn.getsessopt('metrics')

In [100]: out
Out[100]:
[metrics]

 0

+ Elapsed: 0.000365s, mem: 0.0626mb
```

The output is our usual CASResults object with a key that matches the requested option name. In this case, the metrics option is returned as an integer value of zero (corresponding to a Boolean false). You can get the actual value of the metrics option by accessing that key of the CASResults object.

```
In [101]: out.metrics
Out[101]: 0
```

Setting the values of options is done using setsessopt with keyword arguments for the option names. You can specify as many options in setsessopt as you need.

```
In [102]: conn.setsessopt(metrics=True, collate='MVA')
NOTE: Executing action 'sessionProp.setSessOpt'.
NOTE: Action 'sessionprop.setsessopt' used (Total process time):
NOTE:         real time              0.000370 seconds
NOTE:         cpu time               0.000000 seconds (0.00%)
NOTE:         total nodes            1 (32 cores)
NOTE:         total memory           188.99G
NOTE:         memory                 98.19K (0.00%)
Out[102]: + Elapsed: 0.000334s, mem: 0.0959mb
```

Notice that the metrics option takes effect immediately. We now get performance metrics of the action that is printed to the output. Checking the value of collate, you see that it has been set to MVA.

```
In [103]: conn.getsessopt('collate').collate
NOTE: Executing action 'sessionProp.getSessOpt'.
NOTE: Action 'sessionprop.getsessopt' used (Total process time):
NOTE:         real time                 0.000302 seconds
```

```
NOTE:        cpu time          0.000000 seconds (0.00%)
NOTE:        total nodes       1 (32 cores)
NOTE:        total memory      188.99G
NOTE:        memory            49.91K (0.00%)
Out[103]: 'MVA'
```

Conclusion

We have covered a lot of territory in this chapter, but you should now have the tools that you need in order to connect to CAS, call CAS actions, and traverse the results. We also covered the possible error conditions that you might run into, and what to do when they happen. Finally, we demonstrated some of the SWAT client and CAS session options to control certain behaviors of both areas. Now that we have that all out of the way, we can move on to something a little more interesting: data and how to get it into CAS.

---

[1] Technically, these parameters can also be specified by setting environment variables CASHOST and CASPORT, and not specified in the CAS constructor.

[2] The name _self_ is used instead of the more typical self argument to prevent possible name collisions with action parameters.

Chapter 4: Managing Your Data in CAS

Before you can do any sort of analysis in CAS, you need some data to work with. There are two components to data access in CAS: caslibs and CAS tables. Caslibs are definitions that give access to a resource that contains data. These resources can be files that are located in a file system, a database, streaming data from an ESP (Event Stream Processing) server, or other data sources that SAS can access. Caslibs contain all of the connection information as well as authentication and authorization settings. In addition, caslibs are containers for tables that are loaded in the server, effectively enabling you to create namespaces for tables.

When you want to analyze data from one of your caslib resources, you load the data into a CAS table. A CAS table contains columns of data and information about the data in the columns (including column labels, data types, data formats, and so on).

CAS tables and caslibs are the topic of this chapter.

Overview

The subject of caslibs and CAS tables is fairly extensive, especially when you consider the multiple ways of loading and parsing data from various sources. We have attempted to boil it down to one simple diagram to give you an overall view of the process and components involved.

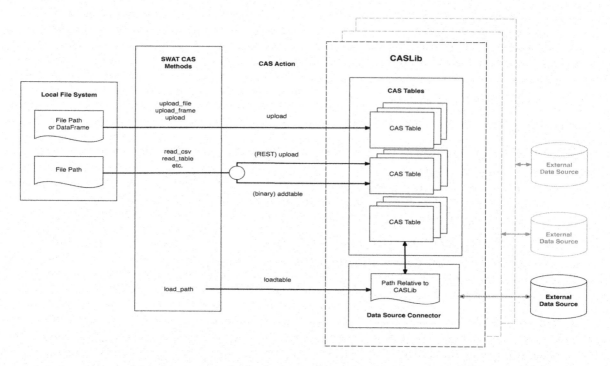

From the preceding diagram, you see that SWAT has multiple methods for loading data, and the CAS actions used to load the data vary as well. Each session can have one or more caslibs, with each connected to a different data source. The caslibs and tables within the caslibs might have session scope or global scope depending on the options that they were created with. These details are covered in the following sections.

Getting Started with Caslibs and CAS Tables

Since all data that is accessed by CAS must be in a caslib, it makes sense to start there when discussing how to get your data into CAS. Depending on your CAS server setup, you might already have one or more caslibs configured and ready to use. To find out what caslibs are available, use the caslibinfo action.

```
In [1]: import swat

In [2]: conn = swat.CAS('server-name.mycompany.com', 5570,
   ...:                    'username', 'password')

In [3]: conn.caslibinfo()
Out[3]:
[CASLibInfo]

                   Name   Type                    Description   \
 0  CASUSER(username)   PATH   Personal File System Caslib
 1           Formats    PATH                   Format Caslib

                   Path Definition   Subdirs   Local   Active   \
 0           /u/username/               1.0     0.0      1.0
 1   /bigdisk/lax/formats/             1.0     0.0      0.0

      Personal   Hidden
 0        1.0      0.0
 1        0.0      0.0


+ Elapsed: 0.000434s, mem: 0.0971mb
```

We can see from this that we have two caslibs defined already. The first caslib points to our home directory. The second caslib is for holding user-defined data formats. Both of these initial caslibs are set up by a system administrator. Depending on your permissions, you might be able to add others as needed. You see that the table describing the caslibs also contains additional information about each caslib.

A human-readable description can be added when creating a caslib as well as information about the breadth and scope of the caslib. The Subdirs column indicates whether subdirectories of the specified path of the caslib can be accessed. A value of 0 means no, and 1 means yes. The Local column indicates whether the caslib is visible in the current session (indicated by 1), or if it is visible by all sessions (indicated by 0). The Active column indicates which caslib is active. When a caslib is active, it is used if a caslib is not explicitly specified during any operation that requires one. The Personal column indicates whether the caslib is specific to the user. These caslibs can be seen only by the current user regardless of whether the caslib is local or global in scope. Finally, the Hidden column indicates whether the caslib should be displayed in caslib listings. The caslib is displayed only when the showhidden parameter is set to True in the caslibinfo action.

Now that we know what caslibs are available to us, let's see what they contain. We have some data files that are stored in the data subdirectory of our home directory, which is pointed to by the caslib Casuser. Let's use the fileinfo action to list the contents of that directory.

```
In [4]: conn.fileinfo('data', caslib='casuser')
Out[4]:
[FileInfo]
```

```
        Permission      Owner   Group                                      Name  \
0       -rw-r--r--      username users                                  iris.csv
1       -rw-r--r--      username users                                  cars.csv
2       -rw-r--r--      username users               sashelp_class.sashdat
3       -rw-r--r--      username users                                 class.csv

        Size Encryption                      Time
0       3716                      18Feb2016:17:25:43
1       42177                     18Feb2016:17:25:49
2       82136           NONE      19Feb2016:17:02:37
3        519                      14Apr2016:10:39:02

+ Elapsed: 0.0165s, user: 0.001s, sys: 0.003s, mem: 0.121mb
```

You'll notice that when we specified the caslib to look in, we used Casuser, but we didn't include the username enclosed in parentheses. The username part can be specified, but it is primarily there to differentiate multiple Casuser caslibs in the listing. You'll also notice that caslib names as well as CAS table names are case-insensitive. In addition, since Casuser is our active caslib, we don't have to specify a caslib option at all.

```
In [5]: conn.fileinfo('data')
Out[5]:
[FileInfo]

        Permission      Owner   Group                                      Name  \
0       -rw-r--r--      username users                                  iris.csv
1       -rw-r--r--      username users                                  cars.csv
2       -rw-r--r--      username users               sashelp_class.sashdat
3       -rw-r--r--      username users                                 class.csv

        Size Encryption                      Time
0       3716                      18Feb2016:17:25:43
1       42177                     18Feb2016:17:25:49
2       82136           NONE      19Feb2016:17:02:37
3        519                      14Apr2016:10:39:02

+ Elapsed: 0.0103s, user: 0.003s, sys: 0.003s, mem: 0.118mb
```

Although you can omit the caslib option, it's generally a good practice to include it. When you create larger programs and start moving code around, your active caslib might not be what was in your original program context.

In addition to the files that are accessible to this caslib, there can also be tables that have already been loaded that are available to the caslib. These can be seen using the tableinfo action.

```
In [6]: out = conn.tableinfo()
NOTE: No tables are available in caslib CASUSER(username) of Cloud
Analytic Services.
Out[6]: + Elapsed: 0.000399s, mem: 0.0749mb
```

At this point, we don't have any tables already loaded. Since we have data files that are located in an area that is accessible to our Casuser caslib, let's load one into a table.

Loading Data into a CAS Table

To load data from a file in a caslib into a CAS table, you use the loadtable action by specifying the file path and the caslib name.

```
In [6]: out = conn.loadtable('data/iris.csv', caslib='casuser')
NOTE: Cloud Analytic Services made the file data/iris.csv available as
table DATA.IRIS in caslib CASUSER(username).

In [7]: out
Out[7]:
[caslib]

 'CASUSER(username)'

[tableName]

 'DATA.IRIS'

[casTable]

 CASTable('DATA.IRIS', caslib='CASUSER(username)')

+ Elapsed: 0.109s, user: 0.075s, sys: 0.036s, mem: 64.9mb
```

You might remember from Chapter 2 that we used the upload method on the CAS connection object to load data. That method loads data from the client side, whereas the loadtable action loads files from the server side. We'll get into more details about the upload method later in this chapter.

The result of the loadtable action includes the table name (tableName), the caslib (caslib), and a CAS table object (casTable). We discuss the CAS table object in much more detail in a later chapter. For now, let's focus on the table name and caslib outputs.

The table name that you get from the loadtable action is generated and is based on the file name that was loaded. You can change the name of the loaded table using the casout option. In the following example, we specify both the name and the caslib that the loaded table is written to:

```
In [8]: out = conn.loadtable('data/iris.csv',
   ...:                      caslib='casuser',
   ...:                      casout=dict(name='mydata',
   ...:                                  caslib='casuser'))

NOTE: Cloud Analytic Services made the file data/iris.csv available as
table MYDATA in caslib CASUSER(username).

In [9]: out
Out[9]:
[caslib]

 'CASUSER(username)'

[tableName]

 'MYDATA'

[casTable]
```

```
CASTable('MYDATA', caslib='CASUSER(username)')
```

```
+ Elapsed: 0.0907s, user: 0.054s, sys: 0.039s, mem: 64.7mb
```

Now that our data is loaded into a table, let's request information about the table from the server. The first action you'll want to use is the tableinfo action.

```
In [10]: conn.tableinfo('data.iris', caslib='casuser')
Out[10]:
[TableInfo]
```

	Name	Rows	Columns	Encoding	CreateTimeFormatted	\
0	DATA.IRIS	150	5	utf-8	02Nov2016:11:54:28	

	ModTimeFormatted	JavaCharSet	CreateTime	ModTime	\
0	02Nov2016:11:54:28	UTF8	1.793707e+09	1.793707e+09	

	Global	Repeated	View	SourceName	SourceCaslib	\
0	0	0	0	data/iris.csv	CASUSER(username)	

	Compressed	Creator	Modifier
0	0	username	

```
+ Elapsed: 0.00101s, user: 0.000999s, mem: 0.104mb
```

From these results, we see that there are 150 rows of data in 5 columns. Another field of particular note is the Global value. This indicates whether the table can be seen in other CAS sessions. In our case, the value is 0, and therefore, it is local to this session only.

Now that we have some information about the table as a whole, let's see what information we can get about the columns. To get information about CAS table columns, you use the columninfo action. Since the tableinfo action gives a broad view of the table information, it needs only a table name and a caslib name. The columninfo action is somewhat more complex and uses a dictionary as a table argument.

```
In [11]: out = conn.columninfo(table=dict(name='data.iris',
    ....:                                 caslib='casuser'))
In [12]: out
Out[12]:
[ColumnInfo]
```

	Column	ID	Type	RawLength	FormattedLength	NFL	NFD
0	sepal_length	1	double	8	12	0	0
1	sepal_width	2	double	8	12	0	0
2	petal_length	3	double	8	12	0	0
3	petal_width	4	double	8	12	0	0
4	species	5	varchar	10	10	0	0

```
+ Elapsed: 0.000751s, mem: 0.168mb
```

From this output, you can see the column names, the data types, the data sizes, and various formatting information.

Now that we know about our data, let's look at the data itself.

Displaying Data in a CAS Table

Of course, the most important thing about the table is the data itself. We can get a sample of the data by using the fetch action. In this case, we use the to=5 parameter to fetch only five rows.

```
In [13]: conn.fetch(table=dict(name='data.iris',
   ....:                        caslib='casuser'),
   ....:            to=5)
Out[13]:
[Fetch]

Selected Rows from Table DATA.IRIS

     sepal_length  sepal_width  petal_length  petal_width  species
0             5.1          3.5           1.4          0.2  setosa
1             4.9          3.0           1.4          0.2  setosa
2             4.7          3.2           1.3          0.2  setosa
3             4.6          3.1           1.5          0.2  setosa
4             5.0          3.6           1.4          0.2  setosa

+ Elapsed: 0.00381s, user: 0.004s, mem: 1.64mb
```

Note that unless you specify sorting options, the order of the data that comes back is not guaranteed to be in the same order that the data was entered in. This is because data can be spread across the CAS grid and the result that you see is the compiled version of all of the results of the nodes on a grid. In the following code, we fetch the data using the sepal_length and sepal_width sort keys to guarantee ordering.

```
In [14]: conn.fetch(table=dict(name='data.iris',
   ....:                        caslib='casuser'),
   ....:            to=5,
   ....:            sortby=['sepal_length', 'sepal_width'])
Out[14]:
[Fetch]

Selected Rows from Table DATA.IRIS

     sepal_length  sepal_width  petal_length  petal_width  species
0             4.3          3.0           1.1          0.1  setosa
1             4.4          2.9           1.4          0.2  setosa
2             4.4          3.0           1.3          0.2  setosa
3             4.4          3.2           1.3          0.2  setosa
4             4.5          2.3           1.3          0.3  setosa

+ Elapsed: 0.0171s, user: 0.014s, sys: 0.003s, mem: 8.58mb
```

Now that we have seen a sample of the data, let's compute some simple statistics.

Computing Simple Statistics

Just to whet your appetite a bit, let's get some summary statistics on the table that we just loaded. We'll delve into running actions on data in later chapters, but it seems a shame to load our first set of data and not do any sort of analysis on it. Let's run the summary action on our table.

```
In [15]: conn.summary(table=dict(name='data.iris',
   ....:                         caslib='casuser'))
Out[15]:
```

```
[Summary]

Descriptive Statistics for DATA.IRIS

          Column  Min  Max      N  NMiss      Mean     Sum       Std  \
0   sepal_length  4.3  7.9  150.0    0.0  5.843333  876.5  0.828066
1    sepal_width  2.0  4.4  150.0    0.0  3.054000  458.1  0.433594
2   petal_length  1.0  6.9  150.0    0.0  3.758667  563.8  1.764420
3    petal_width  0.1  2.5  150.0    0.0  1.198667  179.8  0.763161

     StdErr       Var      USS         CSS         CV     TValue  \
0  0.067611  0.685694  5223.85  102.168333  14.171126  86.425375
1  0.035403  0.188004  1427.05   28.012600  14.197587  86.264297
2  0.144064  3.113179  2583.00  463.863733  46.942721  26.090198
3  0.062312  0.582414   302.30   86.779733  63.667470  19.236588

          ProbT
0  3.331256e-129
1  4.374977e-129
2   1.994305e-57
3   3.209704e-42

+ Elapsed: 0.0266s, user: 0.028s, sys: 0.003s, mem: 1.74mb
```

When you are finished using a table, it can be removed from memory. Let's see how to do that in the next section.

Dropping a CAS Table

If a table is no longer needed, you can remove it by using the droptable action.

```
In [16]: conn.droptable('data.iris', caslib='casuser')
NOTE: Cloud Analytic Services dropped table data.iris from caslib
CASUSER(username).
Out[16]: + Elapsed: 0.000332s, mem: 0.0535mb
```

In some of the previous listings, you might have seen data types that haven't previously been available in a SAS product. CAS has a much richer set of data types than traditional SAS does, we'll look at those next.

CAS Data Types

When parsing the Iris CSV file in the previous examples, the character data was stored as a varchar (variable-width character) column. This means that the values are not padded with extra space like a fixed-width character column. This is just one of the new data types in CAS that aren't available in traditional SAS. Here is a full list of the data types that are available in CAS tables[1].

Name	Description
Double	8-byte IEEE floating point number
Int32	32-bit integer
Int64	64-bit integer
DecQuad	128-bit fixed-decimal value
DecSext	192-bit fixed-decimal value
Char	Fixed-width, blank-padded UTF-8 encoded character data

Name	Description
Varchar	Variable-width UTF-8 encoded character data
Binary	Fixed-width binary data
Varbinary	Variable-width binary data
Date	CAS date value (32-bit integer containing the number of days since January 1, 1960)
Time	CAS time value (64-bit integer containing the number of microseconds since midnight)
Datetime	CAS datetime value (64-bit integer containing the number of microseconds since January 1, 1960)

With all of these data types, it is possible to do much more targeted data processing.

Caslib and CAS Table Visibility

There are two scopes in CAS for caslibs and CAS tables: session (or local) and global. By default, both caslibs and CAS tables are created with session scope. That means that they are visible only in the session that created them. If you need to use them across sessions, you need to specify a parameter indicating the global scope. The addcaslib action uses the session parameter to indicate session or global visibility. The loadtable and addtable actions use the promote parameter to indicate whether the table should be promoted to the global scope. CAS tables can also be promoted after creation by using the promote action. However, note that the promotion of a table is possible only in a global caslib.

The Active Caslib

As mentioned previously, there is one caslib that is considered active at any point in time. To be active means that any table references in actions that are not accompanied by a caslib name are assumed to be in the active caslib. You can use the caslibinfo action to see which caslib is active. In the following output, the Casuser caslib is marked as the active caslib.

```
In [17]: conn.caslibinfo()
Out[17]:
[CASLibInfo]

                    Name  Type                 Description  \
0   CASUSER(username)  PATH  Personal File System Caslib
1            Formats  PATH                 Format Caslib

               Path Definition  Subdirs  Local  Active  \
0            /u/username/           1.0    0.0     1.0
1   /bigdisk/lax/formats/           1.0    0.0     0.0

     Personal  Hidden
0         1.0     0.0
1         0.0     0.0

+ Elapsed: 0.000427s, mem: 0.095mb
```

Alternatively, you can use the getsessopt action to query the caslib option.

```
In [18]: conn.getsessopt('caslib')
Out[18]:
[caslib]
```

```
'CASUSER(username)'

+ Elapsed: 0.000268s, mem: 0.0477mb
```

The active caslib can be set at creation using the activeonadd parameter of addcaslib, or it can be set at any time using the setsessopt action.

```
In [19]: conn.setsessopt(caslib='formats')
NOTE: 'Formats' is now the active caslib.
Out[19]: + Elapsed: 0.000289s, mem: 0.0948mb
```

Regardless of which caslib is active, it's generally a good idea to always specify the caslib that you load a table from. This practice helps avoid errors where the active caslib gets changed at another point in the program.

Let's set the active caslib back to casuser before moving on.

```
In[20]: conn.setsessopt(caslib='casuser')
```

With the information from this chapter so far, you should be able load basic data files into CAS. If you have some data that you want to analyze, you could jump ahead to the chapters that cover the topics that you are interested in. However, if you want to learn about other ways of getting data into CAS, go to the next section.

Uploading Data Files to CAS Tables

In the previous section, we showed how to load a data file from a file-based caslib. But what if you don't have direct access to the file system where the CAS server is running, or you just want to upload data from a file that exists on the client side? The easiest solution is to use the upload method on the CAS connection.

In its simplest form, the upload method just takes a filename, a URL, or a Pandas DataFrame as an argument. The type of data that is in the file is inferred from the file extension, and the CAS table name is automatically generated. At the time of this writing, the file types that are supported by the upload method are sashdat, sas7bdat, XLS, CSV, DTA, JMP, and SPSS. Note that when loading data using the upload method, the table exists only in-memory. The file is not stored anywhere on the server. Let's load the Iris data set from a local file rather than from a file on the server.

```
In [21]: conn.upload('/u/username/data/iris.csv')
NOTE: Cloud Analytic Services made the uploaded file available as table
IRIS in caslib Formats.
NOTE: The table IRIS has been created in caslib Formats from binary data
uploaded to Cloud Analytic Services.
Out[21]:
[caslib]

 'CASUSER'

[tableName]

 'IRIS'

[casTable]
```

```
CASTable('IRIS', caslib='CASUSER(username)')

+ Elapsed: 0.0683s, user: 0.038s, sys: 0.024s, mem: 48.4mb
```

As you can see, the output from the upload method is very similar to that of the loadtable action. We get back a results object that contains a caslib name, a table name, and a CAS table object. We can now query for the table, the column, and data information as we did in the previous section.

In [22]: conn.columninfo(table=dict(name='iris',
    ....:   caslib='casuser'))
Out[22]:
[ColumnInfo]

	Column	ID	Type	RawLength	FormattedLength	NFL	NFD
0	sepal_length	1	double	8	12	0	0
1	sepal_width	2	double	8	12	0	0
2	petal_length	3	double	8	12	0	0
3	petal_width	4	double	8	12	0	0
4	species	5	varchar	10	10	0	0

```
+ Elapsed: 0.000707s, mem: 0.17mb
```

Also, just as with the loadtable action, you can specify a casout option in order to assign a different table name or caslib.

In [23]: conn.upload('/u/username/data/iris.csv',
    ....:   **casout=dict(name='iris2', caslib='casuser'))**
NOTE: Cloud Analytic Services made the uploaded file available as table
IRIS2 in caslib CASUSER(username).
NOTE: The table IRIS2 has been created in caslib CASUSER(username) from
binary data uploaded to Cloud Analytic Services.
Out[23]:
[caslib]

 'CASUSER(username)'

[tableName]

 'IRIS2'

[casTable]

 CASTable(**'IRIS2'**, caslib=**'CASUSER(username)'**)

```
+ Elapsed: 0.0614s, user: 0.037s, sys: 0.021s, mem: 48.4mb
```

So far, we have been using the default data parsing parameters for our CSV file. The upload method supports various options for each of the supported file types. The parameter that is used to specify parsing options is the importoptions parameter. This parameter is the same as in the loadtable action, so we can use the Help from the loadtable action to see what options are available. Here is a partial listing.

In [24]: conn.loadtable?

...

Loads a table from a caslib's data source

```
Parameters
----------
path : string
    specifies the file, directory, or table name.

readahead : boolean, optional
    when set to True, loads the table into memory immediately. By
    default, a table is loaded into memory when it is first used.
    Default: False

importoptions : dict, optional
    specifies the settings for reading a table from a data source.

    importoptions.filetype : string
        Default: auto
        Values: auto, hdat, csv, delimited, excel, jmp, spss, dta,
                esp, lasr, basesas, mva, xls, fmt

    if importoptions.filetype == hdat:

        importoptions.encryptionpassword : string or blob, optional
            specifies a password for encrypting or decrypting stored
            data.

    if importoptions.filetype == csv:

        importoptions.guessrows : int64, optional
            specifies the number of rows to scan in order to determine
            data types for variables. Specify 0 to scan all rows.
            Default: 20
            Note: Value range is 1 <= n < 9223372036854775807

        importoptions.delimiter : string, optional
            specifies the character to use as the field delimiter.
            Default: ,

        importoptions.vars : list of dicts, optional
            specifies the names, types, formats, and other metadata
            for variables.

            importoptions.vars[*].name : string, optional
                specifies the name for the variable.

            importoptions.vars[*].label : string, optional
                specifies the descriptive label for the variable.

... truncated ...
```

Using the importoptions parameter that was previously described, you can parse a tab-delimited file rather than a comma-delimited file by changing the delimiter.

```
In [25]: out = conn.upload('/u/username/data/iris.tsv',
   ....:                   importoptions=dict(filetype='csv',
   ....:                                      delimiter='\t'),
   ....:                   casout=dict(name='iris_tsv',
   ....:                               caslib='casuser'))
```

```
NOTE: Cloud Analytic Services made the uploaded file available as table
IRIS_TSV in caslib CASUSER(username).
NOTE: The table IRIS_TSV has been created in caslib CASUSER(username)
from binary data uploaded to Cloud Analytic Services.
```

In [26]: out
Out[26]:
```
[caslib]

 'CASUSER(username)'

[tableName]

 'IRIS_TSV'

[casTable]

 CASTable('IRIS_TSV', caslib='CASUSER(username)')

+ Elapsed: 0.0918s, user: 0.051s, sys: 0.04s, mem: 64.7mb
```

Now that we have seen how to upload local files, let's examine uploading data from URLs.

Uploading Data from URLs to CAS Tables

Uploading data from a URL works exactly the same way as uploading from a local file. The only difference is that you are specifying a URL as the first parameter of the upload method.

```
In [27]: out = conn.upload('https://raw.githubusercontent.com/'
    ....:                   'sassoftware/sas-viya-programming/'
    ....:                   'master/data/class.csv')
NOTE: Cloud Analytic Services made the uploaded file available as table
CLASS in caslib CASUSER(username).
NOTE: The table CLASS has been created in caslib CASUSER(username) from
binary data uploaded to Cloud Analytic Services.
```

In [28]: out
Out[28]:
```
[caslib]

 'CASUSER(username)'

[tableName]

 'CLASS'

[casTable]

 CASTable('CLASS', caslib='CASUSER(username)')

+ Elapsed: 0.0948s, user: 0.06s, sys: 0.035s, mem: 64.7mb
```

A fact to note about uploading from a URL is that the file is not downloaded by the CAS server. The URL is downloaded to a temporary file on the client side, and then it is uploaded to the server. Although this form of uploading is quick and convenient, you'll want to keep this fact in mind when using it.

Uploading Data from a Pandas DataFrame to a CAS Table

If you already have your data in a Pandas DataFrame and you want to upload it to a CAS table, again, the upload method is the quickest and easiest way. In the case of DataFrames, you give the DataFrame object as the first argument to the upload method rather than a filename. In the following example, we first read a CSV file into a DataFrame, and then we'll upload that DataFrame to CAS.

```
# Read the CSV file with Pandas
In [29]: import pandas as pd

In [30]: df = pd.read_csv('/u/username/data/iris.csv')

# Quick check of data values
In [31]: df.head()
Out[31]:
   sepal_length  sepal_width  petal_length  petal_width species
0           5.1          3.5           1.4          0.2  setosa
1           4.9          3.0           1.4          0.2  setosa
2           4.7          3.2           1.3          0.2  setosa
3           4.6          3.1           1.5          0.2  setosa
4           5.0          3.6           1.4          0.2  setosa

# Upload the DataFrame
In [32]: conn.upload(df)
NOTE: Cloud Analytic Services made the uploaded file available as table
TMPWZJKVO_1 in caslib CASUSER(username).
NOTE: The table TMPWZJKVO_1 has been created in caslib CASUSER(username)
from binary data uploaded to Cloud Analytic Services.
Out[32]:
[caslib]

 'CASUSER(username)'

[tableName]

 'TMPWZJKVO_1'

[casTable]

 CASTable('TMPWZJKVO_1', caslib='CASUSER(username)')

+ Elapsed: 0.0897s, user: 0.059s, sys: 0.031s, mem: 64.7mb

In [33]: conn.fetch(table=dict(name='TMPWZJKVO_1',
   ....:                       caslib='casuser'), to=5)
Out[33]:
[Fetch]

 Selected Rows from Table TMPWZJKVO_1
```

```
    sepal_length  sepal_width  petal_length  petal_width  species
0            5.1          3.5           1.4          0.2   setosa
1            4.9          3.0           1.4          0.2   setosa
2            4.7          3.2           1.3          0.2   setosa
3            4.6          3.1           1.5          0.2   setosa
4            5.0          3.6           1.4          0.2   setosa

+ Elapsed: 0.00321s, user: 0.003s, mem: 1.65mb
```

You'll see that in the case of DataFrames, the table name is always generated since it can't be inferred from a filename. Of course, you can always specify a name manually using the casout argument to the upload method.

Since it is possible to upload data directly from a Pandas DataFrame, you can use any of the Pandas data readers to construct your data and then push the result to CAS. However, although the DataFrame uploader is a simple way to upload data, it has limitations as well. When a DataFrame is uploaded, it gets exported to CSV first, and then the CSV file is uploaded. This works fine for character and numeric data, but if your data includes dates or times, those are always treated as character data by the loadtable action that gets invoked behind-the-scenes. It is possible to create more customized data loaders. That is the topic of the next section.

Using Data Message Handlers

If you can't get your data properly uploaded using the simpler methods such as the loadtable action or the upload method, you might require the heavier duty technique called data message handlers. Data message handlers are Python classes that can handle requests from the CAS server for batches of data. The data message handler classes are used when invoking the addtable action. They set up the list of variable attributes, and they respond to requests from the server for chunks of data.

Although the data message handlers are more powerful than the upload method, they work only with the binary protocol to CAS. You cannot use them with the REST interface. If you use the REST interface, you must stick with the upload method, or you must load server-side tables using the loadtable action.

The SWAT package includes three primary data message handler classes: CASDataMsgHandler, PandasDataFrame, and DBAPI. The CASDataMsgHandler class is an abstract class, which means that it isn't meant to be used directly. It is used only as a subclass to create concrete data message handler classes such as PandasDataFrame and DBAPI.

As you might have suspected from the names, the PandasDataFrame data message handler class supports Pandas DataFrame objects, and the DBAPI data message handler class supports DB-API 2.0 compliant database connection objects. There are several subclasses of the PandasDataFrame class that correspond to many of the parsers and database connections that the Pandas package supplies. These include CSV, Text, HTML, Excel, JSON, SQLQuery, SQLTable, and Clipboard. These classes are convenient classes that bundle both the parsing of data with the data upload in one class. You could also use the Pandas parsers to create your own DataFrame, and then use the generic PandasDataFrame class to upload the result.

All of the data message handler classes are included in the swat.cas.datamsghandlers package. That's quite a lot to enter, so we'll import it as follows so that we can use the dmh alias.

```
In [34]: from swat.cas import datamsghandlers as dmh
```

To see the available data message handler classes, you can use Python's __subclasses__ method. Note that this method prints only the immediate subclasses. Therefore, you must traverse the subclasses as well, in order to see all of the classes.

```
In [35]: dmh.CASDataMsgHandler.__subclasses__()
Out[35]: [swat.cas.datamsghandlers.PandasDataFrame,
          swat.cas.datamsghandlers.DBAPI]

In [36]: dmh.PandasDataFrame.__subclasses__()
Out[36]:
[swat.cas.datamsghandlers.SQLTable,
 swat.cas.datamsghandlers.CSV,
 swat.cas.datamsghandlers.Text,
 swat.cas.datamsghandlers.JSON,
 swat.cas.datamsghandlers.HTML,
 swat.cas.datamsghandlers.SAS7BDAT,
 swat.cas.datamsghandlers.Clipboard,
 swat.cas.datamsghandlers.Excel,
 swat.cas.datamsghandlers.SQLQuery]
```

We've practiced loading the CSV data type. Now let's look at another data type in our next example: HTML.

The HTML Data Message Handler

For this example, we'll look at loading data from an HTML file. The URL that we use is https://www.fdic.gov/bank/individual/failed/banklist.html. This document has a nice table of information about banks that have failed since October 1, 2000. This is an especially good example because the data in this table includes character, numeric, and date-based columns.

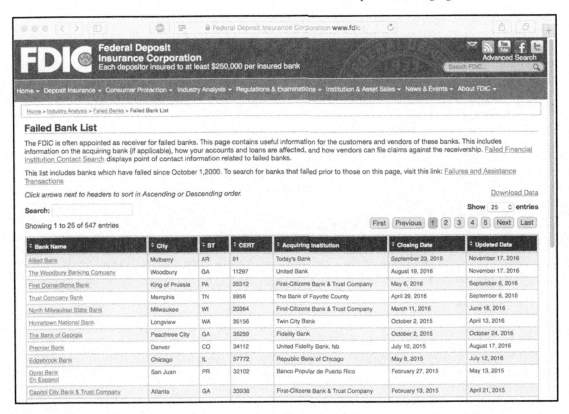

The HTML data message handler has an option to specify which table in the file should be read. In this case, the data table of bank information happens to be the first table in the file. To use the HTML data message handler, you create an instance of it using the URL of the HTML file as the first argument. We also specify index=0 as the index of the table to load, which is also the default.

```
In [37]: htmldmh = dmh.HTML('https://www.fdic.gov/bank/' +
    ....:                    'individual/failed/banklist.html',
    ....:                    index=0)
```

Now that we have a data message handler instance that is bound to some data, we can use it with the addtable action in order to upload the data to CAS. The addtable action takes various parameters that describe the data. These parameters are generated by the data message handler classes. Since the addtable action might not be the only action that uses data messages, the data message handler classes are set up to support various parameter sets. The parameters for the addtable action are accessed in the htmldmh.args.addtable property.

```
In [38]: htmldmh.args.addtable
Out[38]:
{'datamsghandler': <swat.cas.datamsghandlers.HTML at 0x7fd4ba20da20>,
 'reclen': 104,
 'vars': [{'length': 16,
   'name': 'Bank Name',
   'offset': 0,
   'rtype': 'CHAR',
   'type': 'VARCHAR'},
  {'length': 16,
```

```
            'name': 'City',
            'offset': 16,
            'rtype': 'CHAR',
            'type': 'VARCHAR'},
           {'length': 16,
            'name': 'ST',
            'offset': 32,
            'rtype': 'CHAR',
            'type': 'VARCHAR'},
           {'length': 8,
            'name': 'CERT',
            'offset': 48,
            'rtype': 'NUMERIC',
            'type': 'INT64'},
           {'length': 16,
            'name': 'Acquiring Institution',
            'offset': 56,
            'rtype': 'CHAR',
            'type': 'VARCHAR'},
           {'length': 16,
            'name': 'Closing Date',
            'offset': 72,
            'rtype': 'CHAR',
            'type': 'VARCHAR'},
           {'length': 16,
            'name': 'Updated Date',
            'offset': 88,
            'rtype': 'CHAR',
            'type': 'VARCHAR'}]}
```

As you can see from the preceding lengthy listing a lot of information is generated to describe the columns that are uploaded to CAS. You might also notice that there might be more columns in this code than are displayed in the HTML table. That's because some of the columns in the HTML table are hidden by CSS (Cascading Style Sheet) rules. Even though those columns are hidden from view, they still exist in the HTML table and are parsed by Pandas.

To use these generated parameters, we can take advantage of the Python ** operator, which expands a dictionary to keyword parameters in a method call. Since we are using the addtable action, the invocation appears as follows. Note that we must also specify a name for our table, and we specify a caslib name as well in order to be explicit about where the table should be created.

```
In [39]: out = conn.addtable(table='banklist', caslib='casuser',
   ....:                     **htmldmh.args.addtable)

In [40]: out
Out[40]:
[caslib]
```

```
 'CASUSER(username)'

[tableName]

 'BANKLIST'

[casTable]

 CASTable('BANKLIST', caslib='CASUSER(username)')

+ Elapsed: 0.109s, user: 0.003s, mem: 0.56mb
```

The output from addtable action looks just like the output from the loadtable action. We get a table name, a caslib name, and a CASTable object in the results. Now that we have the table loaded into CAS, we can query it in order to verify that it loaded as expected.

```
In [41]: conn.columninfo(table=dict(name='banklist',
    ....:                            caslib='casuser'))
Out[41]:
[ColumnInfo]
```

	Column	ID	Type	RawLength	FormattedLength	\
0	Bank Name	1	varchar	90	90	
1	City	2	varchar	17	17	
2	ST	3	varchar	2	2	
3	CERT	4	int64	8	12	
4	Acquiring Institution	5	varchar	65	65	
5	Closing Date	6	varchar	18	18	
6	Updated Date	7	varchar	18	18	

	NFL	NFD
0	0	0
1	0	0
2	0	0
3	0	0
4	0	0
5	0	0
6	0	0

```
+ Elapsed: 0.000628s, mem: 0.172mb
```

You might notice that even Pandas didn't automatically detect the date columns. You can use the parse_dates option for the Pandas HTML reader to specify where to look for dates in your data. In this case, the date columns are columns 5 and 6. In our data message handler parameters, we add parse_dates=[5, 6] in order to have the date columns entered correctly.

Also, in order to reload the data, you must create a new data message handler object. Once the data from a data message handler has been exhausted, it can't be used again.

```
In [42]: htmldmh = dmh.HTML('https://www.fdic.gov/bank/' +
    ....:                    'individual/failed/banklist.html',
    ....:                    index=0, parse_dates=[5, 6])

In [43]: out = conn.addtable(table='banklist', caslib='casuser',
    ....:                     replace=True,
    ....:                     **htmldmh.args.addtable)
```

```
In [44]: conn.columninfo(table=dict(name='banklist',
    ....:                            caslib='casuser'))
Out[44]:
[ColumnInfo]
```

	Column	ID	Type	RawLength	FormattedLength \
0	Bank Name	1	varchar	90	90
1	City	2	varchar	17	17
2	ST	3	varchar	2	2
3	CERT	4	int64	8	12
4	Acquiring Institution	5	varchar	65	65
5	Closing Date	6	**datetime**	8	20
6	Updated Date	7	**datetime**	8	20

	Format	NFL	NFD
0		0	0
1		0	0
2		0	0
3		0	0
4		0	0
5	**DATETIME**	0	0
6	**DATETIME**	0	0

```
+ Elapsed: 0.000638s, user: 0.001s, mem: 0.175mb
```

There are a couple of things to note about the preceding output. First, columns 5 and 6 now have the datetime type and a DATETIME format. We know that our date parsing option worked. Second, notice the replace=True option in our second call to the addtable action. If a table already exists in CAS with the given name, you receive an error and the existing table is not overwritten. In order for the addtable action to overwrite the existing table, you must supply the replace=True option.

We can fetch a sample of the data to verify that it looks correct. We specify sastypes=False on the fetch call so that it returns the data in the richest form possible.

```
In [45]: conn.fetch(table=dict(name='banklist',
    ....:                       caslib='casuser'),
    ....:           sastypes=False, to=3)
Out[45]:
[[Fetch]
```

Selected Rows from Table BANKLIST

	Bank Name	City	ST	CERT \
0	Allied Bank	Mulberry	AR	91
1	The Woodbury Banking Company	Woodbury	GA	11297
2	First CornerStone Bank	King of Prussia	PA	35312

	Acquiring Institution	Closing Date	Updated Date
0	Today's Bank	2016-09-23	2016-10-17
1	United Bank	2016-08-19	2016-10-17
2	First-Citizens Bank & Trust Company	2016-05-06	2016-09-06

```
+ Elapsed: 0.00369s, user: 0.001s, sys: 0.001s, mem: 1.69mb
```

In addition to parse_dates option, you can specify any of the Pandas read_html options that deal with parsing such as header, index_col, thousands, encoding, and so on.

Now that we have seen one example of how the data message handlers work, let's look at one that is likely to be popular: Excel.

The Excel Data Message Handler

The Excel data message handler works like the HTML data message handler. The only difference is that it uses the Pandas read_excel function "under the covers" rather than the read_html function. For this example, we use the Crop Year 2014 Disaster Declarations from the USDA website:

http://www.fsa.usda.gov/Internet/FSA_File/disaster_cty_list_ytd_14.xls[2]

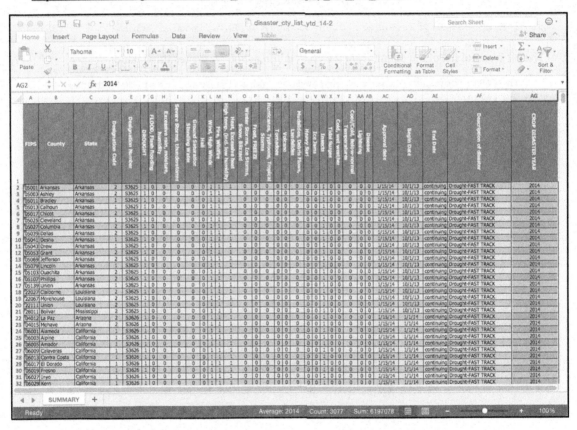

Like the HTML in the previous example, this file has a mixture of data types.

We start by creating a data message handler object, just like in the section about HTML.

```
In [46]: exceldmh = dmh.Excel('http://www.fsa.usda.gov/Internet/' +
   ....:                      'FSA_File/disaster_cty_list_ytd_14.xls')
```

Now we can add the table to the server using the addtable action.

```
In [47]: out = conn.addtable(table='crops', caslib='casuser',
   ....:                     **exceldmh.args.addtable)
```

```
In [48]: out
Out[48]:
[caslib]

 'CASUSER(username)'

[tableName]

 'CROPS'

[casTable]

 CASTable('CROPS', caslib='CASUSER(username)')

+ Elapsed: 0.992s, user: 0.007s, sys: 0.013s, mem: 2.83mb
```

Here is a partial list of the output from the columninfo action on the resulting table:

```
In [49]: conn.columninfo(table=dict(name='crops', caslib='casuser'))
Out[49]:
[ColumnInfo]
```

	Column	ID	Type	RawLength
0	FIPS	1	int64	8
1	County	2	varchar	17
2	State	3	varchar	14
3	Designation Code	4	int64	8
4	Designation Number	5	varchar	5
5	DROUGHT	6	int64	8
6	FLOOD, Flash flooding	7	int64	8
..	...	..	...	...
28	Approval date	29	varchar	0
29	Begin Date	30	datetime	8
30	End Date	31	varchar	10
31	Description of disaster	32	varchar	251
32	CROP DISASTER YEAR	33	int64	8
33	Unnamed: 33	34	varchar	101
34	Unnamed: 34	35	double	8

	FormattedLength	Format	NFL	NFD
0	12		0	0
1	17		0	0
2	14		0	0
3	12		0	0
4	5		0	0
5	12		0	0
6	12		0	0
..	...	...	...	...
28	0		0	0
29	20	DATETIME	0	0
30	10		0	0
31	251		0	0
32	12		0	0
33	101		0	0
34	12		0	0

```
[35 rows x 8 columns]

+ Elapsed: 0.00075s, user: 0.001s, mem: 0.166mb
```

You can see that unlike HTML, the datetime column was automatically detected and put into the correct column type. Again, you can pass any of the Pandas read_excel arguments to the Excel data message handler to modify the behavior of the parsing.

If you already have a Pandas DataFrame or you just want to use the Pandas file reader functions directly, you can advance to the PandasDataFrame data message handler.

The PandasDataFrame Data Message Handler

Most of the data message handlers that are supplied by SWAT are subclasses of the PandasDataFrame data message handler class. This data message handler class handles all of the work in computing the CAS data types, constructing data buffers, and passing them to the server. The subclasses merely have to parse data into a Pandas DataFrame and then pass it to the PandasDataFrame class to handle the transfer of data to the server. Rather than using one of the convenience classes, let's just use the PandasDataFrame class directly.

Just so that you can see what is going on behind the scenes in the Excel data message handler, let's repeat the example from the previous section but parse the Excel file on our own and then pass the result to PandasDataFrame. This exercise provides insight into writing your own data message handlers.

In the following example, we first parse the Excel file into a DataFrame, then we load it into CAS.

```
# Import Pandas
In [50]: import pandas as pd

# Read the Excel file into a DataFrame
In [51]: exceldf = pd.read_excel('http://www.fsa.usda.gov/Internet/' +
    ....:                        'FSA_File/disaster_cty_list_ytd_14.xls')

# Create a PandasDataFrame data message handler
In [52]: exceldmh = dmh.PandasDataFrame(exceldf)

# Add the table to the server
In [53]: out = conn.addtable(table='crops_df', caslib='casuser',
    ....:                     **exceldmh.args.addtable)

In [54]: out
Out[54]:
[caslib]

 'CASUSER(username)'

[tableName]

 'CROPS_DF'

[casTable]

 CASTable('CROPS_DF', caslib='CASUSER(username)')

+ Elapsed: 0.993s, user: 0.032s, sys: 0.006s, mem: 3.07mb
```

As you can see, there are a few extra steps involved in order to do the parsing of the Excel yourself. However, the PandasDataFrame data message handler gives you a lot of power since you can pass any DataFrame to it for loading on the server regardless of its origin.

In addition to files and URLs, Pandas DataFrames have additional methods to import data from databases. We look at these techniques in the following section.

Using Data Message Handlers with Databases

Pandas includes a few methods for importing data from a database, including read_sql_table and read_sql_query. These are used in the SQLTable and SQLQuery data message handler classes, respectively. The easiest way to demonstrate database connectivity is by using SQLite. SQLite is a self-contained SQL database engine that requires no configuration or setup. It can be used "out of the box."

We use the Iris data set again for this example. However, in this case, we load the data into an SQLite database, and then use the SQLTable and SQLQuery data message handlers to load the data from the database. Of course, Python supports many other commercial and non-commercial databases, so this same procedure will work with those as well.

```
# Import csv parser and sqlite3
In [55]: import csv

In [56]: import sqlite3

# Create an in-memory database
In [57]: sqlc = sqlite3.connect('iris.db')

In [58]: cur = sqlc.cursor()

# Define the table
In [59]: cur.execute('''CREATE TABLE iris (sepal_length REAL,
    ....:                                  sepal_width REAL,
    ....:                                  petal_length REAL,
    ....:                                  petal_width REAL,
    ....:                                  species CHAR(10));''')
Out[59]: <sqlite3.Cursor at 0x7fbf3eedd810>

# Parse the iris CSV file and format it as tuples
In [60]: with open('/u/username/data/iris.csv', 'r') as iris:
    ....:     data = csv.DictReader(iris)
    ....:     rows = [(x['sepal_length'],
    ....:              x['sepal_width'],
    ....:              x['petal_length'],
    ....:              x['petal_width'],
    ....:              x['species']) for x in data]

# Load the data into the database
In [61]: cur.executemany('''INSERT INTO iris (sepal_length,
    ....:                                     sepal_width,
    ....:                                     petal_length,
    ....:                                     petal_width,
    ....:                                     species)
    ....:                    VALUES (?, ?, ?, ?, ?);''', rows)
Out[61]: <sqlite3.Cursor at 0x7fbf3eedd810>

In [62]: sqlc.commit()
```

```
# Verify that the data looks correct
In [63]: cur.execute('SELECT * from iris')
Out[63]: <sqlite3.Cursor at 0x7fbf3b9afb90>

In [64]: cur.fetchmany(5)
Out[64]:
[(5.1, 3.5, 1.4, 0.2, 'setosa'),
 (4.9, 3.0, 1.4, 0.2, 'setosa'),
 (4.7, 3.2, 1.3, 0.2, 'setosa'),
 (4.6, 3.1, 1.5, 0.2, 'setosa'),
 (5.0, 3.6, 1.4, 0.2, 'setosa')]
```

Now that we have a database with a table in it, we can connect to the table using the SQLTable data message handler and load the iris table into CAS. To do this, we need to create an SQLAlchemy engine. Then, we pass that engine and the name of the table to SQLTable.

```
# Create the SQLAlchemy database engine
In [65]: eng = dmh.SQLTable.create_engine('sqlite:///iris.db')

# Create the data message handler
In [66]: sqldmh = dmh.SQLTable('iris', eng)

# Load the database table into CAS
In [67]: out = conn.addtable(table='iris_sql', caslib='casuser',
                             **sqldmh.args.addtable)

In [68]: out
Out[68]:
[caslib]

 'CASUSER(username)'

[tableName]

 'IRIS_SQL'

[casTable]

 CASTable('IRIS_SQL', caslib='CASUSER(username)')

+ Elapsed: 0.0585s, user: 0.002s, mem: 0.239mb

# Reality check the data in the server
In [69]: conn.columninfo(table=dict(name='iris_sql',
    ....:                            caslib='casuser'))
Out[69]:
[ColumnInfo]

            Column  ID     Type  RawLength  FormattedLength  NFL  NFD
0     sepal_length   1   double          8               12    0    0
1      sepal_width   2   double          8               12    0    0
2     petal_length   3   double          8               12    0    0
3      petal_width   4   double          8               12    0    0
4          species   5  varchar         10               10    0    0
```

```
+ Elapsed: 0.000665s, mem: 0.155mb

In [70]: conn.fetch(table=dict(name='iris_sql',
    ....:                       caslib='casuser'), to=5)
Out[70]:
[Fetch]

Selected Rows from Table IRIS_SQL

    sepal_length  sepal_width  petal_length  petal_width  species
0            5.1          3.5           1.4          0.2  setosa
1            4.9          3.0           1.4          0.2  setosa
2            4.7          3.2           1.3          0.2  setosa
3            4.6          3.1           1.5          0.2  setosa
4            5.0          3.6           1.4          0.2  setosa

+ Elapsed: 0.00278s, user: 0.002s, mem: 1.62mb
```

Using the SQLQuery data message handler, we can load the result of a SELECT statement in the database. The result may be a subset of a table or the result of a complex merge operation. Since we have only one table in our example database, we'll just use a WHERE clause to subset the data and then upload the data to CAS.

```
# Set up the SQLQuery data message handler with a query
In [71]: sqldmh = dmh.SQLQuery('''SELECT * FROM iris
    ....:                         WHERE species = "versicolor"
    ....:                         AND sepal_length > 6.6''', eng)

# Load the query result into CAS
In [72]: out = conn.addtable(table='iris_sql2', caslib='casuser',
    ....:                     **sqldmh.args.addtable)

In [73]: out
Out[73]:
[caslib]

 'CASUSER(username)'

[tableName]

 'IRIS_SQL2'

[casTable]

 CASTable('IRIS_SQL2', caslib='CASUSER(username)')

+ Elapsed: 0.0121s, user: 0.001s, mem: 0.212mb

# Reality check the result
In [74]: conn.fetch(table=dict(name='iris_sql2',
    ....:                      caslib='casuser'))
Out[74]:
[Fetch]
```

```
Selected Rows from Table IRIS_SQL2

    sepal_length  sepal_width  petal_length  petal_width      species
0            7.0          3.2           4.7          1.4  versicolor
1            6.9          3.1           4.9          1.5  versicolor
2            6.7          3.1           4.4          1.4  versicolor
3            6.8          2.8           4.8          1.4  versicolor
4            6.7          3.0           5.0          1.7  versicolor
5            6.7          3.1           4.7          1.5  versicolor

+ Elapsed: 0.00379s, user: 0.003s, sys: 0.001s, mem: 1.58mb
```

So far, all of the data message handlers that we have looked at use a Pandas DataFrame in the background. That means that all of the data gets loaded into memory before it gets shipped to CAS. For small tables, it's not an issue. But if you want to load large amounts of data, you could run into problems.

There is one data message handler that loads data from a Python DB-API 2.0 compliant database into CAS while just loading one buffer's worth of data from the database in each pass. That is the topic for the next section.

Streaming Data from a Database into a CAS Table

The DBAPI data message handler loads data a little differently than all of the previously discussed data message handlers. It connects to a database and requests just enough data to fill a buffer to pass on to CAS. Then, it sends the data to CAS and refills the buffer with the next set of data from the database. It fills and refills the buffer until all of the data from the query has been exhausted. This method of data loading prevents the data message handler from storing all of the data in memory before loading it into CAS.

In the code below, we load the SQLite database that we created earlier and execute a query on a cursor. The SQLite module and the cursor are used in creating the DBAPI data message handler instance. Then, just as with all of the other data message handlers, the data message handler is used to generate the parameters to the addtable action.

```
# Import SQLite package and load database
In [75]: import sqlite3

In [76]: sqlc = sqlite3.connect('iris.db')

# Perform query
In [77]: c = sqlc.cursor()

In [78]: c.execute('SELECT * FROM iris')
Out[78]: <sqlite3.Cursor at 0x7f44b98f3030>

# Create data message handler with the current query
In [79]: dbdmh = dmh.DBAPI(sqlite3, c, nrecs=10)

# Upload the data to the server
In [80]: conn.addtable(table='iris_db', caslib='casuser',
    ....:                 **dbdmh.args.addtable)
Out[80]:
[caslib]

 'CASUSER(username)'
```

```
[tableName]

 'IRIS_DB'

[casTable]

 CASTable('IRIS_DB', caslib='CASUSER(username)')

+ Elapsed: 0.0462s, user: 0.003s, mem: 0.239mb

# Reality check the data
In [81]: conn.columninfo(table=dict(name='iris_db',
   ....:                            caslib='casuser'))
Out[81]:
[ColumnInfo]
```

	Column	ID	Type	RawLength	FormattedLength	NFL	NFD
0	sepal_length	1	double	8	12	0	0
1	sepal_width	2	double	8	12	0	0
2	petal_length	3	double	8	12	0	0
3	petal_width	4	double	8	12	0	0
4	species	5	varchar	10	10	0	0

```
+ Elapsed: 0.000766s, user: 0.001s, mem: 0.173mb

In [82]: conn.fetch(table=dict(name='iris_db',
                     caslib='casuser'), to=5)
Out[82]:
[Fetch]

 Selected Rows from Table IRIS_DB
```

	sepal_length	sepal_width	petal_length	petal_width	species
0	5.1	3.5	1.4	0.2	setosa
1	4.9	3.0	1.4	0.2	setosa
2	4.7	3.2	1.3	0.2	setosa
3	4.6	3.1	1.5	0.2	setosa
4	5.0	3.6	1.4	0.2	setosa

```
+ Elapsed: 0.00347s, user: 0.003s, mem: 1.58mb
```

You might notice in the preceding code that when we created the DBAPI data message handler, we specified the nrecs keyword argument. Valid on all data message handler classes, this argument specifies the number of records to include in the buffer that is being sent to CAS. In this case, it also specifies the number of rows from the database that can be stored in-memory at one time before being sent to CAS. You can tune this value as needed, but most of the time the default is fine.

Although you can stream as much data into CAS as you need, using this method, if you have very large amounts of data, this method might not be the best way. There is a lot of overhead in getting values from a database, converting them to Python objects, converting them into a format that CAS can read, and then uploading them. Only you can decide whether any of the methods described in the previous sections are right for your use.

So far, in this chapter, we have covered ways of uploading data to CAS from commonly known data formats. If you have data that you want to access from less commonly known sources, you might want to consider writing a custom data message handler. That is covered in the next section.

Writing Your Own Data Message Handlers

Although most people are well-served with the supplied data message handler classes, you might have a custom data format or an unsupported database that you want to use for loading data into CAS. The first thing you need to decide is if using a Python-based data message handler is the appropriate choice. As mentioned in the previous section, there is a lot of overhead in transforming data into and out of Python objects as well as performance limitations of Python's looping constructs. So, if you have a large amount of data to move into CAS, you might want to consider exporting it to CSV or another common format that can be copied to the server and loaded through the loadtable action. However, if you have a reasonable amount of data for this technique and simply want a way to load custom data from Python, then writing your own data message handler could be the solution that you are looking for.

Writing a custom data message handler isn't difficult. Most of the work is already done for you in the CASDataMsgHandler class. This class does all of the low-level communication with the server and creates all of the needed data structures behind the scenes. All you need to do is create the attributes for each of the columns to be uploaded and implement a getrow method that can return a specified row of data from the underlying data store.

Here is a simple example that loads data from a hardcoded structure in the class definition:

```python
class MyDMH(dmh.CASDataMsgHandler):

    def __init__(self):
        self.data = [
            ('Alfred',  'M', 14, 69,   112.5),
            ('Alice',   'F', 13, 56.5, 84),
            ('Barbara', 'F', 13, 65.3, 98),
            ('Carol',   'F', 14, 62.8, 102.5),
            ('Henry',   'M', 14, 63.5, 102.5),
        ]

        vars = [
            dict(name='name', label='Name', type='varchar'),
            dict(name='sex', label='Sex', type='varchar'),
            dict(name='age', label='Age', type='int32'),
            dict(name='height', label='Height', type='double'),
            dict(name='weight', label='Weight', type='double'),
        ]

        super(MyDMH, self).__init__(vars)

    def getrow(self, row):
        try:
            return self.data[row]
        except IndexError:
            return
```

That's all there is to it. The __init__ constructor sets up the data source and the descriptions of the columns of data, and the getrow method returns the requested row of data. When there is no more data, the getrow method returns None. Note that the getrow method requests a row number rather than just the next row because if there is an error in sending a buffer of data, the same row could be requested repeatedly.

In this example, the data and the variable definitions are hardcoded, but you can use any available facilities to generate the data and the variable definitions, as necessary.

Now that we have a new data message handler to work with, let's try it out.

```
# Create an instance of the data message handler
In [83]: mydmh = MyDMH()

# Call addtable using the new data message handler
In [84]: conn.addtable(table='myclass', caslib='casuser',
   ....:                    **mydmh.args.addtable)
Out[84]:
[caslib]

 'CASUSER(username)'

[tableName]

 'MYCLASS'

[casTable]

 CASTable('MYCLASS', caslib='CASUSER(username)')

+ Elapsed: 0.00909s, user: 0.002s, mem: 0.221mb

# Reality check the resulting table
In [85]: conn.columninfo(table=dict(name='myclass',
   ....:                    caslib='casuser'))
Out[85]:
[ColumnInfo]
```

	Column	Label	ID	Type	RawLength	FormattedLength	NFL	NFD
0	name	Name	1	varchar	7	7	0	0
1	sex	Sex	2	varchar	1	1	0	0
2	age	Age	3	int32	4	12	0	0
3	height	Height	4	double	8	12	0	0
4	weight	Weight	5	double	8	12	0	0

```
+ Elapsed: 0.000739s, user: 0.001s, mem: 0.173mb

In [86]: conn.fetch(table=dict(name='myclass',
   ....:                    caslib='casuser'), to=5)
Out[86]:
[Fetch]

 Selected Rows from Table MYCLASS
```

	name	sex	age	height	weight
0	Alfred	M	14.0	69.0	112.5
1	Alice	F	13.0	56.5	84.0
2	Barbara	F	13.0	65.3	98.0
3	Carol	F	14.0	62.8	102.5
4	Henry	M	14.0	63.5	102.5

```
+ Elapsed: 0.00355s, user: 0.004s, mem: 1.58mb
```

As you can see from the preceding output, the data has been uploaded and is of the specified types. Let's take a closer look at how to specify the variable definitions.

Variable Definition Details

In the previous section, we created a custom data message handler that used hardcoded data and variable definitions. If you look at the documentation for the addtable action, you'll see that the variable definition section is slightly different. SWAT simplifies variable definitions somewhat since the buffer that is sent to CAS is also created by the SWAT client. The only required fields for the variable definitions in the vars parameter are name and type. The required field name specifies the name of the column, and type is the name of the CAS data type. Labels and SAS data formats for the columns can also be specified using the parameters label, format, and formattedlength. The remaining parameters in the addtable action should rarely be used.

Adding Data Transformers

Sometimes the data that you are accessing needs to be converted to another form before it can be sent to CAS. This situation is common when dealing with dates and times that might be read in as character data, but they should be converted to the proper numeric value for CAS. You could do this step yourself while reading in the data, but there is also a feature in data message handlers that can do it for you "on the fly." These are called *data transformers*.

Let's use our custom data message handler from the previous section to demonstrate transformers. We're going to add a column to the table called birthdate. The changes in the following code have been emphasized.

```
class MyDMH(dmh.CASDataMsgHandler):

    def __init__(self):
        self.data = [
            ('Alfred',  'M', 14, 69,   112.5, '1987-03-01'),
            ('Alice',   'F', 13, 56.5, 84,    '1988-06-12'),
            ('Barbara', 'F', 13, 65.3, 98,    '1988-12-13'),
            ('Carol',   'F', 14, 62.8, 102.5, '1987-04-17'),
            ('Henry',   'M', 14, 63.5, 102.5, '1987-01-30'),
        ]

        vars = [
            dict(name='name', label='Name', type='varchar'),
            dict(name='sex', label='Sex', type='varchar'),
            dict(name='age', label='Age', type='int32'),
            dict(name='height', label='Height', type='double'),
            dict(name='weight', label='Weight', type='double'),
            dict(name='birthdate', label='Birth Date',
                 type='date', format='DATE', formattedlength=12),
        ]

        super(MyDMH, self).__init__(vars)

    def getrow(self, row):
        try:
            return self.data[row]
```

```
    except IndexError:
        return
```

If we tried to use this class without modifications, it would fail because the last column is defined as a numeric type, but the column's data is a character type. We need to be able to transform the character data to the correct numeric value before it gets sent to CAS. To do that, we can use a utility function from the datamsghandlers module: str2cas_date. The utility functions str2cas_datetime and str2cas_time are also available.

```
class MyDMH(dmh.CASDataMsgHandler):

    def __init__(self):
        self.data = [
            ('Alfred',   'M', 14, 69,    112.5, '1987-03-01'),
            ('Alice',    'F', 13, 56.5, 84,     '1988-06-12'),
            ('Barbara',  'F', 13, 65.3, 98,     '1988-12-13'),
            ('Carol',    'F', 14, 62.8, 102.5, '1987-04-17'),
            ('Henry',    'M', 14, 63.5, 102.5, '1987-01-30'),
        ]

        vars = [
            dict(name='name', label='Name', type='varchar'),
            dict(name='sex', label='Sex', type='varchar'),
            dict(name='age', label='Age', type='int32'),
            dict(name='height', label='Height', type='double'),
            dict(name='weight', label='Weight', type='double'),
            dict(name='birthdate', label='Birth Date',
                type='date', format='DATE', formattedlength=12),
        ]

        transformers = {
            'birthdate': dmh.str2cas_date,
        }

        super(MyDMH, self).__init__(vars, transformers=transformers)

    def getrow(self, row):
        try:
            return self.data[row]
        except IndexError:
            return
```

We can now use our custom data message handler to upload dates in the correct form.

```
In [87]: mydmh = MyDMH()

In [88]: conn.addtable(table='myclass', caslib='casuser',
    ....:              replace=True,
    ....:              **mydmh.args.addtable)
Out[88]:
[caslib]

 'CASUSER(username)'

[tableName]
```

```
 'MYCLASS'

[casTable]

 CASTable('MYCLASS', caslib='CASUSER(username)')

+ Elapsed: 0.0232s, sys: 0.001s, mem: 0.254mb
```

In [89]: conn.columninfo(table=dict(name='myclass',
    ....:   caslib='casuser'))
Out[89]:
[ColumnInfo]

	Column	Label	ID	Type	RawLength	FormattedLength	\
0	name	Name	1	varchar	7	7	
1	sex	Sex	2	varchar	1	1	
2	age	Age	3	int32	4	12	
3	height	Height	4	double	8	12	
4	weight	Weight	5	double	8	12	
5	birthdate	Birth Date	6	date	4	12	

	Format	NFL	NFD
0		0	0
1		0	0
2		0	0
3		0	0
4		0	0
5	DATE	0	0

```
+ Elapsed: 0.00105s, mem: 0.172mb
```

In [90]: conn.fetch(table=dict(name='myclass', caslib='casuser'),
    ....:   sastypes=False)
Out[90]:
[Fetch]

Selected Rows from Table MYCLASS

	name	sex	age	height	weight	birthdate
0	Alfred	M	14	69.0	112.5	1987-03-01
1	Alice	F	13	56.5	84.0	1988-06-12
2	Barbara	F	13	65.3	98.0	1988-12-13
3	Carol	F	14	62.8	102.5	1987-04-17
4	Henry	M	14	63.5	102.5	1987-01-30

```
+ Elapsed: 0.00363s, user: 0.001s, sys: 0.002s, mem: 1.58mb
```

Although we used our custom data message handler to demonstrate data transformers, you can pass a dictionary of functions to any of the data message handler classes that are described in this chapter using the transformers parameter on the constructor.

That's all there is to writing your own data message handlers. You just need to create a subclass CASDataMsgHandler and override the __init__ constructor and the getrow method. The constructor creates the list of variable attributes and sets up the data source, and the getrow method returns a specified row of data. Transformers can be defined in the constructor to convert automatically data values to the appropriate form for CAS. With a custom data message handler, you have the capability to load data from any data source into CAS.

Managing Caslibs

We have used file system path-based caslibs throughout this chapter. These are the most common form of caslib, but there are other types such as HDFS, DNFS, ESP, and Hadoop. Coverage of all of them is beyond the scope of this book, but we cover how to set up and manage a new caslib in this section.

Creating a Caslib

Suppose that you have a collection of data files in a directory called /research/data/ and you want to create a caslib that enables access to only the files (but not the subdirectories) in that directory. The caslib should be accessible by all sessions and should not be the active caslib.

Consulting the documentation for the addcaslib action, you'll see that we need to use the parameters subdirs, session, and activeonadd. We'll also add a description just to be complete. Here is the code:

```
In [91]: conn.addcaslib(path='/research/data',
    ....:                caslib='research',
    ....:                description='Research Data',
    ....:                subdirs=False,
    ....:                session=False,
    ....:                activeonadd=False)
NOTE: Cloud Analytic Services added the caslib 'research'.
Out[91]:
[CASLibInfo]

         Name   Type    Description         Path Definition  \
 0   research   PATH    Research Data       /research/data/

      Subdirs  Local   Active   Personal   Hidden
 0        0.0    0.0      0.0        0.0      0.0

 + Elapsed: 0.00125s, user: 0.001s, mem: 0.12mb
```

As you can see from the output, we now have a new caslib that matches the parameters that we specified. Subdirs is set to 0, which indicates that subdirectories cannot be accessed. Local is set to 0, which means that it can be seen in any session. Note that this setting might require additional permissions for your user account. Active is set to 0, which means that it needs to be specified explicitly in action calls in conjunction with paths and table names.

Setting an Active Caslib

If you later decide that you want to make this caslib the active caslib, you can use the setsessopt action with the caslib parameter.

```
In [92]: conn.setsessopt(caslib='research')
NOTE: 'research' is now the active caslib.
Out[92]: + Elapsed: 0.00039s, mem: 0.085mb

In [92]: conn.caslibinfo(caslib='research')
Out[92]:
[CASLibInfo]
```

	Name	Type	Description	Path Definition	\
0	research	PATH	Research Data	/research/data/	

	Subdirs	Local	**Active**	Personal	Hidden
0	0.0	0.0	**1.0**	0.0	0.0

```
+ Elapsed: 0.000553s, mem: 0.0945mb
```

Dropping a Caslib

If you want to remove a caslib, it's as simple as using the dropcaslib action.

```
In [93]: conn.dropcaslib('research')
NOTE: 'CASUSER(username)' is now the active caslib.
NOTE: Cloud Analytic Services removed the caslib 'research'.
Out[93]: + Elapsed: 0.000631s, sys: 0.001s, mem: 0.0682mb
```

Notice that if you drop a caslib that was the active caslib, the active flag gets set on the previously active caslib. Also, if you drop a global caslib, multiple users might be affected.

Conclusion

We have covered a lot of ground in this chapter about getting your data into CAS. We started with learning what caslibs and CAS tables are. We then used the loadtable action to load data files that are stored on the server. From the client side, we used the upload method on the CAS connection object to upload local files, URLs, and Pandas DataFrames. The next step was to load data from various sources using data message handlers. Finally, we wrote our own custom data message handlers.

We also went through the process of creating and dropping a caslib so that you can create your own.

With all of these techniques, you now have the ability to get data into CAS in various ways and to organize it. In the next chapter, we describe the CASAction and CASTable objects.

[1] Support for data types might vary depending on your version of CAS.

[2] US Department of Agriculture. "Crop Year 2014 Disaster Declarations." US Department of Agriculture Data Catalog. Available http://www.fsa.usda.gov/Internet/FSA_File/disaster_cty_list_ytd_14.xls. Accessed December 6, 2016.

Chapter 5: The CASAction and CASTable Objects

All of the CAS action calls that we have covered so far look like method calls on an object (such as conn.loadtable(…), conn.columninfo(…), and so on). However, looks can be deceiving. Python has the ability to make any object look like a function. All of these action calls are actually instances of CASAction objects that are being called.

Another commonly used object in SWAT is the CASTable object. The CASTable object is the most important object in the SWAT package besides the CAS connection object. It keeps your CAS table settings in one object. Also, it enables you to directly call CAS actions on the table object rather than always having to supply them as a parameter to the action. There are other more advanced features that we discuss in the next chapter.

Both the CASAction and CASTable objects manage parameters using the same methods, which is the reason for discussing them together here. In this chapter, we first look at creating CASAction instances manually and interacting with them before we call the action on the server. Then we'll move on to managing CASTable parameters and running actions on the CASTable objects directly.

Getting Started with the CASAction Objects

One of the actions that we've used so far and that includes several options to play with is the fetch action. Here is a partial listing of the options from the IPython Help facility.

```
In [1]: import swat

In [2]: conn = swat.CAS('server-name.mycompany.com', 5570)

In [3]: conn.fetch?
```

```
Parameters
----------

table : dict or CASTable
    specifies the table name, caslib, and other common parameters.

...

from, from_ : int64, optional
    specifies the ordinal position of the first row to return.
    Default: 1

to : int64, optional
    specifies the ordinal position of the last row to return.
    Default: 20

format : boolean, optional
    when set to True, formats are applied to the variables.
    Default: False

maxrows : int32, optional
    specifies the maximum number of rows to return.
    Default: 1000

sastypes : boolean, optional
    when set to True, converts data to fixed-width character and
    double data types.
    Default: True

sortlocale : string, optional
    Locale to use for comparisons during sort.

sortby : list of dicts, optional
    specifies the variables and variable settings for sorting results.

    sortby[*].name : string
        specifies the variable name to use for sorting.

    sortby[*].order : string, optional
        specifies whether the ascending or descending value for the
        variable is used.
        Default: ASCENDING
        Values: ASCENDING, DESCENDING

    sortby[*].formatted : string, optional
        specifies whether the formatted or raw value for the variable
        is used.
        Default: RAW
        Values: FORMATTED, RAW

usebinary : boolean, optional
    Default: False
```

```
index : boolean, optional
    When set to True, adds a column named Index to the results that is
    to identify each row.
    Default: True

fetchvars : list of dicts, optional
    fetchvars[*].name : string
        specifies the name for the variable.

... truncated ...
```

Until now, we have specified these options only in the action call itself. However, an alternative is to create the CASAction instance manually and then to apply parameters, one at a time. To do this, you simply capitalize the first character of the action name.

```
In [4]: fa = conn.Fetch()

In [5]: type(fa)
Out[5]: swat.cas.actions.table.Fetch

In [6]: type(fa).__bases__
Out[6]: (swat.cas.actions.CASAction,)
```

This instance that we created is equivalent to the instance that you get by accessing conn.fetch(...). It just hasn't been executed yet. Let's call the Fetch instance with a table parameter as we've done in previous examples.

```
In [7]: out = conn.loadtable('data/iris.csv', caslib='casuser')

In [8]: fa(table=dict(name='data.iris', caslib='casuser'), to=5)
Out[8]:
[Fetch]

 Selected Rows from Table DATA.IRIS

     sepal_length  sepal_width  petal_length  petal_width  species
0             5.1          3.5           1.4          0.2  setosa
1             4.9          3.0           1.4          0.2  setosa
2             4.7          3.2           1.3          0.2  setosa
3             4.6          3.1           1.5          0.2  setosa
4             5.0          3.6           1.4          0.2  setosa

+ Elapsed: 0.00368s, user: 0.004s, mem: 1.65mb
```

Of course, the instance is reusable, so we can call it again with other options.

```
In [9]: fa(table=dict(name='data.iris', caslib='casuser'), to=5,
    ....:     sortby=['sepal_length', 'sepal_width'])
Out[9]:
[Fetch]

 Selected Rows from Table DATA.IRIS

     sepal_length  sepal_width  petal_length  petal_width  species
0             4.3          3.0           1.1          0.1  setosa
1             4.4          2.9           1.4          0.2  setosa
```

```
2            4.4          3.0          1.3          0.2   setosa
3            4.4          3.2          1.3          0.2   setosa
4            4.5          2.3          1.3          0.3   setosa

+ Elapsed: 0.0155s, user: 0.012s, sys: 0.003s, mem: 8.58mb
```

As you can see, the call syntax for actions can get verbose rather quickly. An alternative way of setting parameters can improve readability.

The CASAction class defines two methods for setting and getting parameters: set_params and get_params. These methods also exist in the singular forms, set_param and get_param, but they share the exact same syntax. To set parameters on an action instance, you use set_params. The most basic usage of set_params is to specify the parameter name as a string, followed by the parameter value as the next argument. For example, to set the table and to parameters as in the fetch call in the preceding example, we do the following:

```
In [10]: fa.set_params('table', dict(name='data.iris',
    ....:                             caslib='casuser'),
    ....:                 'to', 5)

In [11]: fa
Out[11]: ?.table.Fetch(table=dict(caslib='casuser',
                                   name='data.iris'), to=5)
```

As you can see, when we print the result of the action instance now, the parameters that we set are now embedded in the instance. If we were to call the action instance now, those parameters would automatically be used on the action call to the server.

```
In [12]: fa()
Out[12]:
[Fetch]

 Selected Rows from Table DATA.IRIS

     sepal_length  sepal_width  petal_length  petal_width  species
0             5.1          3.5          1.4          0.2   setosa
1             4.9          3.0          1.4          0.2   setosa
2             4.7          3.2          1.3          0.2   setosa
3             4.6          3.1          1.5          0.2   setosa
4             5.0          3.6          1.4          0.2   setosa

+ Elapsed: 0.00317s, user: 0.002s, mem: 1.64mb
```

In addition to the "name string followed by value" form, you can also set parameters using two-element tuples of name/value pairs or dictionaries of name/value pairs, or just using keyword arguments. Which one you use is a personal choice. Each of the following methods is equivalent to the method that was used to set parameters in the previous example:

```
# Tuples method
In [13]: fa.set_params(('table', dict(name='data.iris',
    ....:                              caslib='casuser')),
    ....:               ('to', 5))

# Dictionary method
In [14]: fa.set_params({'table': dict(name='data.iris',
```

```
    ....:                                    caslib='casuser'),
    ....:                       'to': 5})

# Keyword argument method
In [15]: fa.set_params(table=dict(name='data.iris',
    ....:                          caslib='casuser'),
    ....:             to=5)
```

Although you can mix all of the methods in a single call, to avoid a messy look, it is not recommended.

Even though setting options on a CASAction object in this manner cleans up our syntax, it doesn't solve the problem of nested parameters such as the table parameter. Such parameters still use the nested dictionary syntax that can become difficult to read. The good news is that all of the previously discussed forms of parameter setting, except for the keyword argument method, support a nested key syntax. Let's look at nested parameters in the next section.

Setting Nested Parameters

Rather than setting only top-level parameters, as in our previous examples, we can use a dot-separated notation to indicate subparameters. For example, if we want to set a table name of data.iris and a caslib of casuser, we can use the parameter names table.name and table.caslib as top-level parameter names.

```
In [16]: fa = conn.Fetch()

In [17]: fa.set_params('table.name', 'data.iris',
    ....:             'table.caslib', 'casuser')

In [18]: fa
Out[18]: ?.table.Fetch(table=dict(caslib='casuser', name='data.iris'))
```

As you can see from the preceding output, the dot-separated key names expand into levels of a hierarchy in the parameter structure. We can do this with the sortby parameter as well. There is a little trick to sortby though since it uses a list of dictionaries as its argument. To specify items of a list, you use integers as the key name.

```
In [19]: fa.set_params('sortby.0.name', 'petal_length',
    ....:             'sortby.0.formatted', 'raw',
    ....:             'sortby.1.name', 'petal_width',
    ....:             'sortby.1.formatted', 'raw')

In [20]: fa
Out[20]: ?.table.Fetch(sortby=dict(0=dict(formatted='raw',
                                          name='petal_length'),
                                   1=dict(formatted='raw',
                                          name='petal_width')),
                        table=dict(caslib='casuser', name='data.iris'))
```

Printing the resulting action representation might look a bit odd since the numeric keys are actually inserted into a dictionary rather than a list. However, both lists and numeric-indexed dictionaries work as action parameters equivalently.

We can now call the Fetch instance and see that the parameters set on the instance are now applied.

```
In [21]: fa(to=5)
Out[21]:
```

```
[Fetch]

Selected Rows from Table DATA.IRIS

    sepal_length  sepal_width  petal_length  petal_width  species
0            4.6          3.6           1.0          0.2  setosa
1            4.3          3.0           1.1          0.1  setosa
2            5.0          3.2           1.2          0.2  setosa
3            5.8          4.0           1.2          0.2  setosa
4            4.7          3.2           1.3          0.2  setosa

+ Elapsed: 0.0141s, user: 0.012s, sys: 0.002s, mem: 8.58mb
```

You might notice in the preceding code that we used keyword parameters on the action call itself even when we set parameters in set_params. This enables you to add or override parameters just for that call; those parameters are not embedded in the CASAction instance.

Although the nested parameter syntax is convenient and cleans up the syntax, the only downside is that the names contains periods (.), which are not allowed in keyword parameter names. However, there is yet another way to specify parameters that does enable you to use period-separated names. Let's look at that next.

Setting Parameters as Attributes

Rather than calling a method to set parameters on a CASAction object, you can simply set the attributes directly. This can actually be done at two levels in the action instance: 1) on the params attribute of the action instance, or 2) directly on the action instance. Let's look at the params version first.

In the previous section, we used the set_params method to set top-level and nested action parameters. Using the dot-separated syntax from that section, and applying that parameter name directly to the params attribute of the action instance, we can obtain the same effect.

```
In [22]: fa = conn.Fetch()

In [23]: fa.params.table.name = 'data.iris'

In [24]: fa.params.table.caslib = 'casuser'

In [25]: fa
Out[25]: ?.table.Fetch(table=dict(caslib='casuser',
                                   name='data.iris'))
```

Unfortunately, this won't work with the list syntax of the sortby parameter because Python won't accept a number as an attribute name. However, you can specify list indexes using bracket notation.

```
In [26]: fa.params.sortby[0].name = 'petal_width'

In [27]: fa.params.sortby[0].formatted = 'raw'

In [28]: fa.params.sortby[1].name = 'petal_length'

In [29]: fa.params.sortby[1].formatted = 'raw'

In [30]: fa
Out[30]: ?.table.Fetch(sortby=[dict(formatted='raw',
```

```
                                    name='petal_width'),
                        dict(formatted='raw',
                                name='petal_width')],
              table=dict(caslib='casuser',
                          name='data.iris'))
```

To avoid entering "fa.params.sortby" repeatedly, you can store the sortby parameter in a variable and act on it separately. Since the variable contains a reference to the underlying parameter structure, it embeds the parameters in the action instance.

```
In [31]: sortby = fa.params.table.sortby

In [32]: sortby[0].name = 'petal_length'

In [33]: sortby[0].formatted = 'raw'

In [34]: sortby[1].name = 'petal_width'

In [35]: sortby[1].formatted = 'raw'
```

Although this method might produce the nicest looking syntax for setting parameters, it also has a better chance of failing due to name collisions. The params attribute is a subclass of Python's dictionary. That means that if an action parameter name matches the name of a dictionary method or attribute, you might see some surprising behavior. Here is an example of setting a fictional parameter named pop, which is also a dictionary method.

```
In [36]: fa.params.pop = 'corn'

In [37]: fa
Out[37]: ?.table.Fetch(pop='corn',
                        table=dict(caslib='casuserhdfs',
                                    name='data.iris',
                        sortby=[dict(formatted='raw',
                                      name='petal_length'),
                                dict(formatted='raw',
                                      name='petal_width')]))

In [38]: fa.params.pop
Out[38]: <bound method xadict.pop of {'corn': 'foo', 'table': {'caslib':
'casuserhdfs', 'name': 'data.iris', 'sortby': {0: {'name':
'petal_length', 'formatted': 'raw'}, 1: {'name': 'petal_width',
'formatted': 'raw'}}}}>
```

Although setting the pop parameter works, you'll see that if you try to get the value of the pop parameter, you'll get the dictionary method returned instead. However, if you use the dictionary key syntax (for example, fa.params['pop']), you get the correct value back. This leads us to the second method of setting parameters as attributes. That is, you can set them directly on the CASAction instance.

Everything that we have just covered in setting action parameters on the params attribute also works directly on the CASAction instance. Essentially, it's just a shortcut to not having to enter .params while setting each parameter. It's just a slightly less formal form.

```
In [39]: fa
Out[39]: ?.table.Fetch()
```

```
In [40]: fa.table.name = 'data.iris'

In [41]: fa.table.caslib = 'casuser'

In [42]: fa
Out[42]: ?.table.Fetch(table=dict(caslib='casuser', name='data.iris'))

In [43]: fa(to=5)
Out[43]:
[Fetch]

 Selected Rows from Table DATA.IRIS

     sepal_length  sepal_width  petal_length  petal_width  species
  0           5.1          3.5           1.4          0.2  setosa
  1           4.9          3.0           1.4          0.2  setosa
  2           4.7          3.2           1.3          0.2  setosa
  3           4.6          3.1           1.5          0.2  setosa
  4           5.0          3.6           1.4          0.2  setosa

+ Elapsed: 0.00447s, user: 0.003s, sys: 0.002s, mem: 1.64mb
```

In addition to setting parameters, we can also get, delete, or check the existence of attributes. Let's see how in the next section.

Retrieving and Removing Action Parameters

Just like Python dictionaries, the parameters on CASAction objects can be retrieved and removed. You can also check for the existence of a parameter name. The methods that are used to retrieve action parameters by name are get_params and get_param. To remove parameters, you use del_params or del_param. And finally, to check for the existence of parameters, you use has_params or has_param.

All of the previously mentioned methods accept any number of strings as parameter names. The get_param method returns the value of the parameter, and get_params returns a dictionary of all parameter/value pairs that are requested. The parameter names can be top-level names, or you can specify a subparameter using the dot-separated notation from set_params.

```
In [44]: fa = conn.Fetch(to=5, table=dict(name='data.iris',
    ....:                                 caslib='casuser'))

In [45]: fa
Out[45]: ?.table.Fetch(table=dict(caslib='casuser', name='data.iris'),
                        to=5)

In [46]: fa.get_param('to')
Out[46]: 5

In [47]: fa.get_params('to', 'table.name')
Out[47]: {'table.name': 'data.iris', 'to': 5}
```

To delete action parameters, you simply specify the names of the parameters to delete in either del_param or del_params. Again, the key names can be top-level names or the dot-separated names of subparameters.

```
In [48]: fa.del_params('to', 'table.caslib')
```

```
In [49]: fa
Out[49]: ?.table.Fetch(table=dict(name='data.iris'))
```

Finally, to check the existence of parameters, you use has_params or has_param. In each case, all parameter names that are requested must exist in order for the method to return True.

```
In [50]: fa.has_param('table.caslib')
Out[50]: False

In [51]: fa.has_param('table.name')
Out[51]: True

In [52]: fa.has_param('table.name', 'to')
Out[52]: False
```

It is also possible to retrieve and delete parameters using the attribute syntax. We have already seen an example of getting parameters when we create the intermediate variable for sortby in order to minimize keystrokes. Here are some other examples:

```
In [53]: fa = conn.Fetch(to=5, table=dict(name='data.iris',
   ....:                                  caslib='casuser'))

In [54]: fa.table.name
Out[54]: 'data.iris'

In [55]: fa.table
Out[55]: {'caslib': 'casuserhdfs', 'name': 'data.iris'}

In [56]: del fa.table.caslib

In [57]: fa.table
Out[57]: {'name': 'data.iris'}
```

However, using attribute syntax is unreliable for checking for the existence of a parameter. The parameters dictionary is a bit magical. Whenever you request a key from the dictionary, the parameters dictionary automatically creates the object behind the scenes. Without the magic, the attribute setting method won't work. It would always throw attribute exceptions from Python. Therefore, to check for the existence of parameters, always use has_param or has_params.

Setting parameters and calling CAS actions is pretty much all there is to CASAction objects. Let's move on to something more interesting: the CASTable object. It supports all of the same parameter setting and getting methods of CASAction objects, but it also has the ability to clean up the duplication of code that results when specifying table parameters on action calls.

First Steps with the CASTable Object

The first task we need to do before we work with CASTable objects is to create a data table in CAS. Let's use one of the loadtable examples from the previous chapter that loads some data and returns a CASTable object.

```
In [58]: out = conn.loadtable('data/iris.csv', caslib='casuser')
NOTE: Cloud Analytic Services made the file data/iris.csv available as
table DATA.IRIS in caslib CASUSER(username).
```

```
In [59]: out
Out[59]:
[caslib]

 'CASUSER(username)'

[tableName]

 'DATA.IRIS'

[casTable]

 CASTable('DATA.IRIS', caslib='CASUSER(username)')

+ Elapsed: 0.000495s, user: 0.001s, mem: 0.123mb
```

We have mentioned previously that the CASResults object is a subclass of the Python OrderedDict class. Therefore, any of the keys that are seen in the key/value pairs can be accessed using Python's dictionary syntax.

```
In [60]: out['tableName']
Out[60]: 'DATA.IRIS'

In [61]: out['caslib']
Out[61]: 'CASUSER(username)'

In [62]: out['casTable']
Out[62]: CASTable('DATA.IRIS', caslib='CASUSER(username)')
```

In addition, the CASResults class enables you to access the keys as attributes as long as the key is a valid attribute name and doesn't collide with an existing attribute.

```
In [63]: out.casTable
Out[63]: CASTable('DATA.IRIS', caslib='CASUSER(username)')
```

If you look at the last output from the preceding code, you'll see that the CASTable object points to the DATA.IRIS table in the CASUSER(username) caslib. Also, the CASTable object is automatically bound to the session object that ran the loadtable action. That means that any actions that are executed on the CASTable object also run in that session. It also means that any action sets that get loaded into that session are automatically available on the CASTable object.

We used the tableinfo, columninfo, and fetch actions frequently in the previous chapter. Each time, we specified the table in the action call that was executed on the connection. Rather than doing that, you can execute the actions directly on the CASTable object.

```
In [64]: out.casTable.tableinfo()
Out[64]:
[TableInfo]

          Name  Rows  Columns  Encoding  CreateTimeFormatted  \
 0  DATA.IRIS   150        5     utf-8  03Nov2016:12:07:32

      ModTimeFormatted  JavaCharSet   CreateTime      ModTime  \
 0  03Nov2016:12:07:32         UTF8  1.793794e+09  1.793794e+09
```

```
      Global   Repeated    View     SourceName       SourceCaslib  \
0        0          0        0    data/iris.csv   CASUSER(username)

      Compressed Creator Modifier
0             0   username
```

+ Elapsed: 0.000651s, mem: 0.103mb

In [65]: out.**casTable.columninfo**()
Out[65]:
[ColumnInfo]

```
            Column   ID     Type  RawLength  FormattedLength  NFL  NFD
0     sepal_length    1   double          8               12    0    0
1      sepal_width    2   double          8               12    0    0
2     petal_length    3   double          8               12    0    0
3      petal_width    4   double          8               12    0    0
4          species    5  varchar         10               10    0    0
```

+ Elapsed: 0.00067s, mem: 0.169mb

In [66]: out.**casTable.fetch**(to=5)
Out[66]:
[Fetch]

Selected Rows from Table DATA.IRIS

```
     sepal_length  sepal_width  petal_length  petal_width species
0             5.1          3.5           1.4          0.2  setosa
1             4.9          3.0           1.4          0.2  setosa
2             4.7          3.2           1.3          0.2  setosa
3             4.6          3.1           1.5          0.2  setosa
4             5.0          3.6           1.4          0.2  setosa
```

+ Elapsed: 0.00349s, user: 0.003s, mem: 1.64mb

As you can see, calling actions on a table is much more concise and doesn't require you to know the names of the table or the caslib. We briefly showed you the summary action in the previous chapter as well. Executing the summary action on our table now appears as follows:

In [67]: out.**casTable.summary**()
Out[67]:
[Summary]

Descriptive Statistics for DATA.IRIS

```
            Column  Min  Max      N  NMiss      Mean     Sum       Std  \
0     sepal_length  4.3  7.9  150.0    0.0  5.843333   876.5  0.828066
1      sepal_width  2.0  4.4  150.0    0.0  3.054000   458.1  0.433594
2     petal_length  1.0  6.9  150.0    0.0  3.758667   563.8  1.764420
3      petal_width  0.1  2.5  150.0    0.0  1.198667   179.8  0.763161

      StdErr       Var      USS         CSS         CV     TValue  \
0   0.067611  0.685694  5223.85  102.168333  14.171126  86.425375
1   0.035403  0.188004  1427.05   28.012600  14.197587  86.264297
```

```
2  0.144064  3.113179  2583.00  463.863733  46.942721  26.090198
3  0.062312  0.582414   302.30   86.779733  63.667470  19.236588

            ProbT
0  3.331256e-129
1  4.374977e-129
2   1.994305e-57
3   3.209704e-42

+ Elapsed: 0.0269s, user: 0.026s, sys: 0.004s, mem: 1.74mb
```

Now that you see how easily this works, we can try a new action: correlation.

```
In [68]: out.casTable.correlation()
Out[68]:
[CorrSimple]

 Summary Statistics in Correlation Analysis for DATA.IRIS

          Variable      N      Mean     Sum    StdDev  Minimum  Maximum
0     sepal_length  150.0  5.843333  876.5  0.828066      4.3      7.9
1      sepal_width  150.0  3.054000  458.1  0.433594      2.0      4.4
2     petal_length  150.0  3.758667  563.8  1.764420      1.0      6.9
3      petal_width  150.0  1.198667  179.8  0.763161      0.1      2.5

[Correlation]

 Pearson Correlation Coefficients for DATA.IRIS

          Variable  sepal_length  sepal_width  petal_length  \
0     sepal_length      1.000000    -0.109369      0.871754
1      sepal_width     -0.109369     1.000000     -0.420516
2     petal_length      0.871754    -0.420516      1.000000
3      petal_width      0.817954    -0.356544      0.962757

      petal_width
0        0.817954
1       -0.356544
2        0.962757
3        1.000000

+ Elapsed: 0.0066s, user: 0.003s, sys: 0.008s, mem: 1.73mb
```

From these examples, you can see that any action that takes a table definition as an argument can be executed directly on the CASTable object. Even if the action doesn't take a table parameter, you can call it on the table. The CASTable object acts like a CAS connection object.

```
In [69]: out.casTable.userinfo()
Out[69]:
[userInfo]

 {'anonymous': False,
  'groups': ['users'],
  'hostAccount': True,
  'providedName': 'username',
  'providerName': 'Active Directory',
```

```
          'uniqueId': 'username',
          'userId': 'username'}

+ Elapsed: 0.000232s, mem: 0.0656mb
```

In addition to the action interface, you can also call many of the Pandas DataFrame methods and attributes. For example, rather than using the columninfo action to get column information, you can use the columns and dtypes attributes or the info method. We'll cover a few here. In the next chapter, we discuss the DataFrame compatibility features in more detail.

```
In [70]: out.casTable.columns
Out[70]: Index(['sepal_length', 'sepal_width', 'petal_length',
                 'petal_width', 'species'], dtype='object')

In [71]: out.casTable.dtypes
Out[71]:
sepal_length        double
sepal_width         double
petal_length        double
petal_width         double
species             varchar
dtype: object

In [72]: out.casTable.info()
CASTable('DATA.IRIS', caslib='CASUSER(username)')
Data columns (total 5 columns):
                N    Miss     Type
sepal_length   150   False    double
sepal_width    150   False    double
petal_length   150   False    double
petal_width    150   False    double
species        150   False    varchar
dtypes: double(4), varchar(1)
data size: 8450
vardata size: 1250
memory usage: 8528
```

Even the describe method works the same way as in DataFrame objects complete with the percentiles, include, and exclude options. Of course, with the power of CAS behind this, you can retrieve the statistics computed by the describe method on data sets that are much larger than those that are supported by a conventional Pandas DataFrame.

```
In [73]: out.casTable.describe(include=['all'], percentiles=[.4, .8])
Out[73]:
         sepal_length  sepal_width  petal_length  petal_width    species
count         150          150          150          150          150
unique         35           23           43           22            3
top             5            3          1.5          0.2      virginica
freq           10           26           14           28           50
mean      5.84333        3.054      3.75867      1.19867          NaN
std       0.828066     0.433594      1.76442     0.763161          NaN
min           4.3            2            1          0.1       setosa
40%           5.6            3          3.9         1.15          NaN
50%           5.8            3         4.35          1.3          NaN
80%          6.55          3.4         5.35          1.9          NaN
max           7.9          4.4          6.9          2.5      virginica
```

All of these attributes and methods call CAS actions in the background and reformat the results to the familiar DataFrame output types. So, if you are familiar with Pandas DataFrames, you should feel comfortable working with the CASTable objects this way.

So far, every table that we have used has resulted from a CAS action that loaded the table. But, what if you want to wrap previously loaded tables in a CASTable object? Continue reading the next section.

Manually Creating a CASTable Object

If a table is already loaded in CAS, you can wrap the table in a CASTable object. There is a CASTable method on CAS connection objects that creates CASTable objects that are registered with that connection. So, to create a CASTable object that references our DATA.IRIS table, we do the following.

```
# Create the CASTable object manually
In [74]: newtbl = conn.CASTable('data.iris', caslib='casuser')

# Verify the result
In [75]: newtbl
Out[75]: CASTable('data.iris', caslib='casuser')

In [76]: newtbl.columninfo()
Out[76]:
[ColumnInfo]

          Column  ID     Type  RawLength  FormattedLength  NFL  NFD
0   sepal_length   1   double          8               12    0    0
1    sepal_width   2   double          8               12    0    0
2   petal_length   3   double          8               12    0    0
3    petal_width   4   double          8               12    0    0
4        species   5  varchar         10               10   10    0
```

Now that we have shown the basics of CASTable objects, let's dig deeper into the action and parameter interfaces.

CASTable Action Interface

The action interface on CASTables is just like the action interface on CAS connection objects. The only difference is that if you call an action on a CASTable, any parameter that is marked as a table definition or a table name is automatically populated with the information from the CASTable parameters. We have already seen this in our previous examples with actions such as tableinfo, columninfo, and summary. The tableinfo action takes a table name and a caslib name as parameters, and the columninfo and summary actions take a table definition as a parameter. In either case, they were automatically populated.

We can see the result of this population of parameters by using an action class. As we mentioned at the beginning of this chapter, you can create an instance of an action by capitalizing the action name.

```
# Load the table
In [77]: out = conn.loadtable('data/iris.csv', caslib='casuser')
NOTE: Cloud Analytic Services made the file data/iris.csv available as
table DATA.IRIS in caslib CASUSER(username).

# Store the CASTable object in a new variable
In [78]: iris = out.casTable

# Create an instance of the summary action
```

```
In [79]: summ = iris.Summary()

# Display the summary action definition
In [80]: summ
Out[80]: ?.simple.Summary(__table__=CASTable('DATA.IRIS',
                              caslib='CASUSER(username)'))
```

As you can see, the table is now part of the action object. You can then call the action to verify that it executed on our table.

```
In [81]: summ()
Out[81]:
[Summary]

 Descriptive Statistics for DATA.IRIS

            Column  Min  Max      N  NMiss      Mean    Sum       Std  \
0     sepal_length  4.3  7.9  150.0    0.0  5.843333  876.5  0.828066
1      sepal_width  2.0  4.4  150.0    0.0  3.054000  458.1  0.433594
2     petal_length  1.0  6.9  150.0    0.0  3.758667  563.8  1.764420
3      petal_width  0.1  2.5  150.0    0.0  1.198667  179.8  0.763161

      StdErr       Var      USS         CSS         CV     TValue  \
0   0.067611  0.685694  5223.85  102.168333  14.171126  86.425375
1   0.035403  0.188004  1427.05   28.012600  14.197587  86.264297
2   0.144064  3.113179  2583.00  463.863733  46.942721  26.090198
3   0.062312  0.582414   302.30   86.779733  63.667470  19.236588

          ProbT
0  3.331256e-129
1  4.374977e-129
2   1.994305e-57
3   3.209704e-42

+ Elapsed: 0.00671s, user: 0.007s, sys: 0.002s, mem: 1.73mb
```

As we mentioned previously, just like CASAction objects, CASTable objects support the same parameter setting techniques. Let's look at some examples of managing parameters on CASTable objects.

Setting CASTable Parameters

So far, we've demonstrated how to set the table name and a caslib of CASTable. However, there are many more possible parameters to use on both input and output tables. To see the full listing of possible parameters, use the IPython **?** operator on an existing CASTable object. Here is a partial listing:

```
In [82]: iris?

...

Parameters
----------
name : string or CASTable
    specifies the name of the table to use.
caslib : string, optional
    specifies the caslib containing the table that you want to use
    with the action. By default, the active caslib is used. Specify a
```

```
           value only if you need to access a table from a different caslib.
      where : string, optional
           specifies an expression for subsetting the input data.
      groupby : list of dicts, optional
           specifies the names of the variables to use for grouping
           results.
      groupbyfmts : list, optional
           specifies the format to apply to each group-by variable. To
           avoid specifying a format for a group-by variable, use "" (no
           format).
           Default: []
      orderby : list of dicts, optional
           specifies the variables to use for ordering observations within
           partitions. This parameter applies to partitioned tables or it
           can be combined with groupBy variables when groupByMode is set to
           REDISTRIBUTE.
      computedvars : list of dicts, optional
           specifies the names of the computed variables to create. Specify
           an expression for each parameter in the computedvarsprogram
      parameter.
      computedvarsprogram : string, optional
           specifies an expression for each variable that you included in
           the computedvars parameter.
      groupbymode : string, optional
           specifies how the server creates groups.
           Default: NOSORT
           Values: NOSORT, REDISTRIBUTE
      computedondemand : boolean, optional
           when set to True, the computed variables specified in the
           compVars parameter are created when the table is loaded instead
           of when the action begins.
           Default: False
      singlepass : boolean, optional
           when set to True, the data does not create a transient table in
           the server. Setting this parameter to True can be efficient, but
           the data might not have stable ordering upon repeated runs.
           Default: False
      importoptions : dict, optional
           specifies the settings for reading a table from a data source.

      ... truncated ...
```

Let's create a CASTable object that includes a where parameter to subset the rows, and that also includes the computedvars and computedvarsprogram parameters to create computed columns. We haven't used computedvars or computedvarsprogram previously. The computedvarsprogram parameter is a string that contains code to create the values for the computed columns. The computedvars parameter is a list of the variable names that are created by computedvarsprogram and that show up as computed columns in the table.

One way to think of a CASTable object is as a "client-side view." Even though you are subsetting rows and creating computed columns, you do not modify the table on the server side at all. These parameters are simply stored on the CASTable object and are automatically sent as table parameters when actions are called on the CASTable object. The referenced CAS table is always the same, but any methods or CAS actions that are called on the CASTable object are performed using the view of the data from that object.

```
In [83]: iris = conn.CASTable('data.iris', caslib='casuser',
    ....:                      where='''sepal_length > 6.8 and
    ....:                               species = "virginica"''',
    ....:                      computedvars=['length_factor'],
    ....:                      computedvarsprogram='''length_factor =
    ....:                               sepal_length * petal_length;''')

In [84]: iris
Out[84]: CASTable('data.iris', caslib='casuser',
                   where='sepal_length > 6.8 and
                          species = "virginica"',
                   computedvars=['length_factor'],
                   computedvarsprogram='length_factor =
                          sepal_length * petal_length;')
```

```
# Use the fetchvars= parameter to only fetch specified columns
In [85]: iris.fetch(fetchvars=['sepal_length', 'petal_length',
    ....:                      'length_factor'])
Out[85]:
[Fetch]
```

```
Selected Rows from Table DATA.IRIS

     sepal_length  petal_length  length_factor
0             6.9           5.4          37.26
1             6.9           5.1          35.19
2             7.1           5.9          41.89
3             7.6           6.6          50.16
4             7.3           6.3          45.99
5             7.2           6.1          43.92
6             7.7           6.7          51.59
7             7.7           6.9          53.13
8             6.9           5.7          39.33
9             7.7           6.7          51.59
10            7.2           6.0          43.20
11            7.2           5.8          41.76
12            7.4           6.1          45.14
13            7.9           6.4          50.56
14            7.7           6.1          46.97
```

```
+ Elapsed: 0.0135s, user: 0.01s, sys: 0.007s, mem: 2.55mb
```

CASTable objects can also be used as output tables.

```
In [86]: outtbl = conn.CASTable('summout', caslib='casuser',
    ....:                        promote=True)

In [87]: iris.summary(casout=outtbl)
Out[87]:
[OutputCasTables]

               casLib     Name   Rows  Columns  \
0  CASUSER(username)   summout      5       15

                                   casTable
0  CASTable('summout', caslib='CASUSER(...
```

```
+ Elapsed: 0.0179s, user: 0.012s, sys: 0.011s, mem: 2.72mb
```

In [88]: outtbl.fetch()
Out[88]:
[Fetch]

Selected Rows from Table SUMMOUT

	Column	_Min_	_Max_	_NObs_	_NMiss_	_Mean_	_Sum_	\
0	sepal_length	6.90	7.90	15.0	0.0	7.360000	110.40	
1	sepal_width	2.60	3.80	15.0	0.0	3.126667	46.90	
2	petal_length	5.10	6.90	15.0	0.0	6.120000	91.80	
3	petal_width	1.60	2.50	15.0	0.0	2.086667	31.30	
4	length_factor	35.19	53.13	15.0	0.0	45.178667	677.68	

	Std	_StdErr_	_Var_	_USS_	_CSS_	_CV_	\
0	0.337639	0.087178	0.114000	814.1400	1.596000	4.587485	
1	0.353486	0.091270	0.124952	148.3900	1.749333	11.305524	
2	0.501711	0.129541	0.251714	565.3400	3.524000	8.197898	
3	0.241622	0.062386	0.058381	66.1300	0.817333	11.579305	
4	5.527611	1.427223	30.554484	31044.4416	427.762773	12.235003	

	_T_	_PRT_
0	84.424990	2.332581e-20
1	34.257443	6.662768e-15
2	47.243615	7.680656e-17
3	33.447458	9.278838e-15
4	31.654945	1.987447e-14

```
+ Elapsed: 0.00403s, user: 0.003s, mem: 1.67mb
```

You might notice that the outtbl variable worked with the fetch action even when the CASTable object contained output table parameters (such as promote=True). The CASTable objects are polymorphic and send only the parameters that are appropriate for the current context. In this case, the context was an input table parameter, so the promote=True parameter was removed automatically before the action call was made.

In addition to setting parameters on the constructor, you can also set parameters on existing instances. Just like with CASAction objects, these options can be set using: 1) the function interface, and 2) the attribute/dictionary interface.

Managing Parameters Using the Method Interface

The formal way of setting parameters is to use the set_param, get_param, has_param, and del_param methods. These methods work the same way as they do with CASAction objects.

Just as with CAS action calls, CASTable definitions can be verbose. Here is an example:

```
conn.CASTable('data.iris', caslib='casuser',
                    where='''sepal_length > 6.8 and
                          species = "virginica"''',
                    computedvars=['length_factor'],
                    computedvarsprogram='''length_factor
                      = sepal_length * petal_length;''')
```

This CASTable definition uses only a simple where clause and specifies a computed column. However, readability would be difficult for a table that contains more computed columns and other parameters. We can use the same technique of setting individual parameters from the CASAction section to enhance readability. Let's start with creating a CASTable object with a name and a caslib. Then, we add the where parameter and the computed column parameters separately.

```
In [89]: iris = conn.CASTable('data.iris', caslib='casuser')

In [90]: iris.set_param('where',
            'sepal_length > 6.8 and species = "viginica"')

In [91]: iris.set_param('computedvars', ['length_factor'])

In [92]: iris.set_param('computedvarsprogram',
            'length_factor = sepal_length * petal_length;')

In [93]: iris
Out[93]: CASTable('data.iris', caslib='casuser',
                computedvars=['length_factor'],
                computedvarsprogram='length_factor =
                                    sepal_length * petal_length;',
                where='sepal_length > 6.8 and
                        species = "virginica"')

In [94]: iris.fetch(to=5, fetchvars=['sepal_length', 'petal_length',
                                    'length_factor'])
Out[94]:
[Fetch]

 Selected Rows from Table DATA.IRIS

     sepal_length  petal_length   length_factor
  0           6.9           5.4           37.26
  1           6.9           5.1           35.19
  2           7.1           5.9           41.89
  3           7.6           6.6           50.16
  4           7.3           6.3           45.99

+ Elapsed: 0.0167s, user: 0.015s, sys: 0.004s, mem: 2.48mb
```

All of the forms of set_param on CASAction objects work as well. This includes using two-element tuples, dictionaries, and keyword arguments. Therefore, all of the following are equivalent:

```
# String / value pairs
In [95]: iris.set_params('where', '''sepal_length > 6.8 and
                                species = "virginica"''',
    ....:            'computedvars', ['length_factor'],
    ....:        'computedvarsprogram', '''length_factor =
                                sepal_length * petal_length;''')

# Tuples
In [95]: iris.set_params(('where', '''sepal_length > 6.8 and
                                species = "virginica"'''),
    ....:            ('computedvars', ['length_factor']),
    ....:        ('computedvarsprogram', '''length_factor =
                                sepal_length * petal_length;'''))
```

```
# Keyword arguments
In [96]: iris.set_params(where='''sepal_length > 6.8 and
    ....:                       species = "virginica"''',
    ....:            computedvars=['length_factor'],
    ....:            computedvarsprogram='''length_factor =
    ....:                       sepal_length * petal_length;''')

# Dictionaries
In [97]: iris.set_params({'where': '''sepal_length > 6.8 and
    ....:                       species = "virginica"''',
    ....:            'computedvars': ['length_factor'],
    ....:            'computedvarsprogram': '''length_factor =
    ....:                       sepal_length * petal_length;'''})
```

You can also check for the existence of parameters and then retrieve them just like on CASAction objects.

```
In [98]: iris.has_param('where')
Out[98]: True

In [99]: iris.has_param('groupby')
Out[99]: False

In [100]: iris.get_param('where')
Out[100]: 'sepal_length > 6.8 and species = "virginica"'

In [101]: iris.get_params('where', 'computedvars')
Out[101]: {'computedvars': ['length_factor'],
           'where': 'sepal_length > 6.8 and species = "virginica"'}
```

Finally, you can delete table parameters using del_param or del_params.

```
In [102]: iris
Out[102]: CASTable('data.iris', caslib='casuser',
                   computedvars=['length_factor'],
                   computedvarsprogram='length_factor =
                               sepal_length * petal_length;',
               where='sepal_length > 6.8 and
                       species = "virginica"')

In [103]: iris.del_params('computedvars', 'computedvarsprogram')

In [104]: iris
Out[104]: CASTable('data.iris', caslib='casuser',
                   where='sepal_length > 6.8 and
                           species = "virginica"')
```

You might recall that in addition to a function interface, CASAction objects also enable you to set parameters using an attribute interface. This is true of CASTable objects as well.

Managing Parameters Using the Attribute Interface

CASTable parameters can be changed using an attribute-style interface as well as the previously described function-style interface.

```
In [105]: iris = conn.CASTable('data.iris', caslib='casuser')
In [106]: iris
Out[106]: CASTable('data.iris', caslib='casuser')

In [107]: iris.params.where = '''sepal_length > 6.8 and
    ....:                        species = "virginica"'''

In [108]: iris
Out[108]: CASTable('data.iris', caslib='casuser',
                where='sepal_length > 6.8 and
                    species = "virginica"')
```

If your parameters include lists, you can use array indexing syntax to set them individually.

```
In [109]: iris.params.groupby[0] = 'species'

In [110]: iris.params.groupby[1] = 'sepal_length'

In [111]: iris
Out[111]: CASTable('data.iris', caslib='casuser',
                groupby=['species', 'sepal_length'],
                where='sepal_length > 6.8 and
                    species = "virginica"')
```

Retrieving parameter values and deleting them also work with Python's attribute syntax.

```
In [112]: iris.params.groupby
Out[112]: {0: 'length_factor', 1: 'width_factor'}

In [113]: del iris.params.groupby

In [114]: del iris.params.where

In [115]: iris
Out[115]: CASTable('data.iris', caslib='casuser')
```

You might notice that the groupby parameter is displayed as a dictionary. That is simply because when you add keys of an ordered list individually like we did in the previous example, the underlying structure ends up being a dictionary. When the parameters are passed to CAS, they are converted to an ordered list automatically. So, dictionaries with integer keys are equivalent to lists as far as SWAT is concerned.

Parameters can also be set directly on the CASTable object rather than on the params level. You must be more careful with this form because the chance of name collisions is much greater with other methods and attributes on the CASTable object.

```
In [116]: iris
Out[116]: CASTable('data.iris', caslib='casuser')

In [117]: iris.groupby = ['species']

In [118]: iris.where = '''sepal_length > 6.8 and
```

```
     .....:                    species = "virginica"'''

In [119]: iris
Out[119]: CASTable('data.iris', caslib='casuser',
                groupby=['species'],
                where='sepal_length > 6.8 and species = "virginica"')
```

That covers just about anything you need to do with CASTable parameters. We'll show you how to materialize them in a real table in the server in the next section.

Materializing CASTable Parameters

We mentioned previously that CASTable objects are essentially client-side views of the data in a CAS table. Setting parameters on a CASTable object has no effect on the table in the server. Once you have created a CASTable with all of your computed columns and filters, you might want to materialize them on to the server as an in-memory table so that you can access it from other CASTable references. You can use the partition action to do this. Note that this is not the only use for the partition action, but it works for this case as well. Just as with loadtable, the partition action output has a casTable key that contains a reference to the new CASTable object.

```
In [122]: sub_iris = iris.partition()

In [123]: sub_iris
[caslib]

 'CASUSER(username)'

[tableName]

 '_T_ZX6QZEVP_6FIIJT25_2EYMPQQARS'

[rowsTransferred]

 0

[shuffleWaitTime]

 0.0

[minShuffleWaitTime]

 1e+300

[maxShuffleWaitTime]

 0.0

[averageShuffleWaitTime]

 0.0

[casTable]

CASTable('_T_ZX6QZEVP_6FIIJT25_2EYMPQQARS',
         caslib='CASUSER(username)')
```

```
+ Elapsed: 0.00355s, user: 0.003s, mem: 1.62mb
```

In [124]: sub_iris = sub_iris.casTable

In [125]: sub_iris.fetch()
Out[125]:
[Fetch]

Selected Rows from Table _T_ZX6QZEVP_6FIIJT25_2EYMPQQARS

	sepal_length	sepal_width	petal_length	petal_width	species
0	6.9	3.1	5.4	2.1	virginica
1	6.9	3.1	5.1	2.3	virginica
2	7.1	3.0	5.9	2.1	virginica
3	7.6	3.0	6.6	2.1	virginica
4	7.3	2.9	6.3	1.8	virginica
5	7.2	3.6	6.1	2.5	virginica
6	7.7	3.8	6.7	2.2	virginica
7	7.7	2.6	6.9	2.3	virginica
8	6.9	3.2	5.7	2.3	virginica
9	7.7	2.8	6.7	2.0	virginica
10	7.2	3.2	6.0	1.8	virginica
11	7.2	3.0	5.8	1.6	virginica
12	7.4	2.8	6.1	1.9	virginica
13	7.9	3.8	6.4	2.0	virginica
14	7.7	3.0	6.1	2.3	virginica

```
+ Elapsed: 0.0034s, user: 0.003s, mem: 1.57mb
```

Conclusion

In this chapter, we introduced the CASAction and CASTable objects, and showed you various ways of setting parameters on CASAction and CASTable instances. Depending on your coding style or how your parameters are being generated, you can choose the appropriate method for setting your action parameters. Now that we have seen the basics of the CASAction and CASTable objects, let's move on to advanced usage of the CASTable objects.

Chapter 6: Working with CAS Tables

In the previous chapter, we introduced the CASAction and CASTable objects. We covered the methods of setting parameters and calling actions on a CASTable object, but our coverage only included the basics. In this chapter we continue to work on CASTable objects on a variety of topics, including the DataFrame APIs, exporting data, creating visualizations, fetching and indexing, creating temporary columns, and by group processing.

Using CASTable Objects like a DataFrame

The Pandas DataFrame has taken the elegance of the Python programming language and applied it beautifully to data structures that are used in everyday statistics and data analysis. It supports many basic statistical analyses on data sets that can fit into memory on your computer, and it also defines interesting ways to index data sets using Python's "fancy" indexing syntax.

The CASTable object adopts these same APIs and applies them to tables in CAS. This means that you can use the familiar DataFrame API on CAS tables. The result types that are returned by the CASTable versions of the Pandas DataFrame methods are, in most cases, the same as those that are returned by DataFrame methods of the same name. The primary difference is that the amount of data that is referenced by a CASTable object can be much greater than what can be handled on a single desktop machine.

In the following sections, we start with some methods and attributes that describe the CAS table itself, and then move on to methods for simple statistics and other areas of the DataFrame API.

CAS Table Introspection

Basic information about CAS tables includes the names of the columns, the data types, and the number of rows. Until now, we've used the tableinfo and columninfo CAS actions to get that information. However, we can also use the DataFrame attributes and methods for the same purpose. Probably the most common attribute that is used to get this type of information is the columns attribute. It simply lists the names of all of the columns in the table. We load the Iris data into both a CAS table and a DataFrame for comparison.

```
# Import pandas
In [1]: import pandas as pd

# Read iris.csv into a DataFrame
In [2]: df = pd.read_csv('/u/username/data/iris.csv')

In [3]: df.columns
Out[3]: Index(['sepal_length', 'sepal_width', 'petal_length',
               'petal_width', 'species'], dtype='object')

# Load iris.csv into a CAS table
In [4]: tbl = conn.loadtable('data/iris.csv',
                            caslib='casuser').casTable
NOTE: Cloud Analytic Services made the file data/iris.csv available as
table DATA.IRIS in caslib CASUSER(username).

In [5]: tbl.columns
Out[5]: Index(['sepal_length', 'sepal_width', 'petal_length',
               'petal_width', 'species'], dtype='object')
```

In both cases, you see that the columns attribute returns a Pandas Index object that contains the names of the columns. You can also find out the data types using dtypes.

```
In [6]: df.dtypes
Out[6]:
sepal_length      float64
sepal_width       float64
petal_length      float64
petal_width       float64
species            object
dtype: object

In [7]: tbl.dtypes
Out[7]:
sepal_length       double
sepal_width        double
petal_length       double
petal_width        double
species           varchar
dtype: object
```

In this case, you'll see a small difference. The data types that are supported by DataFrames and those that are supported by CAS tables have different names. The different names don't matter since the Python float64 types is equivalent to the CAS double type. However, if you use the type names for filtering in other parts of the API, you want to use the CAS type names.

You can also get the counts of each data type using the get_dtype_counts method.

```
In [8]: df.get_dtype_counts()
Out[8]:
float64    4
object     1
dtype: int64

In [9]: tbl.get_dtype_counts()
Out[9]:
double     4
varchar    1
dtype: int64
```

To obtain the size or the shape of a CAS table, you use the size and the shape attributes just as in a DataFrame.

```
In [10]: tbl.size
Out[10]: 750

In [11]: tbl.shape
Out[11]: (150, 5)
```

For a quick summary of information about the entire table, you can use the info method.

```
In [12]: tbl.info()
CASTable('DATA.IRIS', caslib='CASUSER(username)')
Data columns (total 5 columns):
                N    Miss     Type
sepal_length   150   False    double
sepal_width    150   False    double
petal_length   150   False    double
petal_width    150   False    double
species        150   False    varchar
dtypes: double(4), varchar(1)
data size: 8450
vardata size: 1250
memory usage: 8656
```

Finally, to get a sample of the data, you can use the head or tail methods. Keep in mind that CAS commonly uses distributed data storage that has no particular sort order, so the values that you get from the head and tail methods are not deterministic unless the table has a specified sort order, which is covered later in this chapter.

```
In [13]: tbl.head(n=3)
Out[13]:
Selected Rows from Table DATA.IRIS

     sepal_length  sepal_width  petal_length  petal_width  species
0           5.1          3.5           1.4           0.2  setosa
1           4.9          3.0           1.4           0.2  setosa
2           4.7          3.2           1.3           0.2  setosa

In [14]: tbl.tail(n=4)
Out[14]:
Selected Rows from Table DATA.IRIS
```

```
       sepal_length  sepal_width  petal_length  petal_width    species
146             6.4          2.8           5.6          2.2  virginica
147             6.3          2.8           5.1          1.5  virginica
148             6.1          2.6           5.6          1.4  virginica
149             7.7          3.0           6.1          2.3  virginica
```

As you can see from the preceding code, the head and tail methods accept the n parameter to indicate the number of records to retrieve (the default is 5). CAS commonly deals with large data sets and you might not want to bring all of the variables back. Using the columns parameter, it is possible to subset the columns that are retrieved.

```
In [15]: tbl.head(columns=['sepal_length', 'petal_length'])
Out[15]:
Selected Rows from Table DATA.IRIS

   sepal_length  petal_length
0           5.1           1.4
1           4.9           1.4
2           4.7           1.3
3           4.6           1.5
4           5.0           1.4
```

Although this part of the DataFrame API is fairly simple, it already shows how easy working with CASTable objects can be. Let's move on to computing some basic statistics.

Computing Simple Statistics

A common DataFrame method that is used to learn about the characteristics of your data is the describe method. Here is a simple example of getting basic summary statistics from a DataFrame and a CASTable, both using the describe method.

```
# Run the describe method on a DataFrame
In [16]: desc = df.describe()

In [17]: desc
Out[17]:
       sepal_length  sepal_width  petal_length  petal_width
count    150.000000   150.000000    150.000000   150.000000
mean       5.843333     3.054000      3.758667     1.198667
std        0.828066     0.433594      1.764420     0.763161
min        4.300000     2.000000      1.000000     0.100000
25%        5.100000     2.800000      1.600000     0.300000
50%        5.800000     3.000000      4.350000     1.300000
75%        6.400000     3.300000      5.100000     1.800000
max        7.900000     4.400000      6.900000     2.500000

In [18]: type(desc)
Out[18]: pandas.core.frame.DataFrame

# Run the describe method on a CASTable
In [19]: casdesc = tbl.describe()
```

```
In [20]: casdesc
Out[20]:
        sepal_length  sepal_width  petal_length  petal_width
count     150.000000   150.000000    150.000000   150.000000
mean        5.843333     3.054000      3.758667     1.198667
std         0.828066     0.433594      1.764420     0.763161
min         4.300000     2.000000      1.000000     0.100000
25%         5.100000     2.800000      1.600000     0.300000
50%         5.800000     3.000000      4.350000     1.300000
75%         6.400000     3.300000      5.100000     1.800000
max         7.900000     4.400000      6.900000     2.500000


In [21]: type(casdesc)
Out[21]: pandas.core.frame.DataFrame
```

As you can see, in both cases, we run the describe method and get back the same results even in the same data type. This might not seem impressive for only 150 records, but how about running it on a larger collection? Our table contains 70 million rows and 46 columns, 35 of which are numeric. Running the describe method on our grid of 48 nodes requires only seconds.

```
In [22]: conn.tableinfo('datasources.megacorp5m')
Out[22]:
[TableInfo]

                       Name      Rows   Columns  Encoding  \
0   DATASOURCES.MEGACORP5M  70732833        46    utf-8

    CreateTimeFormatted      ModTimeFormatted JavaCharSet    CreateTime  \
0   01Mar2016:12:57:08   01Mar2016:12:57:08         UTF8  1.772456e+09

          ModTime  Global  Repeated  View                SourceName  \
0   1.772456e+09       0         0     0  datasources/megacorp5m.csv

    SourceCaslib  Compressed
0      CASTestTmp           0


In [23]: %time mega.describe()
CPU times: user 261 ms, sys: 24 ms, total: 285 ms
Wall time: 12.1 s
Out[23]:
               Date        DateByYear        DateByMonth  \
count  70732833.000000  70732833.000000  70732833.000000
mean      14389.447935     14209.155789     14374.679408
std        2653.775328      2651.783194      2653.766319
min        7305.000000      7305.000000      7305.000000
25%       12460.000000     12419.000000     12450.000000
50%       14605.000000     14245.000000     14579.000000
75%       16517.000000     16437.000000     16496.000000
max       18992.000000     18628.000000     18962.000000

 ...

         StateLatitude     CityLongitude      CityLatitude
count  70732833.000000  70119950.000000  70119950.000000
mean         35.090183       -95.995716        34.365083
std           4.313599        12.363752         5.171787
```

```
min             31.051683      -122.418330        27.800283
25%             31.169358       -97.396111        30.694170
50%             32.615651       -92.289440        33.509170
75%             37.271892       -88.043060        37.775000
max             47.272951       -71.455280        47.606390
```

```
[8 rows x 35 columns]
```

Now that we've seen that we can analyze both small and large quantities of data in the familiar Pandas DataFrame API, let's see what else it can do.

In addition to running the describe method with the default settings, you can use any of the options that it supports including percentiles, include, and exclude to modify the output. Let's go back to the Iris data set and try these options.

The percentiles that you get with the default options are 25%, 50%, and 75%. We can customize those values by passing in float values between 0 and 1 to the percentiles option.

```
In [24]: tbl
Out[24]: CASTable('DATA.IRIS', caslib='CASUSER(username)')

In [25]: tbl.describe(percentiles=[0.3, 0.8])
Out[25]:
         sepal_length  sepal_width  petal_length  petal_width
count    150.000000    150.000000    150.000000    150.000000
mean       5.843333      3.054000      3.758667      1.198667
std        0.828066      0.433594      1.764420      0.763161
min        4.300000      2.000000      1.000000      0.100000
30%        5.250000      2.800000      1.700000      0.400000
50%        5.800000      3.000000      4.350000      1.300000
80%        6.550000      3.400000      5.350000      1.900000
max        7.900000      4.400000      6.900000      2.500000
```

As you can see, we now get the 30% and 80% percentiles in addition to 50%, which always gets computed by the DataFrame method. The include and exclude options enable you to specify the data types that should be included in the analysis. You can specify them as a list of strings that indicate the CAS data types that should be included, or you can use the terms 'numeric', 'character', and 'all' to refer to all numeric types, all character types, and all variables, respectively. The values for this option vary slightly from the DataFrame method since the names of the data types are different between Pandas and CAS, but the form of the option is the same. In either case, the default is to analyze numeric data only.

```
# Analyze only character data in the CAS table
In [26]: tbl.describe(include='character')
Out[26]:
           species
count          150
unique           3
top       virginica
freq            50
```

```
# Analyze all data in the CAS table
In [27]: tbl.describe(include='all')
Out[27]:
        sepal_length sepal_width petal_length petal_width    species
count            150         150          150         150        150
unique            35          23           43          22          3
top                5           3          1.5         0.2  virginica
freq              10          26           14          28         50
mean         5.84333       3.054      3.75867     1.19867        NaN
std         0.828066    0.433594      1.76442    0.763161        NaN
min              4.3           2            1         0.1     setosa
25%              5.1         2.8          1.6         0.3        NaN
50%              5.8           3         4.35         1.3        NaN
75%              6.4         3.3          5.1         1.8        NaN
max              7.9         4.4          6.9         2.5  virginica

# Same as above
In [28]: tbl.describe(include=['numeric', 'character'])
Out[28]:
        sepal_length sepal_width petal_length petal_width    species
count            150         150          150         150        150
unique            35          23           43          22          3
top                5           3          1.5         0.2  virginica
freq              10          26           14          28         50
mean         5.84333       3.054      3.75867     1.19867        NaN
std         0.828066    0.433594      1.76442    0.763161        NaN
min              4.3           2            1         0.1     setosa
25%              5.1         2.8          1.6         0.3        NaN
50%              5.8           3         4.35         1.3        NaN
75%              6.4         3.3          5.1         1.8        NaN
max              7.9         4.4          6.9         2.5  virginica
```

The last option that is supported is called stats. This is not a DataFrame option, but was added to allow statistics that are supported by the summary action to be included in the results as well. It accepts a list of strings, including 'count', 'std', 'min', 'pct', 'max', 'unique', 'top', 'freq', 'nmiss', 'sum', 'stderr', 'var', 'uss', 'cv', 'tvalue', and 'probt'. The value of 'pct' includes all of the percentiles that have been computed. If 'all' is specified, all of the previously mentioned statistics are displayed.

```
In [29]: tbl.describe(stats=['count', 'nmiss', 'sum',
    ....:                     'probt', 'freq'])
Out[29]:
         sepal_length   sepal_width  petal_length  petal_width
count   1.500000e+02  1.500000e+02  1.500000e+02  1.500000e+02
nmiss   0.000000e+00  0.000000e+00  0.000000e+00  0.000000e+00
sum     8.765000e+02  4.581000e+02  5.638000e+02  1.798000e+02
probt  3.331256e-129 4.374977e-129  1.994305e-57  3.209704e-42
freq    1.000000e+01  2.600000e+01  1.400000e+01  2.800000e+01

In [30]: tbl.describe(stats='all')
Out[30]:
         sepal_length   sepal_width  petal_length  petal_width
count   1.500000e+02  1.500000e+02  1.500000e+02  1.500000e+02
unique  3.500000e+01  2.300000e+01  4.300000e+01  2.200000e+01
mean    5.843333e+00  3.054000e+00  3.758667e+00  1.198667e+00
std     8.280661e-01  4.335943e-01  1.764420e+00  7.631607e-01
min     4.300000e+00  2.000000e+00  1.000000e+00  1.000000e-01
```

25%	5.100000e+00	2.800000e+00	1.600000e+00	3.000000e-01
50%	5.800000e+00	3.000000e+00	4.350000e+00	1.300000e+00
75%	6.400000e+00	3.300000e+00	5.100000e+00	1.800000e+00
max	7.900000e+00	4.400000e+00	6.900000e+00	2.500000e+00
nmiss	0.000000e+00	0.000000e+00	0.000000e+00	0.000000e+00
sum	8.765000e+02	4.581000e+02	5.638000e+02	1.798000e+02
stderr	6.761132e-02	3.540283e-02	1.440643e-01	6.231181e-02
var	6.856935e-01	1.880040e-01	3.113179e+00	5.824143e-01
uss	5.223850e+03	1.427050e+03	2.583000e+03	3.023000e+02
cv	1.417113e+01	1.419759e+01	4.694272e+01	6.366747e+01
tvalue	8.642537e+01	8.626430e+01	2.609020e+01	1.923659e+01
probt	3.331256e-129	4.374977e-129	1.994305e-57	3.209704e-42

It is also possible to access the individual statistics through the DataFrame methods count, mean, std, and max. The methods nmiss, sum, stderr, var, uss, cv, tvalue, and probt are also available in order to complete the set that is provided by the summary action. These methods return a Pandas Series object that contains the values for each variable.

```
In [31]: tbl.count()
Out[31]:
sepal_length    150
sepal_width     150
petal_length    150
petal_width     150
species         150
dtype: int64

In [32]: tbl.mean()
Out[32]:
sepal_length    5.843333
sepal_width     3.054000
petal_length    3.758667
petal_width     1.198667
dtype: float64

In [33]: tbl.probt()
Out[33]:
sepal_length    3.331256e-129
sepal_width     4.374977e-129
petal_length    1.994305e-57
petal_width     3.209704e-42
dtype: float64
```

At the time of this writing, not all of the DataFrame methods were supported on the CASTable object. As development of the SWAT package continues, more of the DataFrame methods will likely become available.

Now that we have seen some basic DataFrame operations working on CASTable objects, let's move on to some plotting operations.

Creating Plots from CASTable Data

The CASTable objects support all of the same chart types as the DataFrame object because they use the same code. Plotting is done on the client side, so all of the data being visualized must be downloaded first. The plotting DataFrame methods are mirrored in the CASTable objects, and the data is downloaded automatically. Although these methods are convenient, for iterative work that might require tuning your plots, you probably want to bring the data back to a local DataFrame and use the plotting methods on it to avoid downloading data from the server at each iteration.

The easiest way to generate a plot of data in a CASTable is to use the plot method. We'll use our original Iris data set for this example. The following creates a plot:

```
In [34]: tbl.plot()
Out[34]: <matplotlib.axes.AxesSubplot at 0x7f4b6650c4e0>
```

If you use the Jupyter notebook as your client, your plot should show up in-line. If it doesn't appear in-line, you might try running the following IPython magic command and then do the plot again:

```
In [35]: %matplotlib inline
```

If you are using something other than the Jupyter notebook and the plot doesn't show up, you can try the following:

```
In [36]: from matplotlib.pyplot import show
```

```
In [37]: show()
```

The show function tells Matplotlib, which is the plotting package, to show the figure window. The following screenshot shows the plot that is generated on a Linux machine:

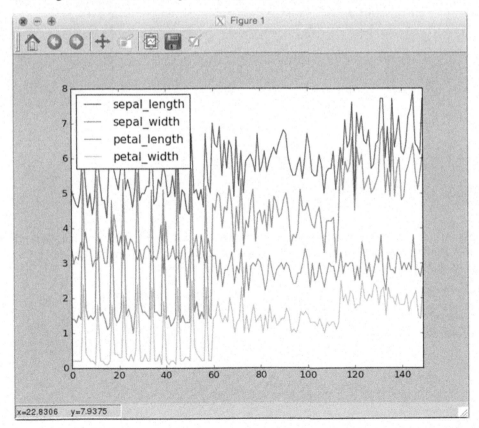

Of course, you can display subsets of columns as well using the standard DataFrame syntax.

```
In [38]: tbl[['sepal_length', 'sepal_width']].plot()
Out[38]: <matplotlib.axes._subplots.AxesSubplot at 0x7fa3efc23240>

In [39]: show()
```

Here is a plot of selected columns from the Iris data set:

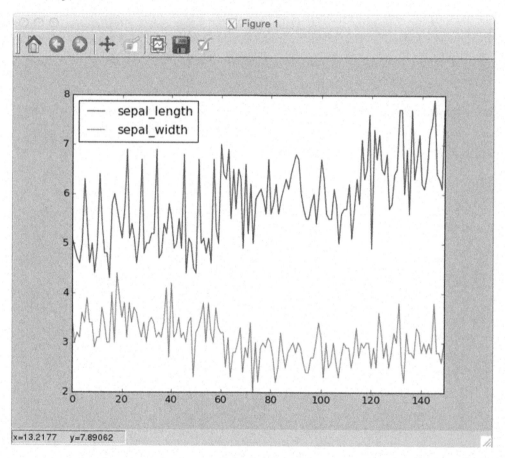

Other chart types include area, bar, horizontal bar, box plot, density, histogram, KDE, and pie. Depending on your version of Pandas, these chart types are accessible in multiple ways. The traditional way is to specify the type of chart in the kind argument of the plot method as follows:

```
In [40]: tbl[['sepal_length', 'sepal_width']].plot(kind='area')
Out[40]: <matplotlib.axes._subplots.AxesSubplot at 0x7f77480ce908>

In [41]: show()
```

Here is an area plot of selected column of the Iris data set:

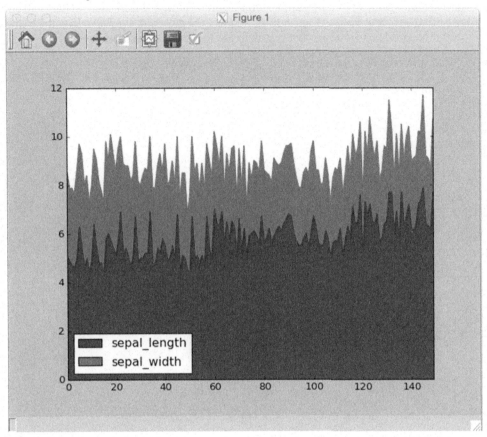

In newer versions of Pandas (releases 0.17.0 and later), you can use the individual chart type attributes on the plot method.

```
In [42]: tbl[['sepal_length', 'sepal_width']].plot.area()
Out[42]: <matplotlib.axes._subplots.AxesSubplot at 0x7f7747ea1fd0>

In [43]: show()
```

Options to the plotting methods can be used to customize the output (see the Pandas documentation for additional details). However, this interface does not provide publication-ready charts. It is primarily for exploration. For highly customized graphics, you should use the Matplotlib package directly.

Exporting CASTables to Other Formats

The data in CAS tables can be saved to all of the formats that are supported by the Pandas DataFrame's export methods. It accomplishes this by fetching the data and using the DataFrame export methods to save the data. Export methods include to_pickle, to_csv, to_hdf, to_sql, to_dict, to_excel, to_json, to_html, to_latex, to_stata, to_msgpack, to_gbq, to_records, to_sparse, to_dense, to_string, and to_clipboard. Keep in mind that all of these methods save the output on the client side. To save the data in a CAS table to a data source, you use the save CAS action.

The save action stores the data in the CAS table to the appropriate format for the caslib where the data is stored. The most basic form is the file-based caslib. You can store the data from a CAS table to either the CSV form or the SASHDAT form in file-based caslibs. To store the data, you simply specify the caslib to which the file should be saved, and you specify the path to the file in the name parameter.

```
In [44]: tbl.save(name='data/irisout.csv', caslib='casuser')
NOTE: Cloud Analytic Services created the file data/irisout.csv in caslib
CASUSER(username).
Out[44]:
[caslib]

 'CASUSER(username)'

[name]

 'data/irisout.csv'

+ Elapsed: 0.0143s, user: 0.004s, mem: 2.14mb

In [45]: tbl.save(name='data/irisout.sashdat', caslib='casuser')
NOTE: Cloud Analytic Services created the file data/irisout.sashdat in
caslib CASUSER(username).
Out[45]:
[caslib]

 'CASUSER(username)'

[name]

 'data/irisout.sashdat'

+ Elapsed: 0.0214s, user: 0.016s, sys: 0.003s, mem: 16.2mb
```

For caslibs with other data sources, see the SAS documentation for the options and parameters that are needed to export the data to a specific data source type.

Sorting, Data Selection, and Iteration

Some of the most basic data operations deal with sorting rows, selecting data based on labels or expressions, and iterating over rows or columns of a table. The following sections introduce techniques for accomplishing each data operation using the CASTable object.

Fetching Data with a Sort Order

As mentioned previously, data in a CAS table might be distributed across a grid, or it can be accessible in ways that do not specify a particular row order. This means that anytime you fetch data from CAS, you can't depend on the order unless you specify a sort order when retrieving it. A sort order can be specified with the sortby parameter on the fetch action, but a different method is used with DataFrames. DataFrame methods preserve order and can be sorted using the sort_values method (or the sort method in older versions of Pandas). To mimic the DataFrame behavior, CASTable objects also support those sorting methods.

The simplest form of sort_values is to specify the names of the columns to sort on. The order is ascending by default.

```
In [46]: tbl.sort_values(['sepal_length', 'sepal_width'])
Out[46]: CASTable('DATA.IRIS',
                   caslib='CASUSER(username)').sort_values(
                       ['sepal_length', 'sepal_width'])
```

There is a subtle point in the preceding code that you might not have noticed if you aren't familiar with Pandas. When you use the sort_values method on a DataFrame, it returns a new DataFrame object with an applied sort order unless you specify the inplace=True option. This is true with CASTable objects as well. The preceding code probably didn't accomplish its sorting goal. Instead, it created a new CASTable object with the sort order applied, but since we didn't save it to a variable, it simply disappeared. We have two choices: we can either use the inplace=True option on sort_values, or specify a variable for storing the returned value. Let's store the value in a variable in the following example:

```
In [47]: sorttbl = tbl.sort_values(['sepal_length', 'sepal_width'])

In [48]: sorttbl
Out[48]: CASTable('DATA.IRIS',
                   caslib='CASUSER(username)').sort_values(
                       ['sepal_length', 'sepal_width'])
```

Now we have a new CASTable object with the sort order applied as indicated by the sort_values(...) that is shown in the string representation above. To clarify, this sorting does nothing on the server side. In fact, nothing was sent to the server when this operation was invoked. The sort_values method call simply binds a sort order to the CASTable object that gets used anytime that the CASTable object is used to retrieve data from that CAS table.

We can now use the head or tail method to retrieve a sample of the data in the specified sort order.

```
In [50]: sorttbl.head(10)
Out[50]:
Selected Rows from Table DATA.IRIS
```

	sepal_length	sepal_width	petal_length	petal_width	species
0	4.3	3.0	1.1	0.1	setosa
1	4.4	2.9	1.4	0.2	setosa
2	4.4	3.0	1.3	0.2	setosa
3	4.4	3.2	1.3	0.2	setosa
4	4.5	2.3	1.3	0.3	setosa
5	4.6	3.1	1.5	0.2	setosa
6	4.6	3.2	1.4	0.2	setosa
7	4.6	3.4	1.4	0.3	setosa
8	4.6	3.6	1.0	0.2	setosa
9	4.7	3.2	1.6	0.2	setosa

```
In [51]: sorttbl.tail(5)
Out[51]:
Selected Rows from Table DATA.IRIS
```

	sepal_length	sepal_width	petal_length	petal_width	species
145	7.7	2.6	6.9	2.3	virginica
146	7.7	2.8	6.7	2.0	virginica
147	7.7	3.0	6.1	2.3	virginica

```
148          7.7          3.8          6.7          2.2  virginica
149          7.9          3.8          6.4          2.0  virginica
```

To change the order to descending, you can specify ascending=False or you can give a list of Booleans to indicate ascending or descending order for each column.

```
In [52]: sorttbl = tbl.sort_values(['sepal_length', 'sepal_width'],
    ....:                           ascending=[False, True])

In [53]: sorttbl
Out[53]: CASTable('DATA.IRIS',
                   caslib='CASUSER(username)').sort_values(
                       ['sepal_length', 'sepal_width'],
                       ascending=[False, True])
```

If we fetch a sample of the data with our mixed descending/ascending sort order, you'll get the following.

```
In [54]: sorttbl.head(10)
Out[54]:
Selected Rows from Table DATA.IRIS
```

	sepal_length	sepal_width	petal_length	petal_width	species
0	7.9	3.8	6.4	2.0	virginica
1	7.7	2.6	6.9	2.3	virginica
2	7.7	2.8	6.7	2.0	virginica
3	7.7	3.0	6.1	2.3	virginica
4	7.7	3.8	6.7	2.2	virginica
5	7.6	3.0	6.6	2.1	virginica
6	7.4	2.8	6.1	1.9	virginica
7	7.3	2.9	6.3	1.8	virginica
8	7.2	3.0	5.8	1.6	virginica
9	7.2	3.2	6.0	1.8	virginica

Now that we have seen how to apply a sort order to a CASTable, we can go to the next set of DataFrame features that pertain to iteration.

Iterating through Columns and Rows

CASTable objects support all of the DataFrame iteration methods. However, you should use the iteration methods judiciously. Although you can iterate through the rows of a CAS table, you probably don't want to do that if your table contains millions of rows. Realistically, you should use iteration methods with CAS tables that contain only summarization data or CAS tables that have a constrained number of records.

Basic Iteration

Iterating through the column names is the most basic form of iteration on a CASTable object. Iterating through columns is done by using the table object itself as the iterator just like with DataFrame objects.

```
In [55]: for col in sorttbl:
    ....:     print(col)
    ....:
sepal_length
sepal_width
petal_length
```

```
petal_width
species
```

Of course, you can also wrap the table in the various Python iteration functions to get a different behavior. For example, you can use the enumerate function to give the index value of each column name, or you can even use the zip function to walk through multiple lists of the same size.

```
In [56]: for i, col in enumerate(sorttbl):
   ....:        print(i, col)
   ....:
0 sepal_length
1 sepal_width
2 petal_length
3 petal_width
4 species

In [57]: for col, dtype in zip(sorttbl, sorttbl.dtypes):
   ....:        print(col, dtype)
   ....:
sepal_length double
sepal_width double
petal_length double
petal_width double
species varchar
```

Iterating over Columns

Much like the basic iterator, the iteritems method iterates over the columns as well. However, in this case, the returned values are a pairing of the column name and a CASColumn object. CASColumn objects are just like CASTable objects except that they reference only a single column. They are analogous to Pandas Series objects and are discussed later in the chapter.

```
In [58]: for col, obj in sorttbl.iteritems():
   ....:        print(col, obj)
   ....:        print('')
   ....:
sepal_length CASColumn('DATA.IRIS',
caslib='CASUSER(username)')['sepal_length'].sort_values(['sepal_length',
'sepal_width'], ascending=[False, True])

sepal_width CASColumn('DATA.IRIS',
caslib='CASUSER(username)')['sepal_width'].sort_values(['sepal_length',
'sepal_width'], ascending=[False, True])

petal_length CASColumn('DATA.IRIS',
caslib='CASUSER(username)')['petal_length'].sort_values(['sepal_length',
'sepal_width'], ascending=[False, True])

petal_width CASColumn('DATA.IRIS',
caslib='CASUSER(username)')['petal_width'].sort_values(['sepal_length',
'sepal_width'], ascending=[False, True])

species CASColumn('DATA.IRIS',
caslib='CASUSER(username)')['species'].sort_values(['sepal_length',
'sepal_width'], ascending=[False, True])
```

Although the previous two iterators can be safely run on large tables (they don't iterate through the data rows), the following two iterators go through all of the rows in a table. The iterrows method returns a tuple that contains the row index and a Pandas Series object that contains the values of the row.

```
In [59]: for row in sorttbl.iterrows():
    ....:     print(row)
    ....:
(0, sepal_length        4.3
sepal_width              3
petal_length           1.1
petal_width            0.1
species             setosa
Name: 0, dtype: object)
(1, sepal_length        4.4
sepal_width            2.9
petal_length           1.4
petal_width            0.2
species             setosa
Name: 1, dtype: object)

 . . .

(149, sepal_length      7.9
sepal_width            3.8
petal_length           6.4
petal_width              2
species           virginica
Name: 149, dtype: object)
```

This method uses a Python generator to appear as if it fetches all of the data and iterates over it. However, the iterrows method pulls the data down in batches (configurable by the n argument) and waits until a new batch is needed before it fetches the next batch. The itertuples method works in a very similar way, but it returns each row as a tuple of values rather than a Series. The row index value can be disabled by passing index=False.

```
In [60]: for row in sorttbl.itertuples():
    ....:     print(row)
    ....:
(0, 4.2999999999999998, 3.0, 1.1000000000000001, 0.1000000000000001,
 'setosa')
(1, 4.4000000000000004, 2.8999999999999999, 1.3999999999999999,
 0.20000000000000001, 'setosa')
(2, 4.4000000000000004, 3.0, 1.3, 0.20000000000000001, 'setosa')

 . . .

(149, 7.9000000000000004, 3.799999999999998, 6.4000000000000004, 2.0,
 'virginica')
```

Now that we've seen how to iterate through our data, let's look at how we can retrieve items from the data.

Techniques for Indexing and Selecting Data

Indexing and selecting data in DataFrames comes in many forms. The loc and iloc attributes enable you to select rows that are based on labels and row indexes. The attributes, at and iat, enable you to select a scalar value at a particular position, given a label and a row index, respectively, paired with a column identifier. The ix attribute supports mixed integer and label access. Finally, using the Python __getitem__ functionality (through the bracket [...] syntax) on the DataFrame itself enables you to select columns and ranges of rows.

Selecting Columns by Label and Position

Probably, the most common way that you see the Pandas DataFrame being indexed is directly on the DataFrame itself. DataFrame objects (and similarly CASTables objects) enable you to select columns either by name or index. To select a single column, you simply index the CASTable using the name of the column.

```
In [61]: col = sorttbl['sepal_width']

In [62]: col
Out[62]: CASColumn('data.iris', caslib='casuser')
            ['sepal_width'].sort_values(['sepal_length',
                                         'sepal_width'],
                              ascending=[False, True])

In [63]: col.head()
Out[63]:
0    3.8
1    2.6
2    2.8
3    3.0
4    3.8
Name: sepal_width, dtype: float64
```

The object that we get back is a CASColumn object. This object is analogous to a Pandas Series. Technically, CAS doesn't support stand-alone columns. The CASColumn object is a specialized subclass of CASTable object that references a single column of the table. As you can see, when you retrieve a column from a CASTable, the resulting CASColumn takes with it all table and sort information that was on the parent CASTable. We cover more advanced uses of CASColumn objects later in the chapter. For now, let's move on to more CASTable indexing.

An alternative way of selecting a column is using the Python attribute syntax. You can specify the name of the column on the CASTable in order to have it return a CASColumn.

```
In [64]: sorttbl.species
Out[64]: CASColumn('DATA.IRIS', caslib='CASUSER(username)')
            ['species'].sort_values(['sepal_length', 'sepal_width'],
                              ascending=[False, True])
```

Although this way of accessing columns is prettier than the bracket syntax, it has some restrictions. The name of the column must be a legal Python attribute name, which cannot collide with any existing attributes or methods on the CASTable object. Although this syntax is appropriate for interactive use, it's much safer to write programs using the bracket syntax.

In addition to retrieving columns from a CASTable, we can also retrieve subsets of a table. To do this, you use a list of columns as the index key.

```
In [65]: widths = sorttbl[['sepal_width', 'petal_width', 'species']]
In [66]: widths
Out[66]: CASTable('DATA.IRIS', caslib='CASUSER(username)')[
             ['sepal_width', 'petal_width', 'species']
         ].sort_values(['sepal_length', 'sepal_width'],
                       ascending=[False, True])

In [67]: widths.head()
Out[67]:
Selected Rows from Table DATA.IRIS

   sepal_width  petal_width    species
0          3.8          2.0  virginica
1          2.6          2.3  virginica
2          2.8          2.0  virginica
3          3.0          2.3  virginica
4          3.8          2.2  virginica
```

If you specify a list of column names (or even a list containing a single column name), you'll get back a new CASTable object that includes only the referenced columns. The data in this table is still the same as the data in the parent table. The local CASTable object simply references the columns that it needs.

Of course, now that we have this new table, we can use any of the previously described CASTable methods on it (including the CAS action and DataFrame methods).

```
In [68]: widths.describe()
Out[68]:
       sepal_width  petal_width
count   150.000000   150.000000
mean      3.054000     1.198667
std       0.433594     0.763161
min       2.000000     0.100000
25%       2.800000     0.300000
50%       3.000000     1.300000
75%       3.300000     1.800000
max       4.400000     2.500000

In [69]: widths.columninfo()
Out[69]:
[ColumnInfo]

        Column  ID     Type  RawLength  FormattedLength  NFL  NFD
0  sepal_width   2   double          8               12    0    0
1  petal_width   4   double          8               12    0    0
2      species   5  varchar         10               10    0    0

+ Elapsed: 0.000839s, sys: 0.001s, mem: 0.188mb
```

In addition to basic column selection such as the examples shown here, you can also use the various accessor properties of DataFrame objects to select columns in other ways. That's covered in the next section.

Selecting Data by Label and Position

Although DataFrames enable you to select rows using the loc, iloc, at, iat, and ix accessors, CAS tables do not have the concept of a row label or an index. These accessors still exist on CASTable objects, but they are limited to column selection only.

Let's use our sorted table from the previous example to select some data points.

```
In [70]: sorttbl
Out[70]: CASTable('DATA.IRIS',
                   caslib='CASUSER(username)').sort_values(
                       ['sepal_length', 'sepal_width'],
                       ascending=[False, True])
```

The loc and iloc data accessors on CASTable objects can select only columns. The loc accessor selects columns by name, whereas the iloc accessor selects columns by index. You must specify an empty slice as the first index parameter.

```
# Select the petal_width column
In [71]: sorttbl.loc[:, 'petal_width'].head()
Out[71]:
0    2.0
1    2.3
2    2.0
3    2.3
4    2.2
Name: petal_width, dtype: float64
```

```
# Select a range of columns
In [72]: sorttbl.loc[:, 'sepal_length':'petal_length'].head()
Out[72]:
Selected Rows from Table DATA.IRIS
```

	sepal_length	sepal_width	petal_length
0	7.9	3.8	6.4
1	7.7	2.6	6.9
2	7.7	2.8	6.7
3	7.7	3.0	6.1
4	7.7	3.8	6.7

```
# Select a list of columns
In [73]: sorttbl.loc[:, ['petal_width', 'sepal_width']].head()
Out[73]:
Selected Rows from Table DATA.IRIS
```

	petal_width	sepal_width
0	2.0	3.8
1	2.3	2.6
2	2.0	2.8
3	2.3	3.0
4	2.2	3.8

The iloc accessor works much like loc except that it uses integer indexes.

```
In [74]: sorttbl.iloc[:, 3].head()
Out[74]:
0    2.0
1    2.3
2    2.0
3    2.3
4    2.2
Name: petal_width, dtype: float64
```

```
In [75]: sorttbl.iloc[:, 0:3].head()
Out[75]:
Selected Rows from Table DATA.IRIS
```

	sepal_length	sepal_width	petal_length
0	7.9	3.8	6.4
1	7.7	2.6	6.9
2	7.7	2.8	6.7
3	7.7	3.0	6.1
4	7.7	3.8	6.7

```
In [76]: sorttbl.iloc[:, [3, 1]].head()
Out[76]:
Selected Rows from Table DATA.IRIS
```

	petal_width	sepal_width
0	2.0	3.8
1	2.3	2.6
2	2.0	2.8
3	2.3	3.0
4	2.2	3.8

Finally, the ix accessor enables you to mix labels and position indexes.

```
In [77]: sorttbl.ix[:, [3, 'sepal_width']].head()
Out[77]:
Selected Rows from Table DATA.IRIS
```

	petal_width	sepal_width
0	2.0	3.8
1	2.3	2.6
2	2.0	2.8
3	2.3	3.0
4	2.2	3.8

```
In [78]: sorttbl.ix[:, 'sepal_width'].head()
Out[78]:
0    3.8
1    2.6
2    2.8
3    3.0
4    3.8
Name: sepal_width, dtype: float64
```

```
In [79]: sorttbl.ix[:, 'sepal_width':-2].head()
Out[79]:
Selected Rows from Table DATA.IRIS

     sepal_width  petal_length
0            3.8           6.4
1            2.6           6.9
2            2.8           6.7
3            3.0           6.1
4            3.8           6.7

In [80]: sorttbl.ix[:, ['sepal_width', 3, 4]].head()
Out[80]:
Selected Rows from Table DATA.IRIS

     sepal_width  petal_width    species
0            3.8          2.0  virginica
1            2.6          2.3  virginica
2            2.8          2.0  virginica
3            3.0          2.3  virginica
4            3.8          2.2  virginica
```

Although the preceding accessors can be useful, they are somewhat limited because the nature of distributed data prevents selection by row index. However, there is a more powerful indexing feature on CASTable objects that allows for various forms of advanced selection of data.

Dynamic Data Selection

Rather than using fixed values of rows and columns to select data, we can create conditions that are based on the data in the table to determine which rows to select. The specification of conditions is done using the same syntax as that used by DataFrame objects. CASColumn objects support Python's various comparison operators and build a filter that subsets the rows in the table. You can then use the result of that comparison to index into a CASTable. It sounds much more complicated than it is, so let's look at an example.

If we want to get a CASTable that contains only values where petal_length is greater than 6.5, we can use the following expression to create our filter:

```
In [81]: expr = sorttbl.petal_length > 6.5
```

This expression creates a computed column that is used in a where expression on the CASTable. This expression can then be used as an index value for a CASTable. Indexing this way essentially creates a Boolean mask. Wherever the expression values are true, the rows of the table are returned. Wherever the expression is false, the rows are filtered out.

```
In [82]: newtbl = sorttbl[expr]

In [83]: newtbl.head()
Out[83]:
Selected Rows from Table DATA.IRIS

     sepal_length  sepal_width  petal_length  petal_width    species
0             7.7          2.6           6.9          2.3  virginica
1             7.7          2.8           6.7          2.0  virginica
```

```
2              7.7            3.8            6.7            2.2  virginica
3              7.6            3.0            6.6            2.1  virginica
```

These two steps are commonly entered on one line.

```
In [84]: newtbl = sorttbl[sorttbl.petal_length > 6.5]
```

```
In [85]: newtbl.head()
Out[85]:
Selected Rows from Table DATA.IRIS

     sepal_length  sepal_width  petal_length  petal_width    species
0             7.7          2.6           6.9          2.3  virginica
1             7.7          2.8           6.7          2.0  virginica
2             7.7          3.8           6.7          2.2  virginica
3             7.6          3.0           6.6          2.1  virginica
```

We can further filter rows out by indexing another comparison expression.

```
In [86]: newtbl2 = newtbl[newtbl.petal_width < 2.2]
```

```
In [87]: newtbl2.head()
Out[87]:
Selected Rows from Table DATA.IRIS

     sepal_length  sepal_width  petal_length  petal_width    species
0             7.7          2.8           6.7          2.0  virginica
1             7.6          3.0           6.6          2.1  virginica
```

Comparisons can be joined using the bitwise comparison operators & (and) and | (or). You must be careful with these operators though due to operator precedence. Bitwise comparison has a higher precedence than comparisons such as greater-than and less-than, so you need to enclose your comparisons in parentheses.

```
In [88]: sorttbl[(sorttbl.petal_length > 6.5) &
   ....:          (sorttbl.petal_width < 2.2)].head()
Out[88]:
Selected Rows from Table DATA.IRIS

     sepal_length  sepal_width  petal_length  petal_width    species
0             7.7          2.8           6.7          2.0  virginica
1             7.6          3.0           6.6          2.1  virginica
```

In all cases, we are not changing anything about the underlying data in CAS. We are simply constructing a query that is executed with the CASTable when it is used as the parameter in a CAS action. You can see what is happening behind the scenes by displaying the resulting CASTable objects.

```
In [89]: sorttbl[(sorttbl.petal_length > 6.5) &
   ....:          (sorttbl.petal_width < 2.2)]
Out[89]: CASTable('data.iris', caslib='casuser',
             computedvars=['_gt_6_', '_and_8_', '_lt_7_'],
             computedvarsprogram='_gt_6_ = (petal_length > 6.5);
                          _lt_7_ = (petal_width < 2.2);
                          _and_8_ = (_gt_6_ and _lt_7_); ',
          where='(_and_8_)')
          [['sepal_length', 'sepal_width',
            'petal_length', 'petal_width',
```

```
                    'species']].sort_values(['sepal_length',
                                             'sepal_width'],
                                     ascending=[False, True])
```

You can also do mathematical operations on columns with constants or on other columns within your comparisons.

```
In [90]: sorttbl[(sorttbl.petal_length + sorttbl.petal_width)
    ....:              * 2 > 17.5].head()
Out[90]:
Selected Rows from Table DATA.IRIS

     sepal_length  sepal_width  petal_length  petal_width    species
0             7.7          2.6           6.9          2.3  virginica
1             7.7          3.8           6.7          2.2  virginica
```

The list of supported operators is shown in the following table:

Operator	Numeric Data	Character Data
+ (add)	✓	✓
- (subtract)	✓	
* (multiply)	✓	
/ (divide)	✓	
% (modulo)	✓	
** (power)	✓	

The supported comparison operators are shown in the following table.

Operator	Numeric Data	Character Data
== (equality)	✓	✓
!= (inequality)	✓	✓
< (less than)	✓	✓
> (greater than)	✓	✓
<= (less than or equal to)	✓	✓
>= (greater than or equal to)	✓	✓

As you can see in the preceding tables, you can do comparisons on character columns as well. It is also possible to use many of the Python string methods on the column values. These methods are accessed through the str attribute of the column, just like in DataFrames.

```
In [91]: sorttbl[sorttbl.species.str.upper().str.startswith('SET')
    ....:              ].head()
Out[91]:
Selected Rows from Table DATA.IRIS

     sepal_length  sepal_width  petal_length  petal_width  species
0             5.8          4.0           1.2          0.2  setosa
1             5.7          3.8           1.7          0.3  setosa
2             5.7          4.4           1.5          0.4  setosa
3             5.5          3.5           1.3          0.2  setosa
4             5.5          4.2           1.4          0.2  setosa
```

The following table shows the string methods that are supported on character columns:

Method	Description
col.str.capitalize	Capitalize the first character, and lowercase the remaining characters.
col.str.contains	Return Boolean values indicating whether the pattern exists in the data values.
col.str.count	Count occurrences of the pattern in each value.
col.str.endswith	Return Boolean values indicating whether the values end with the pattern.
col.str.find	Return the lowest index of the pattern in each value, or return -1 if the pattern is not found.
col.str.index	Is the same as the find method (the preceding entry) except that a ValueError is raised if the pattern is not found.
col.str.len	Compute the length of each value.
col.str.lower	Lowercase the entire column.
col.str.lstrip	Strip the leading spaces.
col.str.repeat	Duplicate the value by the specified number of times.
col.str.rfind	Return the highest index of the pattern in each value, or return -1 if the pattern is not found.
col.str.rindex	Is the same as the rfind method (the preceding entry) except that a ValueError is raised if the pattern is not found.
col.str.rstrip	Strip the trailing whitespace characters.
col.str.slice	Slice a substring from the value.
col.str.startswith	Return Boolean values indicating the value starts with the pattern.
col.str.strip	Strip the leading and trailing whitespace characters.
col.str.title	Capitalize each word in the value, and lowercase the remaining characters.
col.str.upper	Uppercase the value.
col.str.isalnum	Return Boolean values indicating whether the value is all alphanumeric values.
col.str.isalpha	Return Boolean values indicating whether the value is all alphabetic characters.
col.str.isdigit	Return Boolean values indicating whether the value is all digits.
col.str.isspace	Return Boolean values indicating whether the value is all whitespace characters.
col.str.islower	Return Boolean values indicating whether the value is all lowercase.
col.str.isupper	Return Boolean values indicating whether the value is all uppercase.
col.str.istitle	Return Boolean values indicating whether the value is equivalent to the title representation. (See the title method.)

Method	Description
col.str.isnumeric	Return Boolean values indicating whether the value is in a numeric representation.
col.str.isdecimal	Return Boolean values indicating whether the value is in a decimal representation.

In addition to the string column methods, you can also use the following date/time properties on date, time, and datetime columns.

Property	Description
col.dt.year	Return the year of the date/time/datetime.
col.dt.month	Return the month of the date/time/datetime, where January is 1 and December is 12.
col.dt.day	Return the day of the month of the date/time/datetime.
col.dt.hour	Return the hours of the date/time/datetime (0-24).
col.dt.minute	Return the minutes of the date/time/datetime (0-60).
col.dt.second	Return the seconds of the date/time/datetime (0-60).
col.dt.microsecond	Return the microseconds of the date/time/datetime (0-999999).
col.dt.nanosecond	Return the nanoseconds of the date/time/datetime. Since CAS has a resolution of only one microsecond, this property always returns zero.
col.dt.week	Return the week of the year of the date/time/datetime.
col.dt.weekofyear	Is the same as the week property.
col.dt.dayofweek	Return the day of the week of the date/time/datetime. Monday is 0 and Sunday is 6.
col.dt.weekday	Is the same as the dayofweek property.
col.dt.dayofyear	Return the ordinal day of the year of the date/time/datetime.
col.dt.quarter	Return the year's quarter of the date/time/datetime.
col.dt.is_month_start	Boolean indicating whether the date/time/datetime is the first day of the month.
col.dt.is_month_end	Boolean indicating whether the date/time/datetime is the last day of the month.
col.dt.is_quarter_start	Boolean indicating whether the date/time/datetime is the first day of the quarter.
col.dt.is_quarter_end	Boolean indicating whether the date/time/datetime is the last day of the quarter.
col.dt.is_year_start	Boolean indicating whether the date/time/datetime is the first day of the year.
col.dt.is_year_end	Boolean indicating whether the date/time/datetime is the last day of the year.
col.dt.daysinmonth	Returns the number of days in the month of the date/time/datetime.
col.dt.days_in_month	Same as daysinmonth.

Note that when you call any of the previous methods on CAS *time* values, any method that returns a *date-related* component uses the current day. When you call *time-related* methods on a CAS *date*, the values are always zero.

It's easy to create powerful filters that are executed in CAS while still using the Python syntax. However, the similarities to DataFrames don't end there. CASTable objects can also create computed columns and by groups using similar techniques. Those topics are covered in the next section.

Data Wrangling on the Fly

There's a certain amount of "data wrangling" that is required to prepare your data for reporting or modeling. Data wrangling refers to data manipulation, including the transformation of data from one format to another format, BY-group processing, and data aggregation. Such manipulations on large data sets often become bottlenecks to understanding your data, because most of the steps to manipulate data require that you create a new copy of the data or that you move data around the nodes of your cluster. In CAS, several ways are provided to speed up the data wrangling steps such as temporary computed columns and group by processing. Neither requires copying data or moving data.

Creating Computed Columns

Rather than using the CASColumn-based expressions to filter a CASTable object you can also use them to build computed columns. Instead of comparing the result of an expression to another value, you simply set it to a key on the CASTable object. Here is an example that adds the sepal_length and sepal_width and then multiplies the result by 2. The result is a CASColumn object that we set to sepal_factor.

```
In [92]: sorttbl['sepal_factor'] = ((sorttbl.sepal_length +
    ....:                             sorttbl.sepal_width) * 2)

In [93]: sorttbl.head()
Out[93]:
Selected Rows from Table DATA.IRIS
```

	sepal_length	sepal_width	petal_length	petal_width	species	\
0	7.9	3.8	6.4	2.0	virginica	
1	7.7	2.6	6.9	2.3	virginica	
2	7.7	2.8	6.7	2.0	virginica	
3	7.7	3.0	6.1	2.3	virginica	
4	7.7	3.8	6.7	2.2	virginica	

	sepal_factor
0	23.4
1	20.6
2	21.0
3	21.4
4	23.0

The sepal_factor column is a computed column that is not present in the original CAS table. It is a temporary column generated "on the fly" when an action is executed. They exist only for the duration of the action, and are not visible to any other action. Computed columns are efficient because you can use computed columns to dynamically filter or expand the data without actually duplicating the data to create those extra filters or columns. You can create computed columns from other computed columns as well. In the following code, we'll use our previously computed column as part of the expression for a new computed column.

```
In [94]: sorttbl['total_factor'] = sorttbl.sepal_factor + \
    ....:                           sorttbl.petal_width + \
    ....:                           sorttbl.petal_length
```

```
In [95]: sorttbl.head()
Out[95]:
Selected Rows from Table DATA.IRIS
```

	sepal_length	sepal_width	petal_length	petal_width	species	\
0	7.9	3.8	6.4	2.0	virginica	
1	7.7	2.6	6.9	2.3	virginica	
2	7.7	2.8	6.7	2.0	virginica	
3	7.7	3.0	6.1	2.3	virginica	
4	7.7	3.8	6.7	2.2	virginica	

	sepal_factor	**total_factor**
0	23.4	**31.8**
1	20.6	**29.8**
2	21.0	**29.7**
3	21.4	**29.8**
4	23.0	**31.9**

The output from the head method shows that the extra columns are now available on the table. You can even create computed columns that are based on constants or Python expressions (evaluated on the client) rather than on data in the table.

```
In [96]: sorttbl['names'] = 'sepal / petal'
```

```
In [97]: sorttbl.head()
Out[97]:
```

	sepal_length	sepal_width	petal_length	petal_width	species	\
0	7.9	3.8	6.4	2.0	virginica	
1	7.7	2.6	6.9	2.3	virginica	
2	7.7	2.8	6.7	2.0	virginica	
3	7.7	3.0	6.1	2.3	virginica	
4	7.7	3.8	6.7	2.2	virginica	

	sepal_factor	total_factor	names
0	23.4	8.4	**sepal / petal**
1	20.6	9.2	**sepal / petal**
2	21.0	8.7	**sepal / petal**
3	21.4	8.4	**sepal / petal**
4	23.0	8.9	**sepal / petal**

You can use any of the numeric, string, and date/time methods that are described in the filtering section to construct computed columns as well.

```
In [98]: sorttbl['cap_names'] = sorttbl.names.str.title()
```

```
In [99]: sorttbl.head()
Selected Rows from Table DATA.IRIS
```

	sepal_length	sepal_width	petal_length	petal_width	species	\
0	4.3	3.0	1.1	0.1	setosa	
1	4.4	2.9	1.4	0.2	setosa	
2	4.4	3.0	1.3	0.2	setosa	

```
3              4.4            3.2              1.3          0.2  setosa
4              4.5            2.3              1.3          0.3  setosa

     sepal_factor   total_factor          names      cap_names
0            14.6           15.8   sepal / petal   Sepal / Petal
1            14.6           16.2   sepal / petal   Sepal / Petal
2            14.8           16.3   sepal / petal   Sepal / Petal
3            15.2           16.7   sepal / petal   Sepal / Petal
4            13.6           15.2   sepal / petal   Sepal / Petal
```

Now that we have seen that we can filter our data and create computed columns, let's look at the topic of grouping data by data values.

By Group Processing

Many analytic actions and Pandas DataFrame methods support grouping by values in one or more columns in a table. There are a couple of ways to apply by grouping in CASTable objects, one of which is borrowed from the DataFrame API.

The most direct way of applying by groupings to a CASTable object is to use the groupby parameter. We'll start with the Iris table for this example.

```
In [100]: tbl.set_param('groupby', ['species'])

In [101]: tbl
Out[101]: CASTable('DATA.IRIS', caslib='CASUSER(username)',
                    groupby=['species'])
```

Now that we have some grouping variables set, we'll run the summary action.

```
In [102]: tbl.summary(subset=['min', 'max'])
Out[102]:
[ByGroupInfo]

  ByGroupInfo

            species    species_f       _key_
0            setosa       setosa      setosa
1        versicolor   versicolor  versicolor
2         virginica    virginica   virginica

[ByGroup1.Summary]

  Descriptive Statistics for DATA.IRIS

                 Column  Min  Max
  species
  setosa    sepal_length  4.3  5.8
  setosa     sepal_width  2.3  4.4
  setosa    petal_length  1.0  1.9
  setosa     petal_width  0.1  0.6

[ByGroup2.Summary]
```

```
Descriptive Statistics for DATA.IRIS

                 Column  Min  Max
species
versicolor    sepal_length  4.9  7.0
versicolor     sepal_width  2.0  3.4
versicolor    petal_length  3.0  5.1
versicolor     petal_width  1.0  1.8

[ByGroup3.Summary]

Descriptive Statistics for DATA.IRIS

                 Column  Min  Max
species
virginica     sepal_length  4.9  7.9
virginica      sepal_width  2.2  3.8
virginica     petal_length  4.5  6.9
virginica      petal_width  1.4  2.5

+ Elapsed: 0.0082s, user: 0.006s, sys: 0.007s, mem: 1.94mb
```

You see that we now get multiple tables as output rather than just the single table that the summary action produces when running without by groupings. The first table is called ByGroupInfo. This table contains information about all of the by grouping tables that follow. This information is more useful if there are a large number of by groupings and you want to know about them in advance so that you can prepare for the tables as they come from the server. The remaining tables correspond to each of the by groupings.

Each by grouping generates a new output table. The name of the key for that output is the name of the table prefixed by a label ByGroup#, where # is the index of the grouping (starting with 1). Without by grouping applied, the summary action creates a table called Summary. With by grouping applied, the result keys are ByGroup1.Summary, ByGroup2.Summary, and so on.

We mentioned that the DataFrame method for applying by groupings works with CASTable objects as well. The DataFrame groupby method is used to group the data. In the following example, we delete the groupby parameter from the table, and then use the groupby method to apply by groupings instead.

```
In [103]: tbl.del_param('groupby')

In [104]: tbl
Out[104]: CASTable('DATA.IRIS', caslib='CASUSER(username)')

In [105]: grptbl = tbl.groupby(['species'])

In [106]: grptbl
Out[106]: <swat.cas.table.CASTableGroupBy at 0x7f2148e12358>
```

You notice that when using this method, we don't get a CASTable object back. Instead, we get a CASTableGroupBy object. This object corresponds to the Pandas GroupBy object. This object works much like a DataFrame object in many ways. For example, you can still call most DataFrame methods, call CAS actions on it, access columns, and so on, but the CASTableGroupBy object also adds methods for traversing the by-groupings in various ways.

Using the summary action on our grptbl variable shows that we get the same result as when we used the groupby parameter on the CASTable object.

```
In [107]: grptbl.summary(subset=['min', 'max'])
Out[107]:
[ByGroupInfo]

 ByGroupInfo

        species     species_f        _key_
 0       setosa       setosa        setosa
 1   versicolor   versicolor    versicolor
 2    virginica    virginica     virginica

[ByGroup1.Summary]

 Descriptive Statistics for DATA.IRIS

                 Column   Min   Max
 species
 setosa     sepal_length   4.3   5.8
 setosa      sepal_width   2.3   4.4
 setosa     petal_length   1.0   1.9
 setosa      petal_width   0.1   0.6

[ByGroup2.Summary]

 Descriptive Statistics for DATA.IRIS

                   Column   Min   Max
 species
 versicolor   sepal_length   4.9   7.0
 versicolor    sepal_width   2.0   3.4
 versicolor   petal_length   3.0   5.1
 versicolor    petal_width   1.0   1.8

[ByGroup3.Summary]

 Descriptive Statistics for DATA.IRIS

                  Column   Min   Max
 species
 virginica   sepal_length   4.9   7.9
 virginica    sepal_width   2.2   3.8
 virginica   petal_length   4.5   6.9
 virginica    petal_width   1.4   2.5

 + Elapsed: 0.00862s, user: 0.008s, sys: 0.009s, mem: 1.98mb
```

Concatenating By Groups

If you already use Pandas, you might want to combine all of the by-grouping tables into a single DataFrame so that you can continue your workflow, as usual. Fortunately, there is a method on the CASResults object that can be used to combine by-grouping tables into a single DataFrame: concat_bygroups.

```
In [108]: grpsumm = grptbl.summary(subset=['min', 'max'])
```

```
In [109]: grpsumm.concat_bygroups()
Out[109]:
[Summary]

 Descriptive Statistics for DATA.IRIS

                       Column  Min  Max
   species
   setosa        sepal_length  4.3  5.8
   setosa         sepal_width  2.3  4.4
   setosa        petal_length  1.0  1.9
   setosa         petal_width  0.1  0.6
   versicolor    sepal_length  4.9  7.0
   versicolor     sepal_width  2.0  3.4
   versicolor    petal_length  3.0  5.1
   versicolor     petal_width  1.0  1.8
   virginica     sepal_length  4.9  7.9
   virginica      sepal_width  2.2  3.8
   virginica     petal_length  4.5  6.9
   virginica      petal_width  1.4  2.5
```

This method preserves all of the DataFrame index information so that it can be treated just like the output of the native DataFrame methods with by-groups enabled.

If you prefer to keep your by-group tables separate, there are a couple of other methods on the CASResults object that can query specific table names or groups.

Selecting Result Keys by Table Name

Unlike the summary action, some CAS actions return multiple result table names, including the correlation action. We won't explain the correlation action in detail, but we use it in our example to select a particular table name from a result set. We still use our grptbl variable from the previous example as our starting point.

```
In [110]: grpcorr = grptbl.correlation()
```

```
In [111]: grpcorr
Out[111]:
[ByGroupInfo]

 ByGroupInfo

        species    species_f        _key_
   0      setosa       setosa       setosa
   1  versicolor   versicolor   versicolor
   2   virginica    virginica    virginica

[ByGroup1.CorrSimple]
```

```
Summary Statistics in Correlation Analysis for DATA.IRIS

              Variable    N    Mean    Sum    StdDev   Minimum  \
species
setosa     sepal_length  50.0  5.006  250.3  0.352490     4.3
setosa      sepal_width  50.0  3.418  170.9  0.381024     2.3
setosa     petal_length  50.0  1.464   73.2  0.173511     1.0
setosa      petal_width  50.0  0.244   12.2  0.107210     0.1

              Maximum
species
setosa          5.8
setosa          4.4
setosa          1.9
setosa          0.6


[ByGroup1.Correlation]

Pearson Correlation Coefficients for DATA.IRIS

              Variable   sepal_length  sepal_width  petal_length  \
species
setosa     sepal_length    1.000000      0.746780      0.263874
setosa      sepal_width    0.746780      1.000000      0.176695
setosa     petal_length    0.263874      0.176695      1.000000
setosa      petal_width    0.279092      0.279973      0.306308

              petal_width
species
setosa          0.279092
setosa          0.279973
setosa          0.306308
setosa          1.000000

... truncated ...
```

As you can see in the preceding output, the correlation action produces tables that are named CorrSimple and Correlation. These tables appear in each by grouping in the output. If we want to select only the Correlation tables from the output, we can use the get_tables method. This method takes the name of a table and returns a list of all of the tables in the result set with that name. The name of the table should not include the ByGroup#. prefix.

```
In [112]: grpcorr.get_tables('Correlation')
Out[112]:
[Pearson Correlation Coefficients for DATA.IRIS

              Variable   sepal_length  sepal_width  petal_length  \
species
setosa     sepal_length    1.000000      0.746780      0.263874
setosa      sepal_width    0.746780      1.000000      0.176695
setosa     petal_length    0.263874      0.176695      1.000000
setosa      petal_width    0.279092      0.279973      0.306308

              petal_width
species
```

```
setosa          0.279092
setosa          0.279973
setosa          0.306308
setosa          1.000000   , Pearson Correlation Coefficients for DATA.IRIS

                Variable  sepal_length  sepal_width  petal_length  \
species
versicolor  sepal_length      1.000000     0.525911      0.754049
versicolor   sepal_width      0.525911     1.000000      0.560522
versicolor  petal_length      0.754049     0.560522      1.000000
versicolor   petal_width      0.546461     0.663999      0.786668

                petal_width
species
versicolor      0.546461
versicolor      0.663999
versicolor      0.786668
versicolor      1.000000   , Pearson Correlation Coefficients for
DATA.IRIS

                Variable  sepal_length  sepal_width  petal_length  \
species
virginica   sepal_length      1.000000     0.457228      0.864225
virginica    sepal_width      0.457228     1.000000      0.401045
virginica   petal_length      0.864225     0.401045      1.000000
virginica    petal_width      0.281108     0.537728      0.322108

                petal_width
species
virginica       0.281108
virginica       0.537728
virginica       0.322108
virginica       1.000000   ]
```

In the preceding code, you see that we now have a list of DataFrames that correspond to the Correlation tables. You can use the concat function in SWAT to combine the Correlation tables into a single DataFrame.

```
In [113]: swat.concat(grpcorr.get_tables('Correlation'))
Out[113]:
Pearson Correlation Coefficients for DATA.IRIS

                Variable  sepal_length  sepal_width  petal_length  \
species
setosa      sepal_length      1.000000     0.746780      0.263874
setosa       sepal_width      0.746780     1.000000      0.176695
setosa      petal_length      0.263874     0.176695      1.000000
setosa       petal_width      0.279092     0.279973      0.306308
versicolor  sepal_length      1.000000     0.525911      0.754049
versicolor   sepal_width      0.525911     1.000000      0.560522
versicolor  petal_length      0.754049     0.560522      1.000000
versicolor   petal_width      0.546461     0.663999      0.786668
virginica   sepal_length      1.000000     0.457228      0.864225
virginica    sepal_width      0.457228     1.000000      0.401045
virginica   petal_length      0.864225     0.401045      1.000000
virginica    petal_width      0.281108     0.537728      0.322108
```

```
                    petal_width
     species
     setosa             0.279092
     setosa             0.279973
     setosa             0.306308
     setosa             1.000000
     versicolor         0.546461
     versicolor         0.663999
     versicolor         0.786668
     versicolor         1.000000
     virginica          0.281108
     virginica          0.537728
     virginica          0.322108
     virginica          1.000000
```

We've seen how to select specific table names from result sets, but what if we want to select a particular by group? That's covered in the next section.

Selecting a Specific By Group

The CASResults object has a method to select by groups from a result set using the values of the by-grouping variables. This method is called get_group. If you specify a list of values, get_group matches the by-grouping variables as they were specified via the groupby method.

```
In [114]: grpsumm.get_group(['versicolor'])
Out[114]:
[Summary]

 Descriptive Statistics for DATA.IRIS

                     Column  Min  Max
     species
     versicolor  sepal_length  4.9  7.0
     versicolor   sepal_width  2.0  3.4
     versicolor  petal_length  3.0  5.1
     versicolor   petal_width  1.0  1.8
```

You can also use keyword parameters on the get_group method to specify the desired by-grouping variables.

```
In [115]: grpsumm.get_group(species='versicolor')
Out[115]:
[Summary]

 Descriptive Statistics for DATA.IRIS

                     Column  Min  Max
     species
     versicolor  sepal_length  4.9  7.0
     versicolor   sepal_width  2.0  3.4
     versicolor  petal_length  3.0  5.1
     versicolor   petal_width  1.0  1.8
```

The final topic for discussion about by groupings is the case in which a CAS action has support for multiple sets of by groupings.

Handling Multiple Sets of By Groups

Some actions, such as mdsummary, enable you to specify multiple sets of by groups. The output for such actions is similar to what we saw in the examples in the preceding section except that the result keys add another prefix: ByGroupSet#.

```
In [116]: grpmdsumm = \
    .....:        tbl.mdsummary(sets=[dict(groupby=['sepal_length']),
    .....:                            dict(groupby=['petal_length'])])

In [117]: list(grpmdsumm.keys())
Out[117]:
['ByGroupSet1.ByGroupInfo',
 'ByGroupSet1.ByGroup1.MDSummary',
 'ByGroupSet1.ByGroup2.MDSummary',
 'ByGroupSet1.ByGroup3.MDSummary',

 ...

 'ByGroupSet2.ByGroupInfo',
 'ByGroupSet2.ByGroup1.MDSummary',
 'ByGroupSet2.ByGroup2.MDSummary',
 'ByGroupSet2.ByGroup3.MDSummary',

 ...]
```

As you can see from the preceding output, we get a ByGroupSet#.ByGroupInfo table for each by-group set followed by all of the tables for that by-group set. We can extract a particular by-group set from the results using the get_set method.

```
In [118]: grpmdsumm.get_set(1)
Out[118]:
[ByGroupInfo]

ByGroupSet1.ByGroupInfo

     sepal_length  sepal_length_f            _key_
0             5.0               5                5
1             6.0               6                6
2             7.0               7                7
3             4.3             4.3              4.3
4             4.4             4.4              4.4
5             4.5             4.5              4.5
6             4.6             4.6              4.6
7             4.7             4.7              4.7
8             4.8             4.8              4.8
9             4.9             4.9              4.9
..            ...             ...              ...
25            6.7             6.7              6.7
26            6.8             6.8              6.8
27            6.9             6.9              6.9
28            7.1             7.1              7.1
29            7.2             7.2              7.2
30            7.3             7.3              7.3
31            7.4             7.4              7.4
32            7.6             7.6              7.6
33            7.7             7.7              7.7
```

```
34              7.9           7.9              7.9
```

[35 rows x 3 columns]

[ByGroup1.MDSummary]

Descriptive Statistics for DATA.IRIS

```
                      Column   Min   Max      N   NMiss   Mean    Sum  \
sepal_length
5                sepal_length   5.0   5.0   10.0     0.0   5.00   50.0
5                 sepal_width   2.0   3.6   10.0     0.0   3.12   31.2
5                petal_length   1.2   3.5   10.0     0.0   1.84   18.4
5                 petal_width   0.2   1.0   10.0     0.0   0.43    4.3

                    Std      StdErr        Var      USS     CSS  \
sepal_length
5              0.000000    0.000000    0.000000   250.00   0.000
5              0.543241    0.171788    0.295111   100.00   2.656
5              0.834266    0.263818    0.696000    40.12   6.264
5              0.326769    0.103333    0.106778     2.81   0.961

                     CV     TValue         ProbT
sepal_length
5              0.000000        NaN           NaN
5             17.411580  18.161922  2.121189e-08
5             45.340551   6.974502  6.505533e-05
5             75.992719   4.161290  2.443024e-03
```

[ByGroup2.MDSummary]

Descriptive Statistics for DATA.IRIS

```
                      Column   Min   Max     N   NMiss       Mean    Sum  \
sepal_length
6                sepal_length   6.0   6.0   6.0     0.0   6.000000   36.0
6                 sepal_width   2.2   3.4   6.0     0.0   2.733333   16.4
6                petal_length   4.0   5.1   6.0     0.0   4.650000   27.9
6                 petal_width   1.0   1.8   6.0     0.0   1.500000    9.0

                    Std      StdErr        Var      USS       CSS  \
sepal_length
6              0.000000    0.000000    0.000000   216.00   0.000000
6              0.471876    0.192642    0.222667    45.94   1.113333
6              0.403733    0.164823    0.163000   130.55   0.815000
6              0.268328    0.109545    0.072000    13.86   0.360000

                     CV     TValue      ProbT
sepal_length
6              0.000000        NaN        NaN
6             17.263745  14.188635   0.000031
6              8.682421  28.212059   0.000001
6             17.888544  13.693064   0.000037
```

... truncated ...

You see that when using the get_set method, we get back a new CASResults object that corresponds to the output from that particular by-group set. You can then use get_tables, concat_bygroups, or get_group on that result just as we did in the examples in the previous section.

```
In [119]: grpmdsumm.get_set(1).concat_bygroups()
Out[119]:
[MDSummary]
```

Descriptive Statistics for DATA.IRIS

	Column	Min	Max	N	NMiss	Mean	Sum \
sepal_length							
5	sepal_length	5.0	5.0	10.0	0.0	5.000000	50.0
5	sepal_width	2.0	3.6	10.0	0.0	3.120000	31.2
5	petal_length	1.2	3.5	10.0	0.0	1.840000	18.4
5	petal_width	0.2	1.0	10.0	0.0	0.430000	4.3
6	sepal_length	6.0	6.0	6.0	0.0	6.000000	36.0
6	sepal_width	2.2	3.4	6.0	0.0	2.733333	16.4
6	petal_length	4.0	5.1	6.0	0.0	4.650000	27.9
6	petal_width	1.0	1.8	6.0	0.0	1.500000	9.0
7	sepal_length	7.0	7.0	1.0	0.0	7.000000	7.0
7	sepal_width	3.2	3.2	1.0	0.0	3.200000	3.2
...	...	...	...	...	...	...	...
7.6	petal_length	6.6	6.6	1.0	0.0	6.600000	6.6
7.6	petal_width	2.1	2.1	1.0	0.0	2.100000	2.1
7.7	sepal_length	7.7	7.7	4.0	0.0	7.700000	30.8
7.7	sepal_width	2.6	3.8	4.0	0.0	3.050000	12.2
7.7	petal_length	6.1	6.9	4.0	0.0	6.600000	26.4
7.7	petal_width	2.0	2.3	4.0	0.0	2.200000	8.8
7.9	sepal_length	7.9	7.9	1.0	0.0	7.900000	7.9
7.9	sepal_width	3.8	3.8	1.0	0.0	3.800000	3.8
7.9	petal_length	6.4	6.4	1.0	0.0	6.400000	6.4
7.9	petal_width	2.0	2.0	1.0	0.0	2.000000	2.0

```
... truncated ...
```

Conclusion

If you are familiar with Pandas DataFrames, hopefully, the use of much of the API in CASTable objects helps you transition to the world of CAS. We covered the basics of using some of the supported DataFrame methods, using various forms of indexing and iteration, filtering using expressions, creating computed columns, and using by groups. With all of that "under your belt," we can look at some more advanced statistical data in the following chapters.

Chapter 7: Data Exploration and Summary Statistics

Overview

The description of the columns in a table using tabular or visual outputs is typically the first step in a data analysis or a statistical modeling process. In this chapter, you learn how to use CAS to explore and summarize data. Topics include summarizing continuous variables and categorical variables, data transformation, dimensional reduction, and related visualizations using the Python Bokeh package.

Let's start by uploading the Organics Purchase data set from your local directory to CAS. In this example, conn is a CAS object that is connected to a session on a CAS server. For more information about managing your data in CAS, refer to Chapters 4 - 6.

```
In [1]: organics = conn.upload('yourSamplePath/organics.sashdat')
```

We also import the Pandas and Bokeh packages:

```
In [2]: import pandas as pd
   ...: from bokeh.charts import Bar, Scatter, output_file, show, Area
```

Summarizing Continuous Variables

The simple action set provides several useful actions for univariate and multivariate data exploration and summarization. Similar to some action sets that you have learned about in previous chapters, such as builtins and table, the simple action set is also preloaded when you start a new CAS server. Therefore, you can use it on the organics variable, which is a CASTable reference to the data set organics.sashdat that you just uploaded.

Descriptive Statistics

Let's get started with a basic summary action:

```
In [3]: organics.summary()
Out[3]:
[Summary]

      Descriptive Statistics for ORGANICS

              Column     Min      Max            N      NMiss   \
      0       DemAffl     0.00    34.00   1606488.0    82460.0
      1        DemAge    18.00    79.00   1574340.0   114608.0
      2      PromTime     0.00    39.00   1667592.0    21356.0
      3  purchase_3mon  698.44  1188.06  1688948.0        0.0
      4  purchase_6mon 1668.77  2370.87  1688948.0        0.0
      5  purchase_9mon 2624.09  3468.72  1688948.0        0.0
      6 purchase_12mon 3698.92  4684.88  1688948.0        0.0

              Mean           Sum         Std     StdErr           Var   \
      0    8.711893  1.399555e+07    3.421045   0.002699     11.703547
      1   53.797152  8.469501e+07   13.205734   0.010525    174.391404
      2    6.564670  1.094719e+07    4.657008   0.003606     21.687723
      3  950.027539  1.604547e+09   50.067179   0.038525   2506.722438
      4 2049.979250  3.462308e+09   70.731010   0.054425   5002.875812
      5 3070.016785  5.185099e+09   86.588115   0.066627   7497.501651
      6 4189.994798  7.076683e+09  100.009042   0.076954  10001.808545

              USS           CSS          CV       TValue    ProbT
      0  1.407294e+08  1.880160e+07  39.268672   3227.695308    0.0
      1  4.830901e+09  2.745512e+08  24.547273   5111.472302    0.0
      2  1.080310e+08  3.616625e+07  70.940468   1820.333053    0.0
      3  1.528598e+12  4.233721e+09   5.270077  24659.894243    0.0
      4  7.106110e+12  8.449592e+09   3.450328  37665.847454    0.0
      5  1.593100e+13  1.266288e+10   2.820444  46077.679978    0.0
      6  2.966816e+13  1.689252e+10   2.386854  54448.053001    0.0
```

In this example, you execute the summary action to generate descriptive statistics for all the numeric columns in the organics data set. The default statistics that are generated by the summary action are described in the following table:

Statistic	Description
Min	Minimum value
Max	Maximum value
N	Number of observations with nonmissing values
NMiss	Number of observations with missing values
Sum	Sum
Std	Standard Deviation
StdErr	Standard Error
Var	Variable
USS	Uncorrected Sum of Squares
CSS	Corrected Sum of Squares
CV	Coefficient of Variation
TValue	Value of T-statistics for hypothesis testing
ProbT	p-value of the T-statistics

Let's work on a specific set of columns. You can set the inputs parameter of the summary action to obtain the descriptive statistics for specified columns:

```
In [4]: varlist = ['DemAge', 'Purchase_12mon', 'Purchase_6mon']
   ...: organics.summary(inputs=varlist)
Out[4]:
[Summary]

Descriptive Statistics for ORGANICS

            Column      Min      Max            N       NMiss  \
0           DemAge    18.00    79.00    1574340.0    114608.0
1    purchase_12mon  3698.92  4684.88  1688948.0         0.0
2    purchase_6mon   1668.77  2370.87  1688948.0         0.0

          Mean            Sum          Std      StdErr           Var  \
0    53.797152   8.469501e+07    13.205734    0.010525    174.391404
1  4189.994798   7.076683e+09   100.009042    0.076954  10001.808545
2  2049.979250   3.462308e+09    70.731010    0.054425   5002.875812

           USS           CSS          CV       TValue   ProbT
0  4.830901e+09  2.745512e+08   24.547273  5111.472302   0.0
1  2.966816e+13  1.689252e+10    2.386854 54448.053001   0.0
2  7.106110e+12  8.449592e+09    3.450328 37665.847454   0.0
```

This code generates summary statistics only for columns that you have specified: DemAge, Purchase_12mon, and Purchase_6mon. In the next example, we compute the summary statistics for the columns for recent purchase amounts and save the result in a local object.

```
In [5]: varlist = ['Purchase_3mon', 'Purchase_6mon', 'Purchase_9mon',
                    'Purchase_12mon']
   ...: result = organics.summary(inputs=varlist)
```

The result is a CASResults object that contains the log, the performance data, the server information, and the output of the submitted CAS action. For example, you can print out the run time of the preceding summary action:

```
In [6]: print(result.performance.cpu_system_time)
        print(result.performance.cpu_user_time)
Out[6]:
0.766884
0.367944
```

A CAS action might return one or more tables referenced by the keys of the CASResult object. In this example, only one summary table has been returned by the summary action.

```
In [7]: list(result.keys())
Out[7]: ['Summary']
```

Result tables are returned in the form of SASDataFrame objects. Because the SASDataFrame is a subclass of the Pandas DataFrame, it works seamlessly with Pandas and many Python packages that support DataFrames. For example, you can use the stack method to rearrange the output summary table.

```
In [8]: df = result['Summary']
   ...: df.columns

Out[8]: Index(['Column', 'Min', 'Max', 'N', 'NMiss', 'Mean', 'Sum',
       'Std', 'StdErr', 'Var', 'USS', 'CSS', 'CV', 'TValue', 'ProbT'],
       dtype='object')


In [9]: df.index = df['Column']
   ...: stackedDf = df[['Min','Mean','Max']].stack()
   ...: print(stackedDf)

Out[9]:
Column
purchase_3mon    Min      698.440000
                 Mean     950.006638
                 Max     1188.060000
purchase_6mon    Min     1668.770000
                 Mean    2049.989809
                 Max     2370.870000
purchase_9mon    Min     2624.090000
                 Mean    3070.037322
                 Max     3468.720000
purchase_12mon   Min     3704.700000
                 Mean    4190.004978
                 Max     4684.880000
```

You can also use the Bokeh package to generate a bar chart using the summary statistics that are generated by the summary action.

```
In [10]: p = Bar(df, 'Column', values='Mean',
    ...:           color='#1f77b4', agg='mean', title='',
    ...:           xlabel = '', ylabel ='Frequency')
    ...: output_file('visual1.html')

    ...: show(p)
```

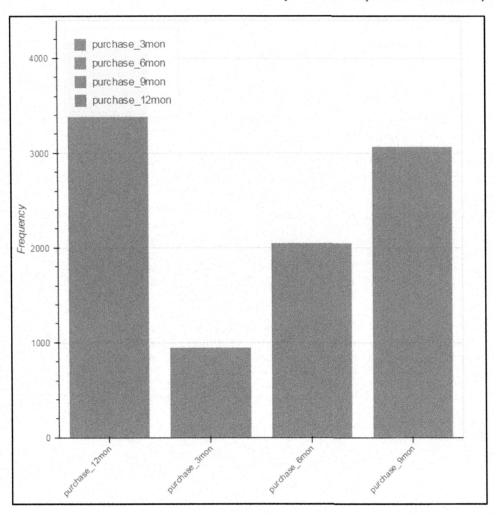

Sometimes it is useful to summarize your data by segments, which is accomplished with the groupby parameter.

```
In [11]: organics.groupby='DemGender'
    ...: result = organics.summary(inputs='DemAge')
```

The groupby parameter groups the data into three segments for DemGender : F, M, or U. Also, it summarizes the column DemAge for each data segment, respectively. The summary statistics are returned in three different DataFrames.

```
In [12]: list(result.keys())
Out[12]: ['ByGroupInfo', 'ByGroup1.Summary', 'ByGroup2.Summary',
          'ByGroup3.Summary']
```

In this case, the summary action also returns a table called ByGroupInfo that provides basic information about the by groups.

```
In [13]: result['ByGroupInfo']
Out[13]:
```

```
ByGroupInfo

    DemGender DemGender_f _key_
0           F           F      F
1           M           M      M
2           U           U      U
```

To merge these tables into one result table, use the CASResults concat_bygroups method. It returns a new CASResults object with all by-group tables that are concatenated.

```
In [14]: result2 = result.concat_bygroups()
    ...: result2['Summary'][['N','Min','Mean','Max','Std']]
```

Out[14]:
```
Descriptive Statistics for ORGANICS

                  N    Min      Mean   Max         Std
DemGender
F          861460.0  18.0  52.880723  79.0  13.546649
M          411768.0  18.0  54.535807  79.0  12.817555
U          301112.0  18.0  55.408884  79.0  12.504695
```

When you specify a group-by variable, the summary action does not require any data shuffle to summarize data by segments. In fact, you can have as many group-by variables as you need. For example, the next action call summarizes DemAge by two columns: DemGender and DemHomeowner.

```
In [15]: varlist='DemAge'
    ...: organics.groupby=['DemGender','DemHomeowner']
    ...: result = organics.summary(inputs=varlist).concat_bygroups()
    ...: result['Summary'][['N','Min','Mean','Max','Std']]
```

Out[15]:
```
Descriptive Statistics for ORGANICS

                              N    Min      Mean   Max         Std
DemGender DemHomeowner
F         No           560471.0  18.0  52.883482  79.0  13.543064
          Yes          300989.0  18.0  52.875587  79.0  13.553343
M         No           267238.0  18.0  54.525262  79.0  12.814615
          Yes          144530.0  18.0  54.555303  79.0  12.823012
U         No           195894.0  18.0  55.414745  79.0  12.504366
          Yes          105218.0  18.0  55.397974  79.0  12.505360
```

In this example, we concatenate the by-group tables and automatically assign the levels of the group-by variables as the indices of the underlying Pandas DataFrame. The index is shown below:

```
In [16]: result['Summary'].index
Out[16]:
MultiIndex(levels=[['F', 'M', 'U'], ['No', 'Yes']],
           labels=[[0, 0, 1, 1, 2, 2], [0, 1, 0, 1, 0, 1]],
           names=['DemGender', 'DemHomeowner'])
```

To remove the grouping variables from the CASTable object, you can use either the Python del statement or the CASTable del_params method. After the grouping variables are removed, the summary action computes summary statistics for the entire data set.

```
In [17]: del organics.groupby
```

You can also use

```
In [18]: organics.del_param('groupby')
```

Histograms

Histograms are another useful visualization tool for summarizing continuous data. A histogram is an estimate of the probability distribution of a continuous variable by *equal-distance binning*. The CAS dataPreprocess action set provides a histogram action. In the next example, we execute the histogram action for the DemAge column:

```
In [19]: result = organics.histogram(
    ...:     reqpacks=[{'nicebinning':False, 'nbins':10}],
    ...:     inputs=['Purchase_3mon']
    ...: )
```

```
In [20]: result['BinDetails']
Out[20]:
```
Bin Details for ORGANICS

	Variable	BinSetId	BinId	BinLowerBnd	BinUpperBnd \
0	purchase_3mon	1	1	698.440	747.402
1	purchase_3mon	1	2	747.402	796.364
2	purchase_3mon	1	3	796.364	845.326
3	purchase_3mon	1	4	845.326	894.288
4	purchase_3mon	1	5	894.288	943.250
5	purchase_3mon	1	6	943.250	992.212
6	purchase_3mon	1	7	992.212	1041.174
7	purchase_3mon	1	8	1041.174	1090.136
8	purchase_3mon	1	9	1090.136	1139.098
9	purchase_3mon	1	10	1139.098	1188.060

	BinWidth	NInBin	Mean	Std	Min	Max \
0	48.962	45	735.920444	11.629722	698.44	747.30
1	48.962	1802	783.902153	10.767204	747.72	796.36
2	48.962	28782	830.094716	12.081154	796.37	845.32
3	48.962	193828	875.761523	13.155664	845.33	894.28
4	48.962	529051	921.156725	13.782269	894.29	943.24
5	48.962	597872	966.341785	13.869978	943.25	992.21
6	48.962	279514	1011.694702	13.360849	992.22	1041.17
7	48.962	53719	1057.383763	12.429201	1041.18	1090.12
8	48.962	4214	1103.745873	11.365814	1090.14	1139.07
9	48.962	121	1151.365785	10.677088	1139.32	1188.06

	MidPoint	Percent
0	722.921	0.002664
1	771.883	0.106694
2	820.845	1.704138
3	869.807	11.476256
4	918.769	31.324292
5	967.731	35.399077
6	1016.693	16.549592
7	1065.655	3.180619

```
8  1114.617   0.249504
9  1163.579   0.007164
```

Each row of the BinDetails output contains the binning information for a specific bin, including the lower and upper bounds, the bin width, and summary statistics per bin such as counts, averages, standard deviations, minimums, maximums and midpoints. You can also use the Bokeh package to create a histogram.

```
In [21]: p = Bar(result['BinDetails'], 'MidPoint', values='Percent',
   ...:             color='#1f77b4', agg='mean', title='', legend=None,
   ...:             xlabel = 'Purchase_3mon',
   ...:             ylabel = 'Percent'
   ...: )
   ...: output_file('bar.html')
   ...: show(p)
```

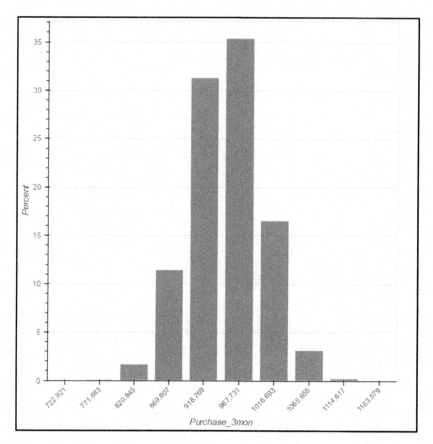

In the preceding example, we set nicebinning to False, which is an option to request coarser upper bounds and lower bounds. Such a calculation usually returns nicer cutpoints for visualization and interpretation. A setting of True for nicebinning generates the following Bokeh visualization:

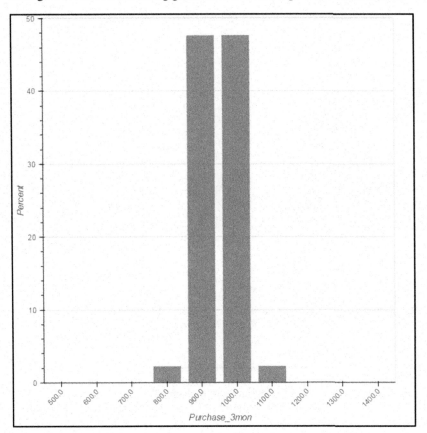

Compared to the previous graph, the nicebinning option allows bounds only at a step size of 100, which is determined automatically by the range of the variable Purchase_3mon. Sometimes you need to increase the number of bins when you use the nicebinning option to get a better understanding of the data. In this example, let us change the number of bins from 10 to 25.

```
In [22]: result= organics.histogram(
    ...:         reqpacks=[{'nicebinning':True, 'nbins':25}],
    ...:         inputs=['Purchase_3mon']
    ...: )

In [23]: p = Bar(result['BinDetails'], 'MidPoint', values='Percent',
    ...:         color='#1f77b4', agg='mean', title='', legend=None,
    ...:         xlabel = 'Purchase_3mon',
    ...:         ylabel = 'Percent'
    ...: )
    ...: output_file('bar.html')
    ...: show(p)
```

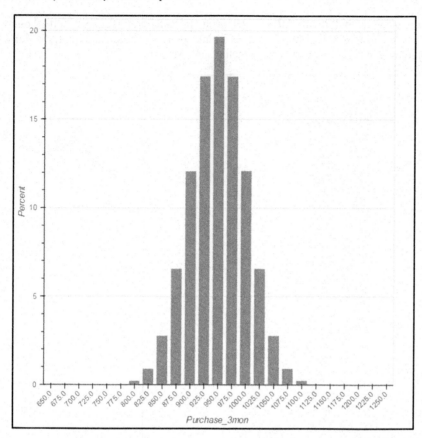

In this example, 25 is chosen as the step size. The histogram action also enables you to set the bins manually. For example, you can force a fixed bin width of 50. In this case, you don't need to specify a number of bins because it is determined automatically.

```
In [24]: result= organics.histogram(
   ...:         reqpacks=[{'binwidth':50}],
   ...:         inputs=['Purchase_3mon']
   ...: )

In [25]: p = Bar(result['BinDetails'], 'MidPoint', values='Percent',
   ...:           color='#1f77b4', agg='mean', title='', legend=None,
   ...:           xlabel='Purchase_3mon',
   ...:           ylabel='Percent'
   ...: )
   ...: output_file('bar.html')
   ...: show(p)
```

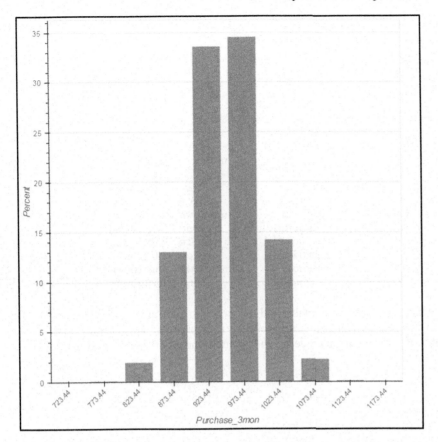

Similar to the summary action, the histogram action also supports group-by processing. You can request a histogram for each data segment that is defined by a set of group-by columns.

```
In [26]: organics.groupby = ['DemGender', 'DemAgeGroup']
    ...: result = organics.histogram(
    ...:     reqpacks=[{'nicebinning':False, 'nbins':20}],
    ...:     inputs=['DemAffl']
    ...: )
    ...: list(result.keys())
Out[26]:
['ByGroupInfo',
 'ByGroup1.BinDetails',
 'ByGroup2.BinDetails',
 'ByGroup3.BinDetails',
 'ByGroup4.BinDetails',
 'ByGroup5.BinDetails',
 'ByGroup6.BinDetails',
 'ByGroup7.BinDetails',
 'ByGroup8.BinDetails',
 'ByGroup9.BinDetails',
 'ByGroup10.BinDetails',
 'ByGroup11.BinDetails',
 'ByGroup12.BinDetails']
```

Except for the ByGroupInfo table, each result table contains the histogram statistics for one by group. The ByGroupInfo table provides an overview of the by-group levels:

```
In [27]: result['ByGroupInfo']
Out[27]:
ByGroupInfo
```

	DemGender	DemGender_f	DemAgeGroup	DemAgeGroup_f	_key_
0	F	F	middle	middle	Fmiddle
1	F	F	senior	senior	Fsenior
2	F	F	unknown	unknown	Funknown
3	F	F	young	young	Fyoung
4	M	M	middle	middle	Mmiddle
5	M	M	senior	senior	Msenior
6	M	M	unknown	unknown	Munknown
7	M	M	young	young	Myoung
8	U	U	middle	middle	Umiddle
9	U	U	senior	senior	Usenior
10	U	U	unknown	unknown	Uunknown
11	U	U	young	young	Uyoung

Next, let's collect the statistics from the output table and use Bokeh to generate a grid of histograms. The all_df dictionary contains the title of each histogram as well as its data. You must generate visualizations, one by one, using the Bokeh bar chart and then define the layout of the grid using the gridplot function from Bokeh.

```
In [28]: all_df = {
    ...:'Gender=Female, AgeGroup=Middle':  result['ByGroup1.BinDetails'],
    ...:'Gender=Female, AgeGroup=Senior':  result['ByGroup2.BinDetails'],
    ...:'Gender=Female, AgeGroup=Unknown': result['ByGroup3.BinDetails'],
    ...:'Gender=Female, AgeGroup=Young' :  result['ByGroup4.BinDetails']
    ...:}
    ...: all_pic = []
    ...:
    ...: for this_title in all_df:
    ...:     this_pic = Bar(all_df[this_title], 'MidPoint', values='Percent',
    ...:         color='#1f77b4', agg='mean', title=this_title, legend=None,
    ...:         xlabel='DemAffl',
    ...:         ylabel='Percent'
    ...:     )
    ...:     all_pic.append(this_pic)
    ...:
    ...: from bokeh.io import gridplot
    ...:
    ...: p = gridplot([[all_pic[0], all_pic[1]],
    ...:               [all_pic[2], all_pic[3]]])
    ...: output_file('grid.html')
    ...: show(p)
```

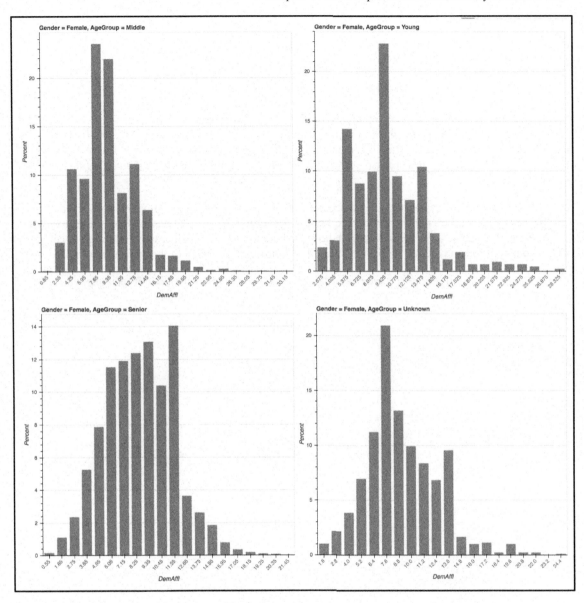

Percentiles

Percentile is another useful tool for numeric data exploration. A percentile is a statistic for indicating a variable that has a given percentage of observations below the percentile value. In CAS, such statistics are available in the percentile action set.

```
In [29]: conn.loadactionset('percentile')
    ...:
    ...: del organics.groupby
    ...: organics.percentile(inputs='DemAge')
NOTE: Added action set 'percentile'.
Out[29]:
[Percentile]
```

Percentiles for ORGANICS

	Variable	Pctl	Value	Converged
0	DemAge	25.0	44.0	1.0
1	DemAge	50.0	54.0	1.0
2	DemAge	75.0	64.0	1.0

By default, the percentile action computes the 25th, the 50th, and the 75th percentiles for the selected columns. The preceding result shows that 25% of the observations of DemAge are less than 44, and half of the observations of DemAge are less than 54. Finally, 75% of the observations of DemAge are less than 64. These three percentiles are also known as the first quartile (Q1), the second quartile (median), and the third quartile (Q3).

The last column of the output table indicates whether the percentile calculation has converged. The CAS percentile action does not sort the data to find the percentiles. Instead, it has a numeric approximation algorithm to estimate the percentile, and the last column indicates whether the algorithm has converged. Two parameters maxiters and epsilon are used to control the accuracy of the approximation.

You can also specify the percentage values directly using the values option. For example, you can get a list of percentiles for percentage from 5% to 90% with a step size of 5% as follows.

```
In [30]: result = organics.percentile(inputs='DemAge', values=list(range(5,95,5)))
    ...: result
Out[30]:
[Percentile]
```

Percentiles for ORGANICS

	Variable	Pctl	Value	Converged
0	DemAge	5.0	32.0	1.0
1	DemAge	10.0	36.0	1.0
2	DemAge	15.0	39.0	1.0
3	DemAge	20.0	41.0	1.0
4	DemAge	25.0	44.0	1.0
5	DemAge	30.0	46.0	1.0
6	DemAge	35.0	48.0	1.0
7	DemAge	40.0	50.0	1.0
8	DemAge	45.0	52.0	1.0
9	DemAge	50.0	54.0	1.0
10	DemAge	55.0	56.0	1.0
11	DemAge	60.0	58.0	1.0
12	DemAge	65.0	60.0	1.0
13	DemAge	70.0	62.0	1.0
14	DemAge	75.0	64.0	1.0
15	DemAge	80.0	66.0	1.0
16	DemAge	85.0	69.0	1.0
17	DemAge	90.0	72.0	1.0

The percentile action supports group-by processing as well:

```
In [31]: organics.groupby = ['DemGender']
    ...: result = organics.percentile(inputs='DemAge', values=list(range(5,95,5)))
```

In this case, we can use the Bokeh package to visually compare the distributions of DemAge across three different levels of the DemGender column.

```
In [32]: df = result.concat_bygroups()['Percentile']
    ...: df.reset_index(level=0, inplace=True)
```

```
In [33]: p = Scatter(df, x='Pctl', y='Value', legend='top_center', marker='DemGender')
    ...: output_file('scatter.html')
    ...: show(p)
```

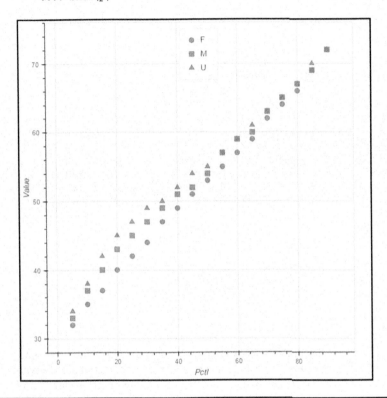

Correlations

The simple action set also provides a correlation action that generates a matrix of Pearson product-moment correlation coefficients for a set of variables.

```
In [34]: organics = conn.CASTable('ORGANICS')
    ...: organics.correlation()
Out[34]:
[CorrSimple]
```

Summary Statistics in Correlation Analysis for ORGANICS

	Variable	N	Mean	Sum	StdDev \
0	DemAffl	1606488.0	8.711893	1.399555e+07	3.421045
1	DemAge	1574340.0	53.797152	8.469501e+07	13.205734
2	PromTime	1667592.0	6.564670	1.094719e+07	4.657008
3	purchase_3mon	1688948.0	950.027539	1.604547e+09	50.067179
4	purchase_6mon	1688948.0	2049.979250	3.462308e+09	70.731010
5	purchase_9mon	1688948.0	3070.016785	5.185099e+09	86.588115
6	purchase_12mon	1688948.0	4189.994798	7.076683e+09	100.009042

```
        Minimum  Maximum
0          0.00    34.00
1         18.00    79.00
2          0.00    39.00
3        698.44  1188.06
4       1668.77  2370.87
5       2624.09  3468.72
6       3698.92  4684.88

[Correlation]

Pearson Correlation Coefficients for ORGANICS

              Variable    DemAffl      DemAge    PromTime   purchase_3mon  \
0              DemAffl   1.000000   -0.137767   -0.029736        0.001571
1               DemAge  -0.137767    1.000000    0.207221       -0.001160
2             PromTime  -0.029736    0.207221    1.000000       -0.000304
3        purchase_3mon   0.001571   -0.001160   -0.000304        1.000000
4        purchase_6mon   0.001686   -0.001008   -0.000564        0.707469
5        purchase_9mon   0.001459   -0.000541   -0.001720        0.578367
6       purchase_12mon   0.000965   -0.000587   -0.002255        0.500961

     purchase_6mon   purchase_9mon   purchase_12mon
0         0.001686        0.001459         0.000965
1        -0.001008       -0.000541        -0.000587
2        -0.000564       -0.001720        -0.002255
3         0.707469        0.578367         0.500961
4         1.000000        0.816600         0.707387
5         0.816600        1.000000         0.866058
6         0.707387        0.866058         1.000000
```

By default, the correlation action uses all of the numeric columns and also computes the univariate statistics for each column as a by-product of computing the Pearson's correlation coefficients. It also provides a simple flag to disable the output of the univariate statistics. To select a set of columns instead of all numeric columns, you must set the inputs option of the correlation action.

```
In [35]: varlist = ['DemAffl', 'DemAge', 'purchase_3mon']
   ...: organics.correlation(inputs=varlist, simple=False)
Out[35]:
[Correlation]

Pearson Correlation Coefficients for ORGANICS

            Variable    DemAffl      DemAge   purchase_3mon
0            DemAffl   1.000000   -0.137767        0.001571
1             DemAge  -0.137767    1.000000       -0.001160
2      purchase_3mon   0.001571   -0.001160        1.000000
```

Summarizing Categorical Variables

In the previous section, we examined some useful actions in the simple, dataPreprocess, and percentile action sets of CAS for summarizing and exploring continuous variables. The simple action set also provides several actions for categorical data analysis, such as these actions: distinct, freq, topk, and crosstab.

Distinct Counts

Before you work on any categorical data, it is useful to first check the cardinality of the data using the distinct action.

```
In [1]: organics = conn.CASTable('ORGANICS')

In [2]: organics.distinct()
Out[2]:
[Distinct]

 Distinct Counts for ORGANICS
```

	Column	NDistinct	NMiss	Trunc
0	ID	1688948.0	0.0	0.0
1	DemAffl	34.0	82460.0	0.0
2	DemAge	63.0	114608.0	0.0
3	DemGender	3.0	0.0	0.0
4	DemHomeowner	2.0	0.0	0.0
5	DemAgeGroup	4.0	0.0	0.0
6	DemCluster	56.0	0.0	0.0
7	DemReg	6.0	0.0	0.0
8	DemTVReg	14.0	0.0	0.0
9	DemFlag1	2.0	0.0	0.0
10	DemFlag2	2.0	0.0	0.0
11	DemFlag3	2.0	0.0	0.0
12	DemFlag4	2.0	0.0	0.0
13	DemFlag5	2.0	0.0	0.0
14	DemFlag6	2.0	0.0	0.0
15	DemFlag7	2.0	0.0	0.0
16	DemFlag8	2.0	0.0	0.0
17	PromClass	4.0	0.0	0.0
18	PromTime	40.0	21356.0	0.0
19	TargetBuy	2.0	0.0	0.0
20	Bought_Beverages	2.0	0.0	0.0
21	Bought_Bakery	2.0	0.0	0.0
22	Bought_Canned	2.0	0.0	0.0
23	Bought_Dairy	2.0	0.0	0.0
24	Bought_Baking	2.0	0.0	0.0
25	Bought_Frozen	2.0	0.0	0.0
26	Bought_Meat	2.0	0.0	0.0
27	Bought_Fruits	2.0	0.0	0.0
28	Bought_Vegetables	2.0	0.0	0.0
29	Bought_Cleaners	2.0	0.0	0.0
30	Bought_PaperGoods	2.0	0.0	0.0
31	Bought_Others	2.0	0.0	0.0
32	purchase_3mon	32944.0	0.0	0.0
33	purchase_6mon	44997.0	0.0	0.0

```
34      purchase_9mon    54032.0    0.0   0.0
35      purchase_12mon   61444.0    0.0   0.0
```

By default, the distinct action calculates two types of information for each column in the table: 1) the number of distinct values, and 2) the number of missing values for both character and numeric columns. Computing the exact distinct counts for the numeric columns and the unique identifiers (such as the ID column in the Organics table) could be slow and could require large memory footprints, but often the exact distinct counts for these columns are not useful because we need to know only whether some variables have distinct levels that exceed a certain threshold. The distinct action provides the option maxnvals to skip the exact counting of the distinct levels for high cardinality variables.

```
In [3]: organics.distinct(maxnvals=500)
Out[3]:
[Distinct]

Distinct Counts for ORGANICS
```

	Column	NDistinct	NMiss	Trunc
0	ID	500.0	0.0	1.0
1	DemAffl	34.0	82460.0	0.0
2	DemAge	63.0	114608.0	0.0
3	DemGender	3.0	0.0	0.0
4	DemHomeowner	2.0	0.0	0.0
5	DemAgeGroup	4.0	0.0	0.0
6	DemCluster	56.0	0.0	0.0
7	DemReg	6.0	0.0	0.0
8	DemTVReg	14.0	0.0	0.0
9	DemFlag1	2.0	0.0	0.0
10	DemFlag2	2.0	0.0	0.0
11	DemFlag3	2.0	0.0	0.0
12	DemFlag4	2.0	0.0	0.0
13	DemFlag5	2.0	0.0	0.0
14	DemFlag6	2.0	0.0	0.0
15	DemFlag7	2.0	0.0	0.0
16	DemFlag8	2.0	0.0	0.0
17	PromClass	4.0	0.0	0.0
18	PromTime	40.0	21356.0	0.0
19	TargetBuy	2.0	0.0	0.0
20	Bought_Beverages	2.0	0.0	0.0
21	Bought_Bakery	2.0	0.0	0.0
22	Bought_Canned	2.0	0.0	0.0
23	Bought_Dairy	2.0	0.0	0.0
24	Bought_Baking	2.0	0.0	0.0
25	Bought_Frozen	2.0	0.0	0.0
26	Bought_Meat	2.0	0.0	0.0
27	Bought_Fruits	2.0	0.0	0.0
28	Bought_Vegetables	2.0	0.0	0.0
29	Bought_Cleaners	2.0	0.0	0.0
30	Bought_PaperGoods	2.0	0.0	0.0
31	Bought_Others	2.0	0.0	0.0
32	purchase_3mon	500.0	0.0	1.0
33	purchase_6mon	500.0	0.0	1.0
34	purchase_9mon	500.0	0.0	1.0
35	purchase_12mon	500.0	0.0	1.0

In this example, the distinct action loops through the data and has early stops for the distinct count calculations for these columns—ID, purchase_3mon, purchase_6mon, purchase_9mon, and purchase_12mon—after their current distinct counts reach 500. Therefore, in the output table, the number of distinct values for these columns are shown as 500. A new column Trunc is added as a binary indicator for whether the distinct count values are exact.

Note that in this data, the categorical variable with the highest cardinality is DemCluster, which has 56 distinct levels. Missing values is another useful item of information that you can access in the distinct action output. In this example, three columns—DemAffl, DemAge and PromTime—have a significant number of missing values.

In the preceding examples, we requested that the output be downloaded to the Python client. You can also store the output of the distinct action in a table on the CAS server. You can then use the head method to download results from the output table.

```
In [4]: result = conn.CASTable('distinctOutput', replace=True)
   ...: organics.distinct(maxnvals=500, casout=result)
   ...: result.head()
Out[4]:
Selected Rows from Table CAS.DISTINCTOUTPUT
```

	Column	_NDis_	_NMiss_	_Truncated_
0	ID	0.0	0.0	1.0
1	DemAffl	34.0	82460.0	0.0
2	DemAge	63.0	114608.0	0.0
3	DemGender	3.0	0.0	0.0
4	DemHomeowner	2.0	0.0	0.0

The columninfo action generates basic information about each column, such as whether it is numeric (double, int32, or int64) or character (char or varchar). The distinct action further computes the cardinality of the columns. It is common to combine these two pieces of information to determine whether a column should be used as a categorical variable or a continuous variable. The following example merges the output tables from the columninfo and distinct actions using the Pandas merge function. Then it selects character columns with no more than 128 levels and numeric columns with no more than 16 levels as categorical variables. Also, it selects numeric columns with more than 16 levels as continuous variables. All other columns are dropped into the Others group.

```
In [5]: out1 = organics.columninfo()['ColumnInfo']
   ...: out2 = organics.distinct(maxnvals=1000)['Distinct']
   ...: out3 = pd.merge(out1, out2, left_on='Column', right_on='Column',
                   how='left')
   ...:
   ...: varlist = { 'cats': [], 'conts': [], 'others' : [] }
   ...:
   ...: for index, row in out3.iterrows():
   ...:     varname = row['Column'].lower()
   ...:     vartype = row['Type'].lower()
   ...:     if vartype == 'char' and row['NDistinct'] <= 128:
   ...:         varlist['cats'].append(varname)
   ...:     elif vartype == 'double' and row['NDistinct'] <= 16:
   ...:         varlist['cats'].append(varname)
   ...:     elif vartype == 'double' and row['NDistinct'] > 16:
   ...:         varlist['conts'].append(varname)
   ...:     else:
   ...:         varlist['others'].append(varname)
```

```
      . . . :
      . . . : print(varlist)

{'conts': ['demaffl', 'demage', 'promtime', 'purchase_3mon',
'purchase_6mon', 'purchase_9mon', 'purchase_12mon'],
 'cats': ['demgender', 'demhomeowner', 'demagegroup', 'demcluster',
'demreg', 'demtvreg', 'demflag1', 'demflag2', 'demflag3', 'demflag4',
'demflag5', 'demflag6', 'demflag7', 'demflag8', 'promclass', 'targetbuy',
'bought_beverages', 'bought_bakery', 'bought_canned', 'bought_dairy',
'bought_baking', 'bought_frozen', 'bought_meat', 'bought_fruits',
'bought_vegetables', 'bought_cleaners', 'bought_papergoods',
'bought_others'],
 'others': ['id']}
```

Frequency

The distinct action computes only the number of distinct levels of a categorical variable. To get the frequency distribution of a categorical variable, you must use the freq action in the simple action set.

```
In [6]: varlist=['TargetBuy']
   ...: organics.freq(inputs=varlist)
Out[6]:
[Frequency]

 Frequency for ORGANICS

        Column CharVar  FmtVar  Level  Frequency
 0   TargetBuy  Bought  Bought      1   418380.0
 1   TargetBuy      No      No      2  1270568.0
```

Note that this method is equivalent to using column indexing first and then calling the freq action:

```
In [7]: organics[['TargetBuy']].freq()
```

The output table of the freq action contains one row for each level of the categorical variable, including:

Column Name	Column Label	Description
Column	Analysis Variable	Column name of the variable in the input data set
CharVar	Character Value	Unformatted value of the variable
FmtVar	Formatted Value	Formatted value of the variable (SAS formats)
Level	Level	Index of the distinct variable value
Frequency	Frequency	Frequency count

Next, let's visualize the result from the freq action. Similar to the data explorations in the previous section, a Bokeh bar chart is used.

```
In [8]: from bokeh.charts import Bar, output_file, show
   ...:
   ...: df = organics['TargetBuy'].freq()
   ...:
   ...: p = Bar(df['Frequency'], 'FmtVar', values='Frequency',
   ...:         color='#1f77b4', agg='mean', title='', legend=None,
   ...:         xlabel='TargetBuy',
   ...:         ylabel='Frequency'
   ...: )
```

```
...: output_file('bar.html')
...: show(p)
```

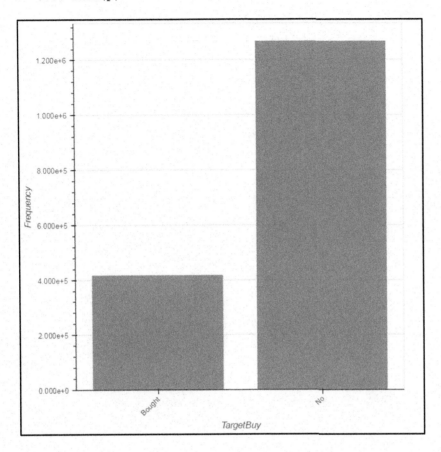

You can request multiple frequency tables in a single freq call by adding more variables to the variable list of the CASTable object.

```
In [9]: organics[['TargetBuy','DemAgeGroup','DemHomeowner']].freq()
Out[9]:
[Frequency]

Frequency for ORGANICS
```

	Column	CharVar	FmtVar	Level	Frequency
0	TargetBuy	Bought	Bought	1	418380.0
1	TargetBuy	No	No	2	1270568.0
2	DemAgeGroup	middle	middle	1	991800.0
3	DemAgeGroup	senior	senior	2	532456.0
4	DemAgeGroup	unknown	unknown	3	114608.0
5	DemAgeGroup	young	young	4	50084.0
6	DemHomeowner	No	No	1	1097860.0
7	DemHomeowner	Yes	Yes	2	591088.0

It is valid to use the freq action on numeric variables as well. The next example uses the freq action to generate a frequency table of the DemAge variable. In this example, the freq action is equivalent to a histogram action with integer binning and a step size set to 1.

```
In [10]: df = organics['DemAge'].freq(includemissing=False)
    ...:
    ...: p = Bar(df['Frequency'], 'FmtVar', values='Frequency',
    ...:         color='#1f77b4', agg='mean', title='', legend=None,
    ...:         xlabel='Age',
    ...:         ylabel='Frequency',
    ...:         bar_width=1,
    ...:         plot_width=1200, plot_height=600
    ...: )
    ...: output_file('bar.html')
    ...: show(p)
```

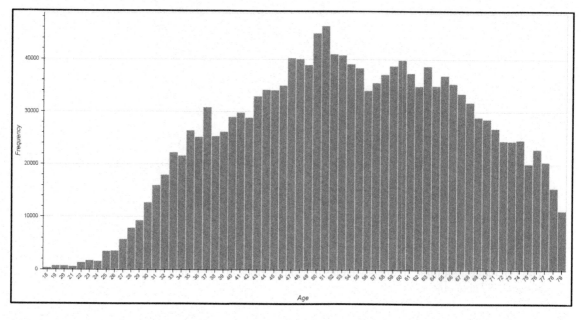

You can see that the age of the customers in this data set has a mode of 51, and it is skewed to the left. The minimum age is 18 and the maximum age is 79. From the distinct action, we also learn that this variable has a lot of missing values. So it is also helpful to enable the includemissing flag to display a missing bar on the bar chart.

```
In [11]: df = organics[['DemAge']].freq(includemissing=True)
    ...:
    ...: p = Bar(df['Frequency'], 'FmtVar', values='Frequency',
    ...:         color='#1f77b4', agg='mean', title='',
    ...:         xlabel='Age',
    ...:         ylabel='Frequency',
    ...:         bar_width=1,
    ...:         plot_width=1200, plot_height=600
    ...: )
    ...: output_file('bar.html')
    ...: show(p)
```

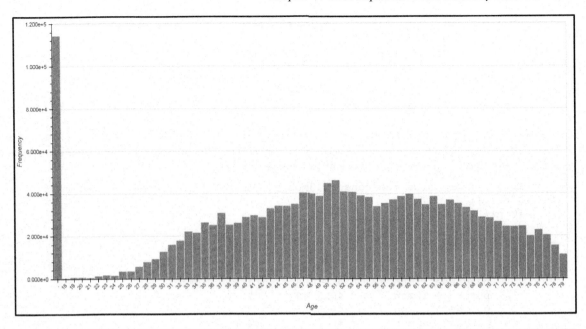

Top K

The freq action returns a complete one-way frequency table. For high cardinality categorical variables, computation of the entire frequency tables might be time-consuming. In this case, the simple action set also provides a topk action to generate partial frequency tables.

```
In [12]: organics['purchase_12mon'].topk(topk=5, bottomk=0)
Out[12]:
[Topk]

Top and Bottom Distinct Values for ORGANICS

            Column       FmtVar  Rank
0  purchase_12mon       4684.88     1
1  purchase_12mon       4653.49     2
2  purchase_12mon       4646.95     3
3  purchase_12mon       4641.13     4
4  purchase_12mon       4631.91     5

[TopkMisc]

Miscellaneous Information on Distinct Values for ORGANICS

            Column      N  TruncatedTopk  TruncatedBtmk  ScoreOther
0  purchase_12mon  61444              0              0         NaN
```

Unlike the freq action, the topk action produces two output tables instead of one output table. The first table contains the top or bottom values of the input variables, and the second table contains a brief report for each input variable. You can loop through the CASResults object to obtain the name of each table and its columns.

```
In [13]: result = organics['purchase_12mon'].topK(topk=5, bottomk=0)
   ...: for df in result:
   ...:     print(df + ' table has: ' +
                   ' '.join(result[df].columns.values))


Topk table has: Column, NumVar, Rank
TopkMisc table has: Column, N, TruncatedTopk, TruncatedBtmk, ScoreOther
```

Similar to the freq action, the topk action can be used to work on more than one variable and to compute both the bottom and top values of the variables. Simply specify the preferred variables when you subset the CASTable object, and specify the topk and bottomk parameters.

```
In [14]: organics[['purchase_12mon','DemAge']].topK(topk=5, bottomk=5)
Out[14]:
[Topk]
```

Top and Bottom Distinct Values for ORGANICS

	Column	FmtVar	Rank
0	purchase_12mon	4684.88	1
1	purchase_12mon	4653.49	2
2	purchase_12mon	4646.95	3
3	purchase_12mon	4641.13	4
4	purchase_12mon	4631.91	5
5	purchase_12mon	3826	61444
6	purchase_12mon	3833	61443
7	purchase_12mon	3849	61442
8	purchase_12mon	3850	61441
9	purchase_12mon	3851	61440
10	DemAge	79	1
11	DemAge	78	2
12	DemAge	77	3
13	DemAge	76	4
14	DemAge	75	5
15	DemAge	.	63
16	DemAge	18	62
17	DemAge	19	61
18	DemAge	20	60
19	DemAge	21	59

[TopkMisc]

Miscellaneous Information on Distinct Values for ORGANICS

	Column	N	TruncatedTopk	TruncatedBtmk	ScoreOther
0	purchase_12mon	61444	0	0	NaN
1	DemAge	63	0	0	NaN

The smallest reported value of DemAge is NaN. By default, the includemissing flag for the topk action is enabled, and missing values are always treated as the lowest machine value by topk. This is the reason NaN is reported as the bottom value of DemAge in the preceding example. To disable reporting NaN as the bottom value, set includemissing to False.

The topk action is not only used to report the smallest and largest values of a variable, but also to report the levels of a categorical variable with the largest or smallest values with respect to another score variable. In the following example, the topk action is used to return the top and bottom rich TV regions with respect to customers' affluence score:

```
In [15]: organics['DemTVReg'].topk(topk=3, bottomk=3,
                                    weight='DemAffl', agg='mean')
```

Out[15]:
[Topk]

Top and Bottom Distinct Values for ORGANICS

	Column	FmtVar	Rank	Score
0	DemTVReg	Unknown	1	8.968397
1	DemTVReg	East	2	8.921506
2	DemTVReg	Yorkshire	3	8.752555
3	DemTVReg	Ulster	14	8.493976
4	DemTVReg	N East	13	8.512684
5	DemTVReg	N West	12	8.533601

[TopkMisc]

Miscellaneous Information on Distinct Values for ORGANICS

	Column	N	TruncatedTopk	TruncatedBtmk	ScoreOther
0	DemTVReg	14	0	0	8.716037

The first result table shows that Unknown, East, and Yorkshire are the top three TV Regions with the highest average affluence scores 8.97, 8.92, and 8.75. TV Regions Ulster, N East, and N West are the bottom three TV Regions with the lowest average affluence scores 8.49, 8.51, and 8.53. The second table also indicates that there are 14 TV Regions in this data set, and the average affluence score for other TV regions (ScoreOther column) is 8.72.

You can also apply aggregators other than sample average in the topk action. For example, let's get the TV regions with the highest and lowest total sales amounts.

```
In [16]: organics['DemTVReg'].topK(topk=3, bottomk=3,
                                    weight='purchase_3mon', agg='sum')
```

Out[16]:
[Topk]

Top and Bottom Distinct Values for ORGANICS

	Column	FmtVar	Rank	Score
0	DemTVReg	London	1	4.468443e+08
1	DemTVReg	Midlands	2	2.255111e+08
2	DemTVReg	S & S East	3	1.765412e+08
3	DemTVReg	Border	14	1.465313e+07
4	DemTVReg	Ulster	13	1.919992e+07
5	DemTVReg	N Scot	12	2.374323e+07

[TopkMisc]

Miscellaneous Information on Distinct Values for ORGANICS

	Column	N	TruncatedTopk	TruncatedBtmk	ScoreOther
0	DemTVReg	14	0	0	6.980542e+08

The aggregators that are supported by the topk action are max, mean, min, n, and sum.

Cross Tabulations

Crosstab is another useful action from the simple action set for categorical data exploration. This action requires a row variable and a col variable to generate a two-way frequency table.

```
In [17]: result = organics.crosstab(row='DemAgeGroup', col='DemGender')
    ...: result
Out[17]:
[Crosstab]

    DemAgeGroup       Col1        Col2        Col3
 0       middle   550240.0    258172.0    183388.0
 1       senior   278312.0    143412.0    110732.0
 2      unknown    61864.0     30172.0     22572.0
 3        young    32908.0     10184.0      6992.0
```

The crosstab output table has a DemAgeGroup column that indicates the levels of the row variable (DemAgeGroup) in the two-way frequency table. However, the levels of the column variable (DemGender) are not displayed in the output table because the crosstab action stores the levels of the row variable in the labels instead of the names of the output columns:

```
In [18]: result['Crosstab'].colinfo
    ...:
Out[18]:
{'Col1': SASColumnSpec(attrs=dict(Template='Col'), dtype='double',
label='F', name='Col1', size=(1, 1), width=8),
 'Col2': SASColumnSpec(attrs=dict(Template='Col'), dtype='double',
label='M', name='Col2', size=(1, 1), width=8),
 'Col3': SASColumnSpec(attrs=dict(Template='Col'), dtype='double',
label='U', name='Col3', size=(1, 1), width=8),
 'DemAgeGroup': SASColumnSpec(attrs=dict(Template='Row'), dtype='varchar',
name='DemAgeGroup', size=(1, 1), width=7)}
```

In Chapter 3, we explained that the output tables of CAS actions are extensions of the DataFrames that are defined by the Pandas package. Such extensions allow the output table to contain extra metadata that is contained in typical SAS data sets. Examples of metadata include the column label, the column format, and the data type. Such information is stored in the colinfo attribute of the output DataFrame.

In the preceding crosstab example, the levels of the row variable are stored in the output column label instead of in the column names mainly because, in some situation, the levels might contain special characters that are not allowed in column names. You can retrieve the levels from the colinfo dictionary, and you can use the rename function to display the complete two-way frequency table:

```
In [19]: df = result['Crosstab']
    ...: labels = {k: v.label for k, v in df.colinfo.items() if v.label}
    ...: df = df.rename(columns = labels)
    ...: df
Out[19]:
    DemAgeGroup          F           M           U
 0       middle   550240.0    258172.0    183388.0
 1       senior   278312.0    143412.0    110732.0
 2      unknown    61864.0     30172.0     22572.0
 3        young    32908.0     10184.0      6992.0
```

Very similar to what the SAS PROC FREQ provides, you can request chi-square tests of homogeneity and measures of associations.

```
In [20]: organics.crosstab(row='DemAgeGroup', col='DemGender',
                           association=True, chisq=True)
Out[20]:
```

[Crosstab]

	DemAgeGroup	Col1	Col2	Col3
0	middle	550240.0	258172.0	183388.0
1	senior	278312.0	143412.0	110732.0
2	unknown	61864.0	30172.0	22572.0
3	young	32908.0	10184.0	6992.0

[Association]

	Statistic	Value	ASE	LowerCL \
0	Gamma	0.022513	0.001227	0.020107
1	Kendall's Tau-B	0.012913	0.000706	0.011529
2	Stuart's Tau-c	0.011092	0.000606	0.009904
3		NaN	NaN	NaN
4	Somers' D C|R	0.013438	0.000735	0.011998
5	Somers' D R|C	0.012408	0.000678	0.011079
6		NaN	NaN	NaN
7	Lambda Asymmetric C|R	0.000000	0.000000	0.000000
8	Lambda Asymmetric R|C	0.000000	0.000000	0.000000
9	Lambda Symmetric	0.000000	0.000000	0.000000
10		NaN	NaN	NaN
11	Uncertainty Coefficient C|R	0.001286	0.000039	0.001210
12	Uncertainty Coefficient R|C	0.001332	0.000040	0.001253
13	Uncertainty Coefficient Symmetric	0.001309	0.000039	0.001231

	UpperCL
0	0.024919
1	0.014296
2	0.012280
3	NaN
4	0.014877
5	0.013737
6	NaN
7	0.000000
8	0.000000
9	0.000000
10	NaN
11	0.001362
12	0.001411
13	0.001386

[ChiSq]

	Statistic	DF	Value	Prob
0	Chi-Square	6.0	4284.485198	0.0
1	Likelihood Ratio Chi-Square	6.0	4334.499685	0.0

A two-way frequency table is usually displayed as a grouped or stacked bar chart. We can use the Bokeh package to visualize the output from the crosstab action.

```
In [21]: from bokeh.charts import Bar, output_file, show
    ...: from bokeh.charts.operations import blend
    ...: from bokeh.charts.attributes import cat, color
    ...:
    ...: result1 = organics.crosstab(row='DemGender', col='DemAgeGroup')
    ...: # rename output columns
    ...: df1 = result1['Crosstab']
    ...: df1.columns = ['DemGender','middle','senior','unknown','young']
    ...:
    ...: bar = Bar(df1,
    ...:           values=blend('middle','senior','unknown','young',
    ...:                        name='counts', labels_name='AgeGroup'),
    ...:           label='DemGender',
    ...:           group='AgeGroup',
    ...:           xlabel='Gender',
    ...:           ylabel='Frequency',
    ...:           legend='top_right')
    ...:
    ...: output_file('bar.html')
    ...: show(bar)
```

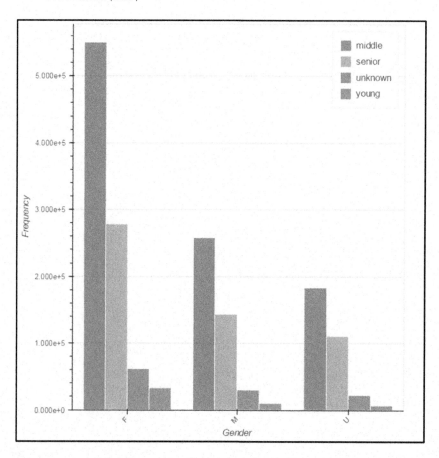

Note that we use the blend function from Bokeh to transform a Pandas DataFrame from a wide format to a long format. Likewise, you can use the Pandas melt function to reshape the data before you call the Bokeh package. You can also replace the group option with the stack option to generate a stacked bar chart instead of a grouped bar chart.

The crosstab action can do more than frequency counts. Similar to the topk action, the crosstab action can be used to specify an aggregation variable for each cell in the two-way table and to specify the type of aggregation. The following example shows how you can compute the total recent three-month sales amounts for the same two-way frequency table that is shown in the preceding example:

```
In [22]: result = organics.crosstab(row='DemAgeGroup', col='DemGender',
                                     weight='purchase_3mon', aggregators='sum')
    ...: df = result['Crosstab']
    ...: labels = {k: v.label for k, v in df.colinfo.items() if v.label}
    ...: df = df.rename(columns = labels)
    ...: df
Out [22]:
   DemAgeGroup              F              M              U
0       middle   5.227447e+08   2.452811e+08   1.742326e+08
1       senior   2.643612e+08   1.362322e+08   1.052163e+08
2      unknown   5.878180e+07   2.866586e+07   2.143959e+07
3        young   3.127620e+07   9.675101e+06   6.640414e+06
```

The results show that the female customers within the middle age group make the largest contribution in terms of purchase amount. Another difference between the crosstab action and the SAS FREQ procedure is that the crosstab action supports binning of numeric variables.

```
In [23]: result = organics.crosstab(row='DemAgeGroup',
                        col='purchase_3mon', colnbins=4, chisq=True)
    ...: df = result['Crosstab']
    ...: labels = {k: v.label for k, v in df.colinfo.items() if v.label}
    ...: df = df.rename(columns = labels)
    ...: df
Out [23]:
   DemAgeGroup   ( 500,  700]   ( 700,  900]   ( 900, 1100]   \
0       middle            1.0       157358.0       833045.0
1       senior            0.0        84901.0       446820.0
2      unknown            0.0        18225.0        96230.0
3        young            0.0         7835.0        42188.0

   (1100, 1300]
0        1396.0
1         735.0
2         153.0
3          61.0

In [24]: result['ChiSq']
Out [24]:
                      Statistic   DF      Value       Prob
0                    Chi-Square   9.0   6.223867   0.717321
1   Likelihood Ratio Chi-Square   9.0   6.641251   0.674414
```

In this case, the row variable DemAgeGroup is a categorical variable, and the column variable purchase_3mon is numeric. The crosstab action uses equal-space binning to discretize the column variable purchase_3mon into four buckets before it computes the two-way frequency table. The p-values of the Chi-square test show that these two variables are not correlated.

Similar to the SAS FREQ procedure, the crosstab action also supports frequency tables with more than two dimensions. You must put the other dimensions into the group-by list. The next example returns a three-way frequency table as a collection of five different two-way frequency tables. For each table, you can also compute the Chi-square likelihood of homogeneity.

```
In [25]: organics.groupby='DemReg'
    ...: result2 = organics.crosstab(row='DemAgeGroup',
    ...:                             col='DemGender',chisq=True)
    ...: for table_name in result2:
    ...:     df = result2[table_name]
    ...:     if 'ChiSq' in table_name:
    ...:         print(df[df['Statistic']=='Chi-Square'])
    ...:
```

```
           Statistic   DF        Value    Prob
DemReg
Midlands   Chi-Square  6.0   2256.130597   0.0
           Statistic   DF        Value            Prob
DemReg
North      Chi-Square  6.0   1096.161298   1.412025e-233
           Statistic   DF        Value            Prob
DemReg
Scottish   Chi-Square  6.0   146.563561    4.120410e-29
              Statistic   DF      Value    Prob
DemReg
South East  Chi-Square  6.0   2959.658738   0.0
              Statistic   DF      Value            Prob
DemReg
South West  Chi-Square  6.0   1137.124002   1.935146e-242
           Statistic   DF        Value            Prob
DemReg
Unknown    Chi-Square  6.0   913.565675    4.385563e-194
```

Variable Transformation and Dimension Reduction

Once you get some ideas about a data set using the data exploration actions that were introduced in the previous two sections, it is often useful to transform some data columns because of "missing-ness" or non-linearity. The datapreprocess action set provides a set of actions for variable imputation, variable binning, and dimension reduction.

```
In [1]: conn.loadactionset('datapreprocess')
    ...: conn.help(actionset='dataPreprocess')
Out[1]:
[dataPreprocess]
```

	Name	Description
0	rustats	Computes robust univariate statistics, centralized moments, and quantiles
1	impute	Performs data matrix (variable) imputation
2	outlier	Performs outlier detection and treatment
3	binning	Categorizes continuous variables into bins
4	discretize	Performs supervised and unsupervised variable discretization
5	catTrans	Groups and encodes categorical variables using unsupervised and supervised grouping techniques

Name	Description
6 histogram	Generates histogram bins and simple bin-based statistics for numeric variables
7 transform	Performs pipelined variable imputation, outlier detection and treatment, functional transformation, binning, and robust univariate statistics to evaluate the quality of the transformation

Variable Binning

We have shown the histogram action, which performs equal-spacing binning on one or multiple columns, and returns lower bounds, upper bounds, and frequencies for the bins for visualization purposes. The histogram action does not actually bin the data and store the binned results. This is accomplished by the binning action from the datapreprocess action set.

```
In [2]: out_data = conn.CASTable('binnedData', replace=True)
   ...:
   ...: result = organics.binning(
   ...:     inputs='purchase_3mon',
   ...:     tech='bucket',
   ...:     casout=out_data,
   ...:     nBinsArray=10
   ...: )
   ...: out_data.head(10)
Out[2]:
Selected Rows from Table BINNEDDATA

     BIN_purchase_3mon
0                  5.0
1                  7.0
2                  6.0
3                  5.0
4                  5.0
5                  4.0
6                  5.0
7                  5.0
8                  7.0
9                  6.0
```

In this example, we perform a bucket binning (which is also known as histogram binning or equal-space binning) on the purchase_3mon column with number of bins equal to 10. You also must specify an output CAS table that contains the binned result. In most of the CAS actions, the option to specify a CAS table is casout. In the preceding example, the result table contains only one column that is the bin assignment (BIN_purchase_3mon).

The result object is a CASResults object that is downloaded to the Python client, and binnedData is actually a CAS table that is stored on the CAS server. If the CAS server is remote, the CAS table is not downloaded to the Python client. You can always print out some observations from the casout table using the head method or the fetch action.

Unlike the histogram action, the binning action produces more than one result table, including VarTransInfo for information about the variable transformations, BinDetails for the actual binning information, and OutputCasTables for the casout table. The last table contains information about the CAS table such as the table name, the library name, the number of observations, and the number of columns.

```
In [3]: result
Out[3]:
[VarTransInfo]

Variable Discretization Information for ORGANICS

          Variable        ResultVar    NBins
0   purchase_3mon   BIN_purchase_3mon   10.0

[BinDetails]

Bin Details for ORGANICS

          Variable  BinId  BinLowerBnd  BinUpperBnd  BinWidth  NInBin  \
0   purchase_3mon       1      698.440      747.402    48.962      45
1   purchase_3mon       2      747.402      796.364    48.962    1802
2   purchase_3mon       3      796.364      845.326    48.962   28782
3   purchase_3mon       4      845.326      894.288    48.962  193828
4   purchase_3mon       5      894.288      943.250    48.962  529051
5   purchase_3mon       6      943.250      992.212    48.962  597872
6   purchase_3mon       7      992.212     1041.174    48.962  279514
7   purchase_3mon       8     1041.174     1090.136    48.962   53719
8   purchase_3mon       9     1090.136     1139.098    48.962    4214
9   purchase_3mon      10     1139.098     1188.060    48.962     121

          Mean         Std       Min       Max
0   735.920444   11.629722    698.44    747.30
1   783.902153   10.767204    747.72    796.36
2   830.094716   12.081154    796.37    845.32
3   875.761523   13.155664    845.33    894.28
4   921.156725   13.782269    894.29    943.24
5   966.341785   13.869978    943.25    992.21
6  1011.694702   13.360849    992.22   1041.17
7  1057.383763   12.429201   1041.18   1090.12
8  1103.745873   11.365814   1090.14   1139.07
9  1151.365785   10.677088   1139.32   1188.06

[OutputCasTables]

                     casLib            Name       Rows  Columns  \
0   CASUSERHDFS(username)   cas.binnedData   1688948         1

                                           casTable
0   CASTable('cas.binnedData', caslib='C...
```

You can specify multiple variables in the binning action, and you can use a different number of bins for each column as well.

```
In [4]: result = organics.binning(
   ...:     inputs=['purchase_3mon', 'purchase_6mon',
                    'purchase_9mon', 'purchase_12mon'],
   ...:     tech='bucket',
   ...:     casout=out_data,
   ...:     nbinsarray=[4, 10, 20, 6]
   ...: );
   ...: out_data.head(10)
Out[4]:
```

```
Selected Rows from Table CAS.BINNEDDATA

     BIN_purchase_12mon   BIN_purchase_3mon   BIN_purchase_6mon   \
0                   3.0                 2.0                 6.0
1                   5.0                 3.0                 7.0
2                   3.0                 3.0                 6.0
3                   3.0                 2.0                 6.0
4                   3.0                 2.0                 4.0
5                   3.0                 2.0                 5.0
6                   3.0                 2.0                 5.0
7                   3.0                 2.0                 5.0
8                   4.0                 3.0                 7.0
9                   4.0                 3.0                 6.0

     BIN_purchase_9mon
0                  9.0
1                 14.0
2                 11.0
3                 10.0
4                 10.0
5                  9.0
6                  8.0
7                 10.0
8                 12.0
9                 12.0
```

The binning action supports three types of binning techniques as follows:

Technique	Description
Bucket	Equal-width binning. Each bin has the same width.
Cutpts	Creates bins according to the user-specified cutpoints.
Quantile	Equal-frequency binning. Each bin has approximately the same number of observations.

The following example shows how to perform a quantile binning of four purchase amount columns. Also, it uses the copyallvars flag to pass all columns from the input table to the casout table.

```
In [5]: out_data2 = s.CASTable('binnedData2', replace=True)
   ...: result = organics.binning(
   ...:         inputs = ['purchase_3mon', 'purchase_6mon',
   ...:                 'purchase_9mon', 'purchase_12mon'],
   ...:         tech = 'Quantile',
   ...:         casout = out_data2,
   ...:         copyallvars = True,
   ...:         nbinsarray = [4, 4, 4, 4]
   ...: )
   ...:
   ...: out_data2.columns

Out[5]:
Index(['ID', 'DemAffl', 'DemAge', 'DemGender', 'DemHomeowner',
       'DemAgeGroup', 'DemCluster', 'DemReg', 'DemTVReg', 'DemFlag1',
       'DemFlag2', 'DemFlag3', 'DemFlag4', 'DemFlag5', 'DemFlag6',
       'DemFlag7', 'DemFlag8', 'PromClass', 'PromTime', 'TargetBuy',
       'Bought_Beverages', 'Bought_Bakery', 'Bought_Canned',
       'Bought_Dairy', 'Bought_Baking', 'Bought_Frozen',
```

```
                 'Bought_Meat', 'Bought_Fruits', 'Bought_Vegetables',
                 'Bought_Cleaners', 'Bought_PaperGoods', 'Bought_Others',
                 'purchase_3mon', 'purchase_6mon', 'purchase_9mon',
                 'purchase_12mon', 'BIN_purchase_12mon', 'BIN_purchase_3mon',
                 'BIN_purchase_6mon', 'BIN_purchase_9mon'],
             dtype='object')
```

You can get some idea about the binned data using the data exploration actions that were introduced previously. For example, you can generate a cross tabulation of two binned purchase amount columns.

```
In [6]: out_data2.crosstab(row='bin_purchase_3mon',
                           col='bin_purchase_12mon')
Out[6]:
[Crosstab]

    BIN_purchase_3mon        Col1        Col2        Col3        Col4
0                   1    203175.0    117851.0     70718.0     30483.0
1                   2    117668.0    124401.0    109169.0     70929.0
2                   3     71142.0    108972.0    124566.0    117614.0
3                   4     30231.0     70984.0    117812.0    203233.0
```

The binning action also provides a few options for cutpoints and observations assignment. The binning options are listed in the following table:

Binning Options	Description	Default Value
binmapping='left' | 'right'	Controls how to map values that fall at the boundary between consecutive bins. left enables you to express the bins with [), [), ..., [] notation. right enables [], (], ..., (] notation.	left
binmissing=True | False	When set to True, bins missing values are stored in a separate bin. The ID for this bin is 0.	False
cutpts=*list*	Specifies the user-provided cutpoints for the cutpts binning technique.	Null
copyallvars=True | False	When set to True, all the variables from the input table are copied to the scored output table.	False
copyvars=*list*	Specifies the names of the variables in the input table to use for identifying scored observations in the output table. The specified variables are copied to the output table.	Null
includeinputvars =True | False	When set to True, the analysis variables from the input table that are specified in the vars parameter are copied to the output table.	False
pctldef=integer	Specifies the percentile definition to use. The definitions are numbered from 1 to 5. The default value, 0, specifies not to use a percentile definition.	0
pctlmaxniters=integer	Specifies the maximum number of iterations for percentile computation.	
pctltol=double	Specifies the tolerance for percentile computation.	1e-05

Another difference between the binning action and the histogram action is that the binning action can generate SAS DATA step code that represents the binning model. This code can be downloaded and saved for later use in scoring new observations. You can also apply the code to score a CAS table directly. Such DATA step code is often called score code when it is used to represent a data transformation or an analytical model.

The next example requests the score code for a bucket binning of the purchase_3mon variable, and then saves the score code into a local result table. Also, you can convert the score code that is stored in result['CodeGen'] into a text file using Pandas.

```
In [7]: result = organics.binning(
   ...:       inputs='purchase_3mon',
   ...:       tech='bucket',
   ...:       casout=out_data,
   ...:       code={'comment':True, 'tabform':True},
   ...:       nBinsArray=10
   ...: )
   ...:
   ...: # score code is saved in this table
   ...: # df = result['CodeGen']
```

Variable Imputation

The impute action from the datapreprocess action set manages missing values. You can use the distinct action to check which columns have missing values.

```
In [8]: df = organics.distinct()['Distinct']
   ...: df[df['NMiss'] > 0]
Out[8]:
```

Distinct Counts for CAS.ORGANICS

	Analysis Variable	Number of Distinct Values	Number of Missing Values	Truncated or Not
1	DemAffl	34	82460	0
2	DemAge	63	114608	0
18	PromTime	40	21356	0

Let's run the impute action for the promotion time variable.

```
In [9]: organics[['PromTime']].impute()
Out[9]:
[ImputeInfo]
```

Imputation Information for ORGANICS

	Variable	ImputeTech	ResultVar	N	NMiss	\
0	PromTime	Mean	IMP_PromTime	1667592.0	21356.0	

	ImputedValueContinuous
0	6.56467

The result table of the impute action contains information about the treatment of missing values for each specified variable. PromTime is a numeric variable and, by default, the impute action selects sample mean as the value to fill the observations with missing PromTime.

The preceding example only suggests the imputation method but won't actually change the data. You must specify a casout table for the impute action in order to create a new data set with imputed values.

```
In [10]: out_data = s.CASTable('cas.imputedData1', replace=True)
    ...:
    ...: impute1 = organics[['PromTime']].Impute()
    ...: impute1.methodcontinuous = 'Median'
    ...: impute1.copyallvars = True
    ...: impute1.casout = out_data
    ...: impute1()
Out[10]:
[ImputeInfo]

 Imputation Information for ORGANICS

     Variable ImputeTech     ResultVar          N      NMiss   \
 0   PromTime     Median   IMP_PromTime   1667592.0   21356.0

     ImputedValueContinuous
 0                      5.0


[OutputCasTables]

                 casLib          Name      Rows   Columns  \
 0   CASUSERHDFS(username)   imputedData1   1688948        37

                                 casTable
 0   CASTable('imputedData1', caslib='CAS...
```

In this example, we create a CASAction object impute1, add a casout table to the impute action, and request that all columns to be copied from the input table to the casout table. Also, the imputation technique is changed from mean to median. The impute action also enables you to specify the value to impute.

```
In [11]: impute1.methodcontinuous = 'Value'
    ...: impute1.valuescontinuous = [0]
    ...: impute1()
Out[11]:
[ImputeInfo]

 Imputation Information for ORGANICS

     Variable ImputeTech     ResultVar          N      NMiss   \
 0   PromTime      Value   IMP_PromTime   1667592.0   21356.0

     ImputedValueContinuous
 0                      0.0


[OutputCasTables]

                 casLib          Name      Rows   Columns  \
 0   CASUSERHDFS(username)   imputedData1   1688948        37

                                 casTable
 0   CASTable('imputedData1', caslib='CAS...
```

The methodcontinuous option and the methodnominal option define the imputation treatment for continuous and categorical variables. The default imputations are mean and mode.

The following table lists techniques for continuous variables:

Technique	Description
MAX	Replaces missing values with the maximum value.
MEAN	Replaces missing values with the mean.
MEDIAN	Replaces missing values with the median.
MIDRANGE	Replaces missing values with the mean of the maximum value and the minimum value.
MIN	Replaces missing values with the minimum value.
RANDOM	Replaces missing values with uniform random numbers.
VALUE	Replaces missing values with the values that are specified in the valuescontinuous parameters.

The following table lists techniques for categorical variables:

Technique	Description
MODE	Replaces missing values with the mode.
VALUE	Replaces missing values with the values that are specified in the valuesnominal parameters.

Similar to other actions in the datapreprocess action set, the impute action also generates score code that you can download so that you can repeat the imputation for a new data source.

```
In [12]: impute1.techforcont = 'Median'
   ...: impute1.code = {'comment':True}
   ...: impute1()['CodeGen']
Out[12]:

                        Score code for Impute action
                                  SASCode
0    /*---------------------------------------------------------------------
1    SAS Code Generated by Cloud Analytic Server for Impute Action
2    Date : 07Mar2016:11:12:45
3    Number of variables : 1
4    ---------------------------------------------------------------------*/
5
6    _igby_ = 0;
7    _tnn_ntrans_ = 1;
8
9    _fuzcmp_ = 0.000000000100;
10
11   array _tnn_vnames_{1} imp_PromTime ;
12
13   array _vnn_names_{1} PromTime ;
14
15   array _tnn_ntransvars_{1} _temporary_ (1 );
```

```
                         Score code for Impute action
                                   SASCode
16
17   array _tv_nn_indices_{1} _temporary_ (1 );
18
19   imp_PromTime = .;
20
21   array _tnn_imputetype_{1} _temporary_ (2 );
22
23
24   array _tnn_imputeuniquevals_{1} _temporary_ (5 );
25
26
27   /*---------Iterate and score----------------*/
28
29   /*---------Count variables----------------*/
30   _ct_ = 0;
31   _impct_ = 0;
32
33   do _i_ = 1 to _tnn_ntrans_;
34   do _j_ = 1 to _tnn_ntransvars_{_i_};
35
36   if (_tnn_imputetype_{_i_} ~= 0) then
37   _impct_ + 1;
38   _ct_ + 1;
39   _numval_ = _vnn_names_{_tv_nn_indices_{_ct_}};
40
41   /*-------Apply Imputation phase--------------*/
42   if missing(_numval_) then
43   do;
44   if _tnn_imputetype_{_i_} = 0 then
45   goto _impute_done1_;
46   else _numval_ = _tnn_imputeuniquevals_{1 *_igby_ + _impct_};
47   end;
48   _impute_done1_:;
49   _tnn_vnames_{_ct_} = _numval_;
50   end;
51   end;
52
53   drop _igby_ _tnn_ntrans_ _fuzcmp_ _ct_ _impct_ _i_ _j_ _numval_ ;
```

Conclusion

In this chapter, we introduced actions in the simple and dataPreprocess action sets for data exploration, data summarization, and basic variable transformation. These actions enable you to learn about your data using different techniques to summarize continuous and categorical variables. You can also apply variable transformation such as binning and imputation to reshape your data. Now that you understand your data, let's move on to Chapter 8 and Chapter 9 for building analytic models.

Chapter 8: Modeling Continuous Variables

In this chapter, we explore several commonly used predictive models for a continuous dependent variable, including linear regressions, generalized linear models, and regression trees. The data set that is used in this chapter is the Cars data set available in the sas-viya-programming repository of the sassoftware account on GitHub. Upload the data set directly from GitHub using the upload method on the CAS connection, as follows:

```
In [1]: cars = conn.upload('https://raw.githubusercontent.com/sassoftware/'
                           'sas-viya-programming/master/data/cars.csv').casTable
```

```
In [1]: cars.tableinfo()
Out[1]:
[TableInfo]

    Name  Rows  Columns Encoding CreateTimeFormatted  \
 0  CARS   428       15    utf-8  09Nov2016:10:32:02

       ModTimeFormatted JavaCharSet    CreateTime       ModTime  \
 0  09Nov2016:10:32:02        UTF8  1.794307e+09  1.794307e+09

    Global  Repeated  View SourceName SourceCaslib  Compressed  \
 0       1         0     0                                    0

    Creator Modifier
 0  username
In [2]: cars.columninfo()
Out[2]:
[ColumnInfo]

           Column            Label  ID    Type  RawLength  \
 0           Make                    1    char         13
 1          Model                    2    char         40
 2           Type                    3    char          8
 3         Origin                    4    char          6
 4      DriveTrain                    5    char          5
 5           MSRP                    6  double          8
 6        Invoice                    7  double          8
 7      EngineSize  Engine Size (L)   8  double          8
 8      Cylinders                    9  double          8
 9     Horsepower                   10  double          8
```

```
10        MPG_City        MPG (City)    11    double              8
11     MPG_Highway     MPG (Highway)    12    double              8
12         Weight       Weight (LBS)    13    double              8
13      Wheelbase      Wheelbase (IN)   14    double              8
14         Length        Length (IN)    15    double              8
```

```
      FormattedLength  Format   NFL   NFD
0                  13              0     0
1                  40              0     0
2                   8              0     0
3                   6              0     0
4                   5              0     0
5                   8  DOLLAR      8     0
6                   8  DOLLAR      8     0
7                  12              0     0
8                  12              0     0
9                  12              0     0
10                 12              0     0
11                 12              0     0
12                 12              0     0
13                 12              0     0
14                 12              0     0
```

Linear Regressions

Linear regression is one of the most widely used statistical models for predictive modeling. The basic idea of a predictive model is to establish a function $y = f(x_1, x_2, \cdots, x_K)$ to predict the value of the dependent variable y that is based on the values of the predictors $X_1, X_2, \cdots, X_K$. Linear regression assumes that the function f is a linear combination of the predictors and an error term ε.

$$y = a + b_1 x_1 + b_2 x_2 + \cdots + b_K x_K + \varepsilon$$

Usually, we assume that ε follows a normal distribution with mean zero and variance σ^2. The parameters to be estimated in a linear model include the intercept α, the slopes $b_1, b_2, \cdots, b_K$, and the variance of the error term σ^2. These parameters are estimated using the least squares method.

The regression action set provides a glm action, which fits linear regression models using the least squares method. You must load the action set before you use the glm action.

```
In [3]: conn.loadactionset('regression')
   ...: conn.help(actionset='regression')


NOTE: Added action set 'regression'.
Out[3]:
Regression
                                regression
      Name                         Description
0 glm       Fits linear regression models using the method of least squares
1 genmod    Fits generalized linear regression models
2 logistic  Fits logistic regression models
```

Let's build a simple regression model using the Cars data to predict MSRP using the city miles per gallon (MPG) of the cars:

```
In [4]: cars.glm(
   ...:      target = 'MSRP',
   ...:      inputs = ['MPG_City']
   ...: )
Out[4]:
[ModelInfo]

Model Information

           RowId        Description  Value
0           DATA        Data Source   CARS
1    RESPONSEVAR  Response Variable   MSRP

[NObs]

Number of Observations

     RowId                    Description  Value
0    NREAD  Number of Observations Read   428.0
1    NUSED  Number of Observations Used   428.0

[Dimensions]

Dimensions

          RowId          Description  Value
0      NEFFECTS    Number of Effects      2
1        NPARMS  Number of Parameters     2

[ANOVA]

Analysis of Variance

     RowId           Source     DF            SS            MS  \
0    MODEL            Model    1.0  3.638090e+10  3.638090e+10
1    ERROR            Error  426.0  1.248507e+11  2.930768e+08
2    TOTAL  Corrected Total  427.0  1.612316e+11           NaN

        FValue          ProbF
0    124.13436  1.783404e-25
1          NaN           NaN
2          NaN           NaN

[FitStatistics]

Fit Statistics

        RowId Description         Value
0        RMSE    Root MSE  1.711949e+04
1     RSQUARE    R-Square  2.256437e-01
2      ADJRSQ    Adj R-Sq  2.238260e-01
3         AIC         AIC  8.776260e+03
4        AICC        AICC  8.776316e+03
```

```
    5            SBC       SBC    8.354378e+03
    6    TRAIN_ASE         ASE    2.917073e+08

[ParameterEstimates]

Parameter Estimates

         Effect    Parameter    DF        Estimate           StdErr        tValue    \
    0  Intercept    Intercept     1    68124.606698    3278.919093    20.776544
    1   MPG_City     MPG_City     1    -1762.135298     158.158758   -11.141560

             Probt
    0  1.006169e-66
    1  1.783404e-25

[Timing]

Task Timing

                    RowId                  Task       Time     RelTime
    0              SETUP     Setup and Parsing    0.027544    0.626975
    1        LEVELIZATION          Levelization    0.007532    0.171444
    2      INITIALIZATION    Model Initialization    0.000371    0.008444
    3               SSCP      SSCP Computation    0.003291    0.074909
    4            FITTING         Model Fitting    0.000367    0.008352
    5            CLEANUP               Cleanup    0.002385    0.054286
    6              TOTAL                 Total    0.043932    1.000000
```

The ParameterEstimates table contains the estimation of parameters for the linear regression model. In the preceding example, the model returned by the glm action is shown as follows:

$$MSRP = 68124.606698 + -1762.135298 \times MPG\_CITY$$

The result tables also contain useful information about the model definition and model fitting. The following table summarizes the result tables.

Table Name	Description
NObs	The number of observations that are read and used. Missing values are excluded, by default.
Dimension	The dimension of the model, including the number of effects and the number of parameters.
ANOVA	The Analysis of Variance table that measures the overall model fitting.
FitStatistics	The fit statistics of the model such as R-Square and root mean square error.
ParameterEstimates	The estimation of the regression parameters.
Timing	A timing of the subtasks of the glm action call.

Compared to the data exploration actions introduced in Chapter 7, the glm action requires a more complex and deeper parameter structure. In this case, it might be more convenient to define a new model first and then specify the model parameters, step-by-step. In other words, the first linear regression shown in the preceding example can be rewritten as follows:

```
linear1 = cars.Glm()
linear1.target = 'MSRP'
linear1.inputs = ['MPG_City']
linear1()
```

This approach enables you to reuse the code when you need to change only a few options of the glm action. For example, to display only the parameter estimation table, you specify the names of the output table in the display option and rerun the linear1 model:

```
In [4]: linear1.display.names = ['ParameterEstimates']
   ...: linear1()
Out[4]:
ParameterEstimates
                          Parameter Estimates
   Effect  Parameter DF   Estimate      StdErr        tValue         Probt
0 Intercept Intercept 1  68124.606698 3278.919092 20.776543969 1.006169E-66
1 MPG_City  MPG_City  1  -1762.135298  158.15875785 -11.14156005 1.783404E-25
```

So far, we have only used the glm action example to estimate the parameters of the linear regression model. We haven't used the model to predict MSRP values of the cars. For prediction, you must specify an output table using the output option. You can also delete the display.names option in order to request all result tables:

```
In [5]: del linear1.display.names
   ...: result1 = conn.CASTable('cas.MSRPPrediction')
   ...: result1.replace = True
   ...: linear1.output.casout = result1
   ...: linear1.output.copyvars = 'all';
   ...: linear1()

Out[5]:

...output clipped...

[OutputCasTables]

                     casLib                 Name Label  Rows  Columns  \
0   CASUSERHDFS(username)  MSRPPrediction              428       16

                                     casTable
0   CASTable('MSRPPrediction', caslib='C...
```

In the preceding example, a new CAS table MSRPPredicton is defined and then used in the output option. When you submit the code, the glm action first fits a linear regression model, and then it uses the fitted model to score the input data. Also, it creates the new CAS table MSRPPrediction that contains the predicted MSRP values. The copyvars='all' option requests that the glm action copy all columns from the CARS table to the MSRPPrediction table.

In the preceding example, the output column name for predicted MSRP is not specified. The glm action automatically chooses Pred as the name.

You can summarize the predicted values using the summary action from the simple action set.

```
In [6]: result1[['pred']].summary()
Out[6]:
[Summary]

 Descriptive Statistics for MSRPPREDICTION

     Column         Min           Max        N  NMiss           Mean  \
  0    Pred -37603.511169   50503.25372  428.0    0.0    32774.85514

             Sum           Std       StdErr           Var           USS  \
  0  14027638.0   9230.448198   446.170554   8.520117e+07   4.961347e+11

             CSS          CV      TValue          ProbT
  0  3.638090e+10   28.163201   73.458131   2.182203e-244
```

The glm action can generate additional columns besides the predicted values. The following table summarizes the statistical outputs that the glm action can generate.

Option	Description
pred	The predicted value. If you do not specify any output statistics, the predicted value is named Pred, by default.
resid	The residual, which is calculated as ACTUAL minus PREDICTED.
cooksd	The Cook's D influence statistic.
covratio	The standard influence of the observation on covariance of betas. The COVRATIO statistic measures the change in the determinant of the covariance matrix of the estimates by deleting the current observation.
dffits	The scaled measure of the change in the predicted value for the ith observation and is calculated by deleting the ith observation. A large value indicates that the observation is very influential in its neighborhood of the X space.
h	The leverage of the observation.
lcl	The lower bound of a confidence interval for an individual prediction.
ucl	The upper bound of a confidence interval for an individual prediction.
lclm	The lower bound of a confidence interval for the expected value of the dependent variable.
uclm	The upper bound of a confidence interval for the expected value of the dependent variable.
likedist	The likelihood displacement.
press	The ith residual divided by 1 - h, where h is the leverage, and where the model has been refit without the ith observation
rstudent	The studentized residual with the current observation deleted.
stdi	The standard error of the individual predicted value.
stdp	The standard error of the mean predicted value.
stdr	The standard error of the residual.
student	The studentized residuals, which are the residuals divided by their standard errors.

The following example adds the residual values (observed MSRP values minus predicted MSRP values) and the confidence intervals of the prediction to the output table:

```
In [7]: result2 = conn.CASTable('cas.MSRPPrediction2', replace=True)
   ...: linear1.output.casout = result2
   ...: linear1.output.pred  = 'Predicted_MSRP'
   ...: linear1.output.resid = 'Residual_MSRP'
   ...: linear1.output.lcl = 'LCL_MSRP'
   ...: linear1.output.ucl = 'UCL_MSRP'
   ...: linear1()
```

The output table MSRPPredcition2 is a CAS table that is saved on the CAS server. You have several ways to fetch or download a table from the CAS server. Since the CARS data is relatively small, you can pull all observations from MSRPPredcition2 directly to the Python client using the to_frame method. Then you can use some visualization package in Python such as Bokeh to observe and understand the model outcome.

```
In [8]: from bokeh.charts import Scatter, output_file, show
   ...: out1 = result2.to_frame()
   ...: p = Scatter(out1, x='Residual_MSRP', y='Predicted_MSRP',
                     color='Origin', marker='Origin')
   ...: output_file('scatter.html')
   ...: show(p)
```

The following figure shows a scatter plot of the predicted MSRP values and residuals.

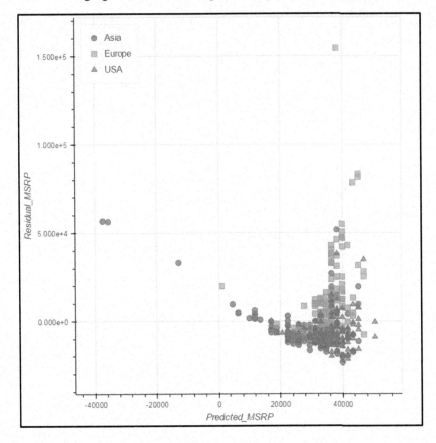

You can see that the model predicted large negative MSRP values for three observations. Let's print out these observations to find out what happens:

```
In [9]: result2[['Predicted_MSRP', 'MSRP', 'MPG_City', 'Make',
                 'Model']].query('Predicted_MSRP < 0').to_frame()
Out[9]:
Selected Rows from Table MSRPPREDICTION3

     Predicted_MSRP      MSRP  MPG_City     Make  \
0     -12933.617000   20140.0      46.0    Honda
1     -35841.375871   20510.0      59.0   Toyota
2     -37603.511169   19110.0      60.0    Honda

                                      Model
0      Civic Hybrid 4dr manual (gas/electric)
1                    Prius 4dr (gas/electric)
2                 Insight 2dr (gas/electric)
```

All of these cars are fuel efficient with relatively high MPG_City. If you generate a scatter plot of the dependent variable MSRP and the predictor variable MPG_City, you can see that the data has some extreme outliers with high MSRP values or high city MPG that might not fit into the linear relationship assumption between these two variables.

```
In [10]: p = Scatter(out1, x='MPG_City', y='MSRP',
                     color='Origin', marker='Origin')
    ...: output_file('scatter.html')
    ...: show(p)
```

The following figure shows a scatter plot of MPG_City and MSRP.

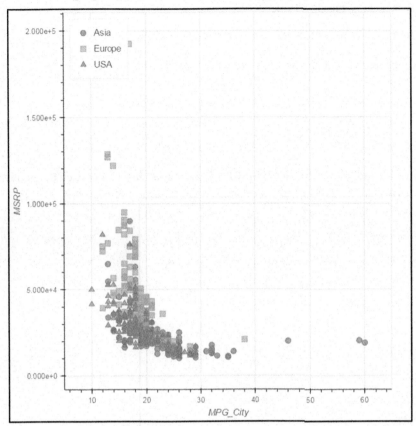

Outliers are observed when MSRP values are higher than $100,000 or MPG City is higher than 40.

Linear regression models are sensitive to outliers. There are several treatments for outliers to improve the prediction accuracy of a linear regression model. The simplest approach is to remove the outliers. In the next example, let's add a filter to remove cars with MPG_City that is greater than 40 or MSRP that is greater than 100,000. The R-Square of the model is actually improved from 0.22 to 0.34.

```
In [11]: cars.where = 'MSRP < 100000 and MPG_City < 40'
    ...:
    ...: result2 = conn.CASTable('cas.MSRPPrediction2')
    ...: result2.replace = True
    ...:
    ...: linear2 = cars.Glm()
    ...: linear2.target = 'MSRP'
    ...: linear2.inputs = ['MPG_City']
    ...: linear2.output.casout = result2
    ...: linear2.output.copyVars = 'ALL';
    ...: linear2.output.pred = 'Predicted_MSRP'
    ...: linear2.output.resid = 'Residual_MSRP'
    ...: linear2.output.lcl = 'LCL_MSRP'
    ...: linear2.output.ucl = 'UCL_MSRP'
    ...: linear2()
```

You can also use the DataFrame API of the CASTable cars to apply a filter. The preceding model can also be defined using the query method of the CASTable:

```
linear2 = cars.query('MSRP < 100000 and MPG_City < 40').Glm()
```

You can see that we have a better residual plot after the outliers are removed from the model.

```
In [12]: out2 = result2.to_frame()
   ...: p = Scatter(out2, x='Predicted_MSRP', y='Residual_MSRP',
                     color='Origin', marker='Origin')
   ...: output_file('scatter.html')
   ...: show(p)
```

The following figure shows a scatter plot of predicted MSRP values and residuals, after excluding outliers.

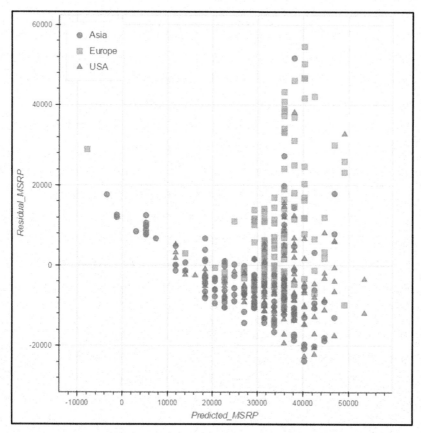

Let's continue to improve the linear regression model for prediction MSRP by adding more predictors to the model. In this example, we add three categorical predictors Origin, Type, and DriveTrain, and two more continuous predictors Weight and Length. The categorical predictors must be specified in both the inputs and the nominals parameters. The R-Square statistic is improved again (0.63).

```
In [13]: nomList = ['Origin','Type','DriveTrain']
   ...: contList = ['MPG_City','Weight','Length']
   ...:
   ...: linear3 = CASTable('cars').Glm()
```

```
    ...: linear3.target = 'MSRP'
    ...: linear3.inputs = nomList + contList
    ...: linear3.nominals = nomList
    ...: linear3.display.names = ['FitStatistics','ParameterEstimates']
    ...: linear3()
```

Out [13]:
[FitStatistics]

Fit Statistics

	RowId	Description	Value
0	RMSE	Root MSE	1.201514e+04
1	RSQUARE	R-Square	6.284172e-01
2	ADJRSQ	Adj R-Sq	6.176727e-01
3	AIC	AIC	8.483996e+03
4	AICC	AICC	8.485013e+03
5	SBC	SBC	8.106765e+03
6	TRAIN_ASE	ASE	1.399787e+08

[ParameterEstimates]

Parameter Estimates

	Effect	Origin	Type	DriveTrain	Parameter	DF \
0	Intercept				Intercept	1
1	Origin	Asia			Origin Asia	1
2	Origin	Europe			Origin Europe	1
3	Origin	USA			Origin USA	0
4	Type		Hybrid		Type Hybrid	1
5	Type		SUV		Type SUV	1
6	Type		Sedan		Type Sedan	1
7	Type		Sports		Type Sports	1
8	Type		Truck		Type Truck	1
9	Type		Wagon		Type Wagon	0
10	DriveTrain			All	DriveTrain All	1
11	DriveTrain			Front	DriveTrain Front	1
12	DriveTrain			Rear	DriveTrain Rear	0
13	MPG_City				MPG_City	1
14	Weight				Weight	1
15	Length				Length	1

	Estimate	StdErr	tValue	Probt
0	-23692.980669	16261.000069	-1.457043	1.458607e-01
1	2191.206289	1479.756700	1.480788	1.394218e-01
2	17100.937866	1779.533025	9.609790	7.112423e-20
3	0.000000	NaN	NaN	NaN
4	26154.719438	10602.173003	2.466921	1.403098e-02
5	-1016.065543	3083.503255	-0.329517	7.419315e-01
6	2481.367175	2359.814614	1.051509	2.936366e-01
7	21015.571095	3065.180416	6.856226	2.572647e-11
8	-12891.562541	3592.436933	-3.588529	3.722560e-04
9	0.000000	NaN	NaN	NaN
10	-7669.535987	1987.120548	-3.859623	1.316520e-04
11	-7699.083608	1722.883863	-4.468719	1.016332e-05
12	0.000000	NaN	NaN	NaN
13	-496.308946	266.606023	-1.861582	6.336879e-02

```
14      9.171343     1.914672  4.790032  2.325015e-06
15    162.893307    82.088679  1.984358  4.787420e-02
```

A linear regression model with categorical effects still assumes homogeneity of variance (that is, the random errors for all observations have the same variance). In the preceding example, this means that the variation of MSRP values is approximately the same across different origins, types, or drive trains. Sometimes data can be heterogeneous. For example, cars from different origins might have different MSRP values as well as different variation in MSRP values.

```
In [14]: cars = conn.CASTable('cars')
    ...: out = cars.groupby('Origin')[['MSRP']].summary()
    ...: out.concat_bygroups()['Summary'][['Column','Mean','Var','Std']]
    ...:
Out[14]:
Descriptive Statistics for CARS

         Column          Mean          Var          Std
Origin
Asia     MSRP    24741.322785  1.281666e+08  11321.069675
Europe   MSRP    48349.796748  6.410315e+08  25318.600464
USA      MSRP    28377.442177  1.371705e+08  11711.982506
```

The output from the summary action shows that cars from Europe not only have higher MSRP values but also a greater variance. The sample standard deviation of MSRP values for the European cars doubles compared to the sample standard deviation of the MSRP values for the cars from Asia and USA. One easy remedy for variance heterogeneity is to fit multiple models, one for each segment of the data. For the glm action, you can fit multiple models with the groupby option:

```
In [15]: cars = conn.CASTable('cars')
    ...: cars.groupby = ['Origin']
    ...: cars.where = 'MSRP < 100000 and MPG_City < 40'
    ...: nomList = ['Type','DriveTrain']
    ...: contList = ['MPG_City','Weight','Length']
    ...: groupBYResult = conn.CASTable('MSRPPredictionGroupBy')
    ...:
    ...: linear4 = cars.Glm()
    ...: linear4.target = 'MSRP'
    ...: linear4.inputs = nomList + contList
    ...: linear4.nominals = nomList
    ...: linear4.display.names = ['FitStatistics','ParameterEstimates']
    ...: linear4.output.casout = groupBYResult
    ...: linear4.output.copyVars = 'ALL';
    ...: linear4.output.pred = 'Predicted_MSRP'
    ...: linear4.output.resid = 'Residual_MSRP'
    ...: linear4.output.lcl = 'LCL_MSRP'
    ...: linear4.output.ucl = 'UCL_MSRP'
    ...: linear4()
    ...:
    ...: out = groupBYResult.to_frame()
    ...: p = Scatter(out, x='Predicted_MSRP', y='Residual_MSRP',
                     color='Origin', marker='Origin')
    ...: output_file('scatter.html')
    ...: show(p)
```

The following figure shows a scatter plot of predicted MSRP values and residuals with three linear regression models fit for each origin (Asia, Europe, and USA):

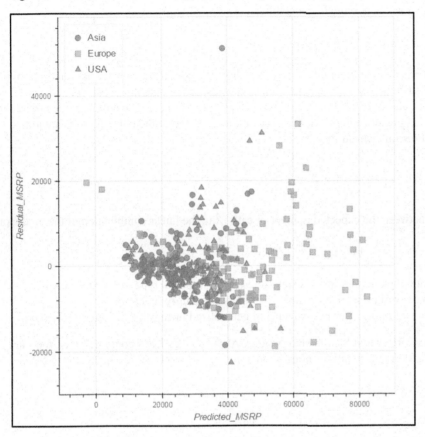

Extensions of Ordinary Linear Regression

The key assumptions of an ordinary linear regression are 1) the expected value of the dependent variable can be predicted using a linear combination of a set of predictors, and 2) the error distribution function of ε follows a normal distribution. The second assumptions might not be valid for some applications such as estimating the number of calls received within a time interval in a call center. Generalized linear models (GLM) and regression trees are popular types of generalization of ordinary linear regression to fit data that does not follow a normal distribution.

Generalized Linear Models

In generalized linear models, the dependent variable Y is assumed to follow a particular probability distribution, and the expected value of Y is predicted by a function of the linear combination of the predictors,

$$E(y) = f(x_1, x_2, \cdots, x_K) = f(a + b_1 x_1 + b_2 x_2 + \cdots + b_K x_K)$$

where $E(y)$ is the expected values of $Y, x_1, x_2, \cdots, x_K$ are the observed values of the predictors $X_1, X_2, \cdots, X_K$, and $b_1, b_2, \cdots, b_K$ are the unknown parameters. It is more common to express a GLM model by linking the expected values of Y o the linear combination of predictors,

$$g\left[E(y)\right] = a + b_1 x_1 + b_2 x_2 + \cdots + b_K x_K$$

The link function $g()$ is the inverse function of $f()$. The probability distribution of Y is usually from the exponential family of distribution, such as normal, binomial, exponential, gamma, Poisson, and zero-inflated distributions. The choice of the link function usually depends on the assumption of the probability distribution. For example, for call center data, it is common to assume that the number of calls within a time interval follows a Poisson distribution

$$P\left(k \; calls \; in \; interval\right) = \frac{\lambda^k e^{-\lambda}}{k!}, k = 0, 1, 2 \ldots$$

and a log link function between the expected number of calls λ to the linear combination of the predictors.

$$\log(\lambda) = a + b_1 x_1 + b_2 x_2 + \cdots + b_K x_K$$

It is also worthwhile to mention that ordinary linear regression is a special type of GLM, where the target variable follows a normal distribution, and the link function is an identity function $E(y) = a + b_1 x_1 + b_2 x_2 + \cdots + b_K x_K$. For more details of generalized linear models, refer to [1] and [2].

Generalized linear models are available in the regression CAS action set. Let's continue to use the Cars data example and build a simple generalized linear model to predict MSRP values of cars using MPG_City.

```
In [1]: cars = conn.CASTable('cars')
   ...: genmodModel1 = cars.Genmod()
   ...: genmodModel1.model.depvars = 'MSRP'
   ...: genmodModel1.model.effects = ['MPG_City']
   ...: genmodModel1.model.dist = 'gamma'
   ...: genmodModel1.model.link = 'log'
   ...: genmodModel1()

NOTE: Convergence criterion (GCONV=1E-8) satisfied.
Out[1]:
[ModelInfo]

 Model Information

         RowId           Description                      Value
0        DATA            Data Source                       CARS
1  RESPONSEVAR      Response Variable                      MSRP
2        DIST           Distribution                      Gamma
3        LINK          Link Function                        Log
4        TECH  Optimization Technique  Newton-Raphson with Ridging

[NObs]

 Number of Observations

   RowId                    Description  Value
0  NREAD  Number of Observations Read  428.0
```

```
1  NUSED  Number of Observations Used  428.0
```

[ConvergenceStatus]

Convergence Status

```
                                Reason  Status   MaxGradient
0  Convergence criterion (GCONV=1E-8) s...       0  1.068483e-09
```

[Dimensions]

Dimensions

	RowId	Description	Value
0	NDESIGNCOLS	Columns in Design	2
1	NEFFECTS	Number of Effects	2
2	MAXEFCOLS	Max Effect Columns	1
3	DESIGNRANK	Rank of Design	2
4	OPTPARM	Parameters in Optimization	3

[FitStatistics]

Fit Statistics

	RowId	Description	Value
0	M2LL	-2 Log Likelihood	9270.853164
1	AIC	AIC (smaller is better)	9276.853164
2	AICC	AICC (smaller is better)	9276.909768
3	SBC	SBC (smaller is better)	9289.030533

[ParameterEstimates]

Parameter Estimates

	Effect	Parameter	ParmName	DF	Estimate	StdErr	\
0	Intercept	Intercept	Intercept	1	11.307790	0.059611	
1	MPG_City	MPG_City	MPG_City	1	-0.047400	0.002801	
2	Dispersion	Dispersion	Dispersion	1	5.886574	0.391526	

	ChiSq	ProbChiSq
0	35983.929066	0.000000e+00
1	286.445370	2.958655e-64
2	NaN	NaN

[Timing]

Task Timing

	RowId	Task	Time	RelTime
0	SETUP	Setup and Parsing	0.008891	0.257967
1	LEVELIZATION	Levelization	0.005668	0.164454
2	INITIALIZATION	Model Initialization	0.000360	0.010446
3	SSCP	SSCP Computation	0.001076	0.031220
4	FITTING	Model Fitting	0.014661	0.425389
5	CLEANUP	Cleanup	0.002235	0.064853
6	TOTAL	Total	0.034465	1.000000

In the preceding example, we fit a generalized linear model using gamma distribution and the log link function because MSRP values of cars are nonnegative continuous values. The type of distribution is usually determined by the range and the shape of the data. For example, exponential, gamma, and inverse Gaussian distributions are popular choices for fitting nonnegative continuous values such as MSRP values of cars, sales revenue, insurance claim amounts, and so on. Binomial and multinomial distributions are a valid distribution assumption to fit an integer response. In the next example, we fix a multinomial regression model to predict the number of cylinders of the vehicles that are based on MPG_City.

```
In [2]: genmodModel1.model.depvars = 'Cylinders'
   ...: genmodModel1.model.dist = 'multinomial'
   ...: genmodModel1.model.link = 'logit'
   ...: genmodModel1.model.effects = ['MPG_City']
   ...: genmodModel1.display.names = ['ModelInfo', 'ParameterEstimates']
   ...: genmodModel1()
   ...:
NOTE: Convergence criterion (GCONV=1E-8) satisfied.
Out[2]:
```

[ModelInfo]

Model Information

	RowId	Description \
0	DATA	Data Source
1	RESPONSEVAR	Response Variable
2	NLEVELS	Number of Response Levels
3	DIST	Distribution
4	LINKTYPE	Link Type
5	LINK	Link Function
6	TECH	Optimization Technique

	Value
0	CARS
1	Cylinders
2	7
3	Multinomial
4	Cumulative
5	Logit
6	Newton-Raphson with Ridging

[ParameterEstimates]

Parameter Estimates

	Effect	Parameter	ParmName	Outcome	Cylinders	DF \
0	Intercept	Intercept	Intercept_3	3	3.0	1
1	Intercept	Intercept	Intercept_4	4	4.0	1
2	Intercept	Intercept	Intercept_5	5	5.0	1
3	Intercept	Intercept	Intercept_6	6	6.0	1
4	Intercept	Intercept	Intercept_8	8	8.0	1
5	Intercept	Intercept	Intercept_10	10	10.0	1
6	MPG_City	MPG_City	MPG_City		NaN	1

	Estimate	StdErr	ChiSq	ProbChiSq
0	-60.329075	4.829533	156.042532	8.286542e-36
1	-21.461149	1.584887	183.361936	8.941488e-42

```
2 -21.233691  1.575766  181.579751  2.190306e-41
3 -16.632445  1.337275  154.693103  1.634032e-35
4 -10.988487  1.139470   92.997190  5.236863e-22
5 -10.314220  1.186541   75.562638  3.539969e-18
6   1.013934  0.077371  171.734698  3.092446e-39
```

In the preceding example, the cumulative logit link function is used for the multinomial model. For a generalized linear model using multinomial distribution, we estimate where an observation (a car) can fall into one of the seven possible number of cylinders (Cylinder=3, 4, 5, 6, 8, 10, 12). In this case, the cumulative log link assume a logit link function between the cumulative probabilities and the linear combination of the predictors:

$$\Pr(\text{Cylinders} = 3) = f(-60.329075 + 1.013934 \times \text{MPG\_City})$$

$$\Pr(\text{Cylinders} = 3) + \Pr(\text{Cylinders} = 4) = f(-21.461149 + 1.013934 \times \text{MPG\_City})$$

......

$$\Pr(\text{Cylinders} = 3) + \cdots + \Pr(\text{Cylinders} = 10) = f(-10.314220 + 1.013934 \times \text{MPG\_City})$$

where $f(u) = \dfrac{\exp(u)}{1 + \exp(u)}$ is the standard inverse logit link function. You can use the parameter estimates to score new observation directly. For example, when a car has MPG_CITY = 20, the chance that this car is 4-cylinder is about 23.5%:

$$\Pr(\text{Cylinders} = 4 \mid \text{MPG\_CITY} = 20) = f(-21.461149 + 1.013934 \times 20) - f(-60.329075 + 1.013934 \times 20) = 0.235$$

Similar to the glm action in the same regression action set, the genmod action generates the predictions from the generalized linear model. Instead of using the parameter estimates from the preceding formulas to manually compute the predictions, you can use genmod to score a data set using the output options.

```
In [3]: result = conn.CASTable('CylinderPredicted', replace=True)
   ...: genmodModel1.output.casout = genmodResult
   ...: genmodModel1.output.copyVars = 'ALL';
   ...: genmodModel1.output.pred = 'Prob_Cylinders'
   ...: genmodModel1()
   ...: result[['Prob_Cylinders','_level_','Cylinders','MPG_City']].head(24)
   ...:
NOTE: Convergence criterion (GCONV=1E-8) satisfied.
Out[3]:
```

Selected Rows from Table CYLINDERPREDICTED

	Prob_Cylinders	_LEVEL_	Cylinders	MPG_City
0	1.928842e-19	3.0	6.0	17.0
1	1.442488e-02	4.0	6.0	17.0
2	1.804258e-02	5.0	6.0	17.0
3	6.466697e-01	6.0	6.0	17.0
4	9.980702e-01	8.0	6.0	17.0
5	9.990158e-01	10.0	6.0	17.0
6	5.316706e-19	3.0	6.0	18.0
7	3.877857e-02	4.0	6.0	18.0
8	4.820533e-02	5.0	6.0	18.0

9	8.345697e-01	6.0	6.0	18.0
10	9.992990e-01	8.0	6.0	18.0
11	9.996427e-01	10.0	6.0	18.0
12	8.460038e-17	3.0	4.0	23.0
13	8.652192e-01	4.0	4.0	23.0
14	8.896126e-01	5.0	4.0	23.0
15	9.987558e-01	6.0	4.0	23.0
16	9.999956e-01	8.0	4.0	23.0
17	9.999978e-01	10.0	4.0	23.0
18	4.039564e-18	3.0	6.0	20.0
19	2.346085e-01	4.0	6.0	20.0
20	2.778780e-01	5.0	6.0	20.0
21	9.745742e-01	6.0	6.0	20.0
22	9.999077e-01	8.0	6.0	20.0
23	9.999530e-01	10.0	6.0	20.0

You can generate the predictions for a car with MPG_CITY = 20 from the last six rows of the preceding output table:

$$\Pr\left(\text{Cylinders} = 3 \mid \text{MPG\_CITY} = 20\right) = 4.039564e - 18 \approx 0$$

$$\Pr\left(\text{Cylinders} = 4 \mid \text{MPG\_CITY} = 20\right) = 0.2346085 - 0 = 0.2346085$$

$$\Pr\left(\text{Cylinders} = 5 \mid \text{MPG\_CITY} = 20\right) = 0.2778780 - 0.2346085 = 0.04327$$

$$\Pr\left(\text{Cylinders} = 6 \mid \text{MPG\_CITY} = 20\right) = 0.9745742 - 0.2778780 = 0.696696$$

$$\Pr\left(\text{Cylinders} > 6 \mid \text{MPG\_CITY} = 20\right) = 1 - 0.9745742 < 0.03$$

Using the multinomial model, a car with MPG_CITY = 20 is most likely a 6-cylinder (69.7%) or 4-cylinder car (23.5%), and the chance that it has more than 6 cylinders is less than 3%.

The following table lists the output result tables from the genmod action. You can use the display option to include or exclude a result table when fitting a generalized linear model using the genmod action.

Table Name	Description
ModelInfo	Basic information about the model such as the data source, the response variable, the distribution and link functions, and the optimization technique.
NObs	The number of observations that are read and used. Missing values are excluded, by default.
ConvergenceStatus	The convergence status of the parameter estimation.
Dimension	The dimension of the model, including the number of effects and the number of parameters.
FitStatistics	The fit statistics of the model such as log likelihood (multiplied by -2), AIC, AICC, and SBC.
ParameterEstimates	The estimation of the model parameters.
Timing	A timing of the subtasks of the GLM action call.

Regression Trees

Similar to decision tree models, regression trees are machine learning algorithms that use recursive partitioning to segment the input data set and to make predictions within each segment of the data. In this section, we briefly introduce how to use the tree models that are available in the decisiontree action set to build predictive models for continuous response. For information about decision tree and tree family models, see Chapter 9.

A regression tree usually follows these steps:

1. Grows a tree as deep as possible based on a splitting criterion and the training data.
2. Prunes back some nodes on the tree based on an error function on the validation data.
3. For each leaf (terminal node), build a simple model to predict the continuous dependent variable. The most common approach is to use the local sample average of the dependent variable.

Let's first load the decisiontree action set:

```
In [4]: conn.loadactionset('decisiontree')
   ...: conn.help(actionset='decisiontree')
NOTE: Added action set 'decisiontree'.
Out[4]:
decisionTree
```

```
                              decisionTree
          Name                         Description
0   dtreeTrain    Train Decision Tree
1   dtreeScore    Score A Table Using Decision Tree
2   dtreeSplit    Split Tree Nodes
3   dtreePrune    Prune Decision Tree
4   dtreeMerge    Merge Tree Nodes
5   dtreeCode     Generate score code for Decision Tree
6   forestTrain   Train Forest
7   forestScore   Score A Table Using Forest
8   forestCode    Generate score code for Forest
9   gbtreeTrain   Train Gradient Boosting Tree
10  gbtreeScore   Score A Table Using Gradient Boosting Tree
11  gbtreecode    Generate score code for Gradient Boosting Trees
```

The dtreetrain action fits decision tree model for a categorical dependent variable or regression tree model for a continuous dependent variable. Let's build a regression tree model using MPG_City to predict MSRP values of cars. In this example, we create the simplest regression tree that splits the root node into only two leaves (splitting the entire data into two partitions).

```
In [5]: cars = conn.CASTable('cars')
   ...:
   ...: output1 = conn.CASTable('treeModel1')
   ...: output1.replace = True;
   ...:
   ...: tree1 = cars.Dtreetrain()
   ...: tree1.target = 'MSRP'
   ...: tree1.inputs = ['MPG_City']
   ...: tree1.casout = output1
   ...: tree1.maxlevel = 2
   ...: tree1()
   ...:
   ...: output1[['_NodeID_', '_Parent_','_Mean_','_NodeName_','_PBLower0_',
                 '_PBUpper0_']].head()
   ...:
Out[5]:
[Fetch]
```

```
Selected Rows from Table TREEMODEL1

     _NodeID_   _Parent_         _Mean_   _NodeName_   _PBLower0_   \
  0       0.0       -1.0    32774.855140    MPG_City          NaN
  1       1.0        0.0    22875.341584        MSRP         20.0
  2       2.0        0.0    41623.092920        MSRP         10.0

     _PBUpper0_
  0        NaN
  1       60.0
  2       20.0
```

In the preceding example, the decision tree model is saved to the CAS table treeModel1. This table is stored on the CAS server You must use the fetch or head method to download the table to the Python client. The tree model table contains three observations, one for each node in the tree, including the root node. We fetch information only from the tree model table such as the unique IDs of the nodes and parents (_NodeID_ and _Parent_), the local sample means of the dependent variable (_Mean_), the splitting variable (_NodeName_), and the splitting points (_PBLower0_ and _PBUpper0_). The tree model table treeModel1 also contains other useful information such as the size of the node, the splitting criterion, and so on.

We can read about how the root node is split from the preceding table. The value of the_NodeName_ column in the first row shows that the root node is split by MPG_City, and the values of the _PBLower0_ and _PBUpper0_ columns show us that Node 1 contains the observations with MPG_CITY in (20,60], and Node 2 contains the observations with MPG_CITY in [10,20]. Note that in the CAS tree models, the splitting points such as MPG_CITY = 20 in this case are assigned to the child node with smaller values of MPG_City.

Based on this information, a tree structure follows for the first decision tree example:

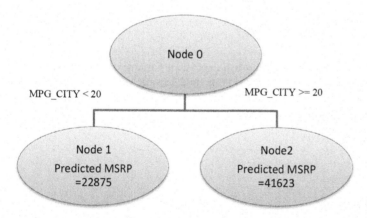

The splitting criteria of the CAS decision tree model are listed in the following table:

Parameter	Description
crit = 'ftest'	Uses the p-values of F test to select the best split.
crit = 'variance'	Uses the best split that produce the largest reduction of sum of squared errors. For regression trees, the sum of squared errors is equivalent to the variable of the data.
crit = 'chaid'	Uses adjusted significance testing (Bonferroni testing) to select the best split.

Pruning a tree model is a necessary step to avoid overfitting when you use the regression tree model to score new data (validation data). In the preceding example, we grow only the simplest tree structure, so there is no need to prune it back. If you have created a deeper tree and you have validation data, you can use the dtreeprune action to prune a given tree model.

```
data2 = conn.CASTable('your_vadliatoin_data')
output2 = conn.CASTable('pruned_tree')
data2.dtreeprune(modelTable=output1, casout=output2)
```

The last step for completing a regression tree model is to use the pruned tree model to score your data. This is done by the dtreescore action.

```
data2.dtreescore(modelTable=output2)
```

Conclusion

In this chapter, we first introduced the linear regression model and discussed some best practices to improve the modeling fitting of a linear regression. Then we introduced the generalized linear model that is available in the regression action set and the actions in the decisiontree action set to build a regression tree model. For more information on these see the following references.

[1] Neter, John, et al. 1996. *Applied Linear Statistical Models*. Vol. 4. Chicago: Irwin.

[2] McCullagh, Peter, and John A. Nelder. 1989. *Generalized Linear Models*. Vol. 37. CRC Press.

Chapter 9: Modeling Categorical Variables

In Chapter 8, we introduced linear regressions, generalized linear models and regression trees for modeling continuous response variables. In this chapter, we focus on applications in which the response variable is categorical, such as organic food that is purchased in a supermarket (Bought, Not), blood press status (High, Normal, Low), and credit card application status (Accepted, Rejected). Logistic regressions and decision trees are introduced in the first two sections for a binary response variable, which is a response variable with only two qualitative outcomes. In the last section, we introduce random forests, gradient boosting trees, and neural networks, which can fit a categorical response variable with more than two distinct outcomes.

We continue to use the Organics data set for this chapter. Again, we assume that a CAS server is already set up and the data sets have been loaded to the CAS server

```
In [1]: organics.tableinfo()
Out[1]:
[TableInfo]

        Name      Rows   Columns  Encoding  CreateTimeFormatted  \
0   ORGANICS   1688948        36     utf-8  09Nov2016:10:32:06

     ModTimeFormatted JavaCharSet    CreateTime       ModTime  \
0  09Nov2016:10:32:06        UTF8  1.794307e+09  1.794307e+09

   Global  Repeated  View  SourceName  SourceCaslib  Compressed  \
0       1         0     0           0                           0

   Creator  Modifier
0  username
```

Logistic Regression

Similar to the linear regression models introduced in Chapter 8, logistic regression uses the linear combination of one or more predictors to build a predictive model for the response outcomes. Unlike linear regressions, the prediction of interest in a logistic regression is not a continuous outcome with a range from negative to positive infinity. Instead, we are interested in predicting the probabilities of the outcome levels of the response variable. Examples are the probability of buying or not buying organic food from a supermarket or the probability of a credit card application that is accepted or rejected. For a binary response variable, the two distinct outcome levels are usually called the event level and the non-event level.

$$P_{event} + P_{non-event} = 1$$

We simply need to predict P_{event}, the event probability for the response variable, which always takes values in $[0, 1]$. Logistic regression originates from the logistic transformation, which maps a continuous input from $(-\infty, \infty)$ to an output between 0 and 1.

$$f(x) = \frac{1}{1 + e^{-k(x - x_0)}}$$

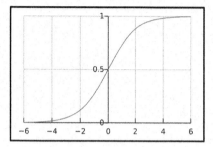

Similarly, a logistic regression model uses the logistic transformation to link the linear combination of one or more predictors to the probability of event level as follows:

$$P_{event} = \frac{1}{1 + e^{-t}}$$

where t is a linear combination of the predictors:

$$t = a + b_1 x_1 + b_2 x_2 + \cdots + b_K x_K$$

The inverse form of the transformation also indicates that a logistic regression is a non-linear model:

$$G(P_{event}) = log\left(\frac{P_{event}}{1 - P_{event}}\right) = a + b_1 x_1 + b_2 x_2 + \cdots + b_K x_K$$

where the function $G(P_{event})$ is often called the logit link function. The ratio $P_{event}/1 - P_{event}$ is also known as the odds ratio. When a logit link function is used, we assume that the predictors have a linear relationship with the log of the odds ratio. Logistic regression can be extended by using other link functions as well, such as probit, cloglog, and negative cloglog.

Logistic regression models are available in the regression action set. First, you must load the action set.

```
In [2]: conn.loadactionset('regression')
```

Now let's build a simple logistic regression for the Organics data to predict whether consumers would like to buy organic food. The response variable in this data is called TargetBuy.

```
In [2]: organics.logistic(
   ...:         target = 'TargetBuy',
   ...:         inputs = ['DemAge', 'Purchase_3mon', 'Purchase_6mon']
   ...: )
```

```
NOTE: Convergence criterion (GCONV=1E-8) satisfied.
```
Out[2]:
```
[ModelInfo]
```

Model Information

	RowId	Description	Value
0	DATA	Data Source	ORGANICS
1	RESPONSEVAR	Response Variable	TargetBuy
2	DIST	Distribution	Binary
3	LINK	Link Function	Logit
4	TECH	Optimization Technique	Newton-Raphson with Ridging

```
[NObs]
```

Number of Observations

	RowId	Description	Value
0	NREAD	Number of Observations Read	1688948.0
1	NUSED	Number of Observations Used	1574340.0

```
[ResponseProfile]
```

Response Profile

	OrderedValue	Outcome	TargetBuy	Freq	Modeled
0	1	Bought	Bought	387600.0	*
1	2	No	No	1186740.0	

```
[ConvergenceStatus]
```

Convergence Status

	Reason	Status	MaxGradient
0	Convergence criterion (GCONV=1E-8) s...	0	4.419888e-08

```
[Dimensions]
```

Dimensions

	RowId	Description	Value
0	NDESIGNCOLS	Columns in Design	4
1	NEFFECTS	Number of Effects	4
2	MAXEFCOLS	Max Effect Columns	1
3	DESIGNRANK	Rank of Design	4
4	OPTPARM	Parameters in Optimization	4

```
[GlobalTest]
```

Testing Global Null Hypothesis: BETA=0

	Test	DF	ChiSq	ProbChiSq
0	Likelihood Ratio	3	149251.090674	0.0

```
[FitStatistics]

Fit Statistics

     RowId                  Description          Value
0    M2LL              -2 Log Likelihood   1.608090e+06
1    AIC       AIC (smaller is better)    1.608098e+06
2    AICC     AICC (smaller is better)    1.608098e+06
3    SBC       SBC (smaller is better)    1.608147e+06

[ParameterEstimates]

Parameter Estimates

               Effect       Parameter          ParmName  DF  Estimate  \
0           Intercept       Intercept         Intercept   1   1.755274
1              DemAge          DemAge            DemAge   1  -0.057438
2      purchase_3mon   purchase_3mon     purchase_3mon   1  -0.000002
3      purchase_6mon   purchase_6mon     purchase_6mon   1   0.000039

        StdErr          ChiSq        ProbChiSq
0     0.057092     945.232627    1.442299e-207
1     0.000158  131358.158671    0.000000e+00
2     0.000055       0.000866    9.765250e-01
3     0.000039       0.990883    3.195267e-01

[Timing]

Task Timing

                RowId                 Task       Time    RelTime
0               SETUP    Setup and Parsing   0.017694   0.058605
1         LEVELIZATION          Levelization   0.027966   0.092627
2       INITIALIZATION   Model Initialization   0.000611   0.002024
3                SSCP      SSCP Computation   0.017766   0.058843
4              FITTING         Model Fitting   0.233353   0.772892
5              CLEANUP              Cleanup   0.002567   0.008502
6                TOTAL                Total   0.301922   1.000000
```

In the preceding example, we build a logistic regression to predict the probability of buying organic food (Pr(TargetBuy = Bought)) using three continuous predictors Age, Recent 3 Month Purchase Amount, and Recent 6 month Purchase Amount. You can also add categorical predictors to the logistic regression. They must be specified in both the inputs argument and the nominals argument.

```
In [3]: organics.logistic(
   ...:     target = 'TargetBuy',
   ...:     inputs = ['DemAge', 'Purchase_3mon', 'Purchase_6mon', 'DemGender',
   ...:               'DemHomeowner'],
   ...:     nominals = ['DemGender', 'DemHomeowner'],
   ...:     display = {'names': ['ParameterEstimates']}
   ...: )

NOTE: Convergence criterion (GCONV=1E-8) satisfied.
Out[3]:
```

[ParameterEstimates]

Parameter Estimates

	Effect	DemGender	DemHomeowner	Parameter \
0	Intercept			Intercept
1	DemAge			DemAge
2	purchase_3mon			purchase_3mon
3	purchase_6mon			purchase_6mon
4	DemGender	F		DemGender F
5	DemGender	M		DemGender M
6	DemGender	U		DemGender U
7	DemHomeowner		No	DemHomeowner No
8	DemHomeowner		Yes	DemHomeowner Yes

	ParmName	DF	Estimate	StdErr	ChiSq \
0	Intercept	1	0.353349	0.059586	35.165819
1	DemAge	1	-0.056478	0.000162	120824.157416
2	purchase_3mon	1	0.000009	0.000057	0.024229
3	purchase_6mon	1	0.000037	0.000040	0.819283
4	DemGender_F	1	1.817158	0.007381	60608.910532
5	DemGender_M	1	0.857905	0.008216	10904.528993
6	DemGender_U	0	0.000000	NaN	NaN
7	DemHomeowner_No	1	0.000320	0.004226	0.005725
8	DemHomeowner_Yes	0	0.000000	NaN	NaN

	ProbChiSq
0	3.027918e-09
1	0.000000e+00
2	8.763032e-01
3	3.653900e-01
4	0.000000e+00
5	0.000000e+00
6	NaN
7	9.396871e-01
8	NaN

In the preceding example, we also use the display option to select only the parameter estimate output table. For each categorical predictor, the logistic action constructs dummy indicators for the distinct levels of the predictor, and uses them as linear terms. For example, if a consumer is 30 years old, has purchased the amount $1,200 and $500 for the last six months and three months, respectively, is male, and currently does not own a home, the predicted probability of buying organic food is 39.65%.

$$t = 0.3533 - 0.056 \times 30 + 0.000008864 \times 500 + 0.00003651 \times 1200 + 0.8579 + 0.0003197 = -0.42024$$

$$P_{event} = \frac{1}{1+e^{-t}} = 39.65\%$$

The following table summarizes the output tables that are returned by the logistic action.

Table Name	Description
NObs	The number of observations that are read and used. Missing values are excluded, by default.
ResponseProfile	The frequency distribution of the response variable. The event level is marked with an asterisk (*).
ConvergenceStatus	The convergence status of the parameter estimation.
Dimension	The dimension of the model, including the number of effects and the number of parameters.
GlobalTest	A likelihood ratio test that measures the overall model fitting.
FitStatistics	The fit statistics of the model such as log likelihood (multiplied by 2), AIC, AICC and BIC.
ParameterEstimates	The estimation of the logistic regression parameters.
Timing	A timing of the subtasks of the GLM action call.

In Python, you can define the logistic model first and add options, step-by-step, which enables you to reuse a lot of code when you need to change only a few options in a logistic model. The preceding logistic action code can be rewritten as follows:

```
In [4]: all_preds = ['DemAge', 'Purchase_3mon', 'Purchase_9mon', 'DemGender',
                      'DemHomeowner']
   ...: all_cats = ['DemGender', 'DemHomeowner']
   ...:
   ...: model1 = organics.Logistic()
   ...: model1.nominals = all_cats
   ...: model1.target = 'TargetBuy'
   ...: model1.inputs = all_preds
   ...: model1.display.names = ['ParameterEstimates']
   ...:
   ...: model1()
```

In the preceding example, first, we define a new logistic model model1, and then add the class effect list (model1.nominals), the response variables (model1.target), and the effect list (model1.inputs), step-by-step. The logistic action, by default, uses the logit link function but you can always override it with your own event selection. In the following example, we reuse the model1 definition from the previous example and change the link function to PROBIT:

```
In [5]: model1.link = 'PROBIT'
   ...: model1.display.names = ['ResponseProfile', 'ParameterEstimates']
   ...: model1()

NOTE: Convergence criterion (GCONV=1E-8) satisfied.
Out[5]:
[ResponseProfile]

 Response Profile

    OrderedValue Outcome TargetBuy      Freq Modeled
 0             1  Bought    Bought   387600.0       *
 1             2      No        No  1186740.0

[ParameterEstimates]
```

```
Parameter Estimates
```

	Effect	DemGender	DemHomeowner	Parameter	\
0	Intercept			Intercept	
1	DemAge			DemAge	
2	purchase_3mon			purchase_3mon	
3	purchase_9mon			purchase_9mon	
4	DemGender	F		DemGender F	
5	DemGender	M		DemGender M	
6	DemGender	U		DemGender U	
7	DemHomeowner		No	DemHomeowner No	
8	DemHomeowner		Yes	DemHomeowner Yes	

	ParmName	DF	Estimate	StdErr	ChiSq	\
0	Intercept	1	0.447991	0.072359	38.330834	
1	DemAge	1	-0.056478	0.000162	120823.996353	
2	purchase_3mon	1	0.000071	0.000049	2.074100	
3	purchase_9mon	1	-0.000026	0.000029	0.811013	
4	DemGender_F	1	1.817162	0.007381	60609.158117	
5	DemGender_M	1	0.857905	0.008216	10904.528278	
6	DemGender_U	0	0.000000	NaN	NaN	
7	DemHomeowner_No	1	0.000318	0.004226	0.005669	
8	DemHomeowner_Yes	0	0.000000	NaN	NaN	

	ProbChiSq
0	5.971168e-10
1	0.000000e+00
2	1.498183e-01
3	3.678210e-01
4	0.000000e+00
5	0.000000e+00
6	NaN
7	9.399814e-01
8	NaN

The logistic regression models that we have built so far train the model without actually using the model to make a prediction (that is, estimating $P(event)$). You must specify an output table for the logistic action in order to score the observations in the input table. By default, the casout table contains only the predictions, but you can use the copyvars option to copy some columns from the input table to the casout table. You can use copyvars='all' to copy all columns to the casout table.

```
In [6]: result1 = conn.CASTable('predicted', replace=True)
   ...: model1.output.casout = result1
   ...: model1.output.copyvars = 'all'
   ...: del model1.display
   ...: model1()
```

The logistic action generates one more result tables when a casout table is created. This table contains basic information about the casout table such as the name, the library, and the dimensions of the table.

```
[OutputCasTables]
```

	casLib	Name	Label	Rows	Columns	\
0	CASUSERHDFS(username)	predicted		1688948	37	

```
                            casTable
    0   CASTable('predicted', caslib='CASUSE...
```

You can print out the column names of the output table to see what new columns have been added. By default, the logistic action creates a new column _PRED_ for the estimated event probability.

```
In [7]: result1.columns
Out[7]:
Index(['_PRED_', 'ID', 'DemAffl', 'DemAge', 'DemGender',
       'DemHomeowner', 'DemAgeGroup', 'DemCluster', 'DemReg',
       'DemTVReg', 'DemFlag1', 'DemFlag2', 'DemFlag3', 'DemFlag4',
       'DemFlag5', 'DemFlag6', 'DemFlag7', 'DemFlag8', 'PromClass',
       'PromTime', 'TargetBuy', 'Bought_Beverages', 'Bought_Bakery',
       'Bought_Canned', 'Bought_Dairy', 'Bought_Baking',
       'Bought_Frozen', 'Bought_Meat', 'Bought_Fruits',
       'Bought_Vegetables', 'Bought_Cleaners', 'Bought_PaperGoods',
       'Bought_Others', 'purchase_3mon', 'purchase_6mon',
       'purchase_9mon', 'purchase_12mon'],
      dtype='object')
```

You can use the data summary actions in the simple action set to look at the model output. For example, let's compare the average predicted probability of buying organic foods across different levels of DemGender:

```
In [8]: result1.crosstab(row='DemGender', weight='_PRED_', aggregators='mean')

Out[8]:
[Crosstab]

     DemGender      Col1
  0          F   0.343891
  1          M   0.165559
  2          U   0.076981
```

From the preceding output, it looks like female customers are more likely to purchase organic food, and the customers who didn't provide gender information are not interested in buying organic food. The ratio (0.343891/0.076981) between these two groups is approximately 5, which means female customers are five times more likely to purchase organic foods than the customers who didn't provide gender information.

The logistic action generates additional model diagnosis outputs. The following table summarizes the columns that a logistic action can generate as output.

Option	Description
pred	The predicted value. If you do not specify any output statistics, the predicted value is named _PRED_, by default.
resraw	The raw residual.
xbeta	The linear predictor.
stdxbeta	The standard error of the linear predictor.
lcl	The lower bound of a confidence interval for the linear predictor.
ucl	The upper bound of a confidence interval for the linear predictor.
lclm	The lower bound of a confidence interval for the mean.
uclm	The upper bound of a confidence interval for the mean.
h	The leverage of the observation.

Option	Description
reschi	The Pearson chi-square residual.
stdreschi	The standardized Pearson chi-square residual.
resdev	The deviance residual.
reslik	The likelihood residual (likelihood displacement).
reswork	The working residual.
difdev	The change in the deviance that is attributable to deleting the individual observation.
difchisq	The change in the Pearson chi-square statistic that is attributable to deleting the individual observation.
cbar	The confidence interval displacement, which measures the overall change in the global regression estimates due to deleting the individual observation.
alpha	The significance level used for the construction of confidence intervals.

Similar to the code argument in the glm action for linear regression, SAS DATA step code can also be used to save a logistic model. You can score new data sets using the DATA step code in Python (using the runcode action from the datastep action set) or in a SAS language environment such as Base SAS or SAS Studio.

```
In [9]: # example 4 score code
   ...: result = organics.logistic(
   ...:     target = 'TargetBuy',
   ...:     inputs = ['DemAge', 'Purchase_3mon', 'Purchase_6mon'],
   ...:     code = {}
   ...: )
NOTE: Convergence criterion (GCONV=1E-8) satisfied.

In [10]: result['_code_']
Out[10]:
Score Code

                                      SASCode
0          /*--------------------------------...
1                  Generated SAS Scoring Code
2                   Date: 09Nov2016:13:33:15
3          --------------------------------...
4
5          drop _badval_ _linp_ _temp_ _i_ _j_;
6                              _badval_  = 0;
7                              _linp_    = 0;
8                              _temp_    = 0;
9                              _i_       = 0;
10                             _j_       = 0;
11
12             array _xrow_0_0_{4} _temporary_;
13         array _beta_0_0_{4} _temporary_ (...
14                      -0.05743797902413
15                      -1.6172314911858E-6
16                      0.00003872414134);
17
18                 if missing(purchase_3mon)
19                     or missing(DemAge)
20                 or missing(purchase_6mon)
```

```
21                                      then do;
22                                  _badval_ = 1;
23                              goto skip_0_0;
24                                        end;
25
26      do _i_=1 to 4; _xrow_0_0_{_i_} = ...
27
28                           _xrow_0_0_[1] = 1;
29
30                      _xrow_0_0_[2] = DemAge;
31
32          _xrow_0_0_[3] = purchase_3mon;
33
34          _xrow_0_0_[4] = purchase_6mon;
35
36                            do _i_=1 to 4;
37      _linp_ + _xrow_0_0_{_i_} * _be...
38                                        end;
39
40                                    skip_0_0:
41      label P_TargetBuy = 'Predicted: T...
42      if (_badval_ eq 0) and not missin...
43                  if (_linp_ > 0) then do;
44          P_TargetBuy = 1 / (1+exp(-_...
45                              end; else do;
46          P_TargetBuy = exp(_linp_) /...
47                                        end;
48                            end; else do;
49                              _linp_ = .;
50                      P_TargetBuy = .;
51                                        end;
52
```

CAS also provides several useful data set options that can interact with an analytical action. For example, to build multiple logistic regressions (one for each level of a categorical variable), you can simply use the groupby option for the Organics data set.

```
In [11]: organics.groupby = ['DemGender']
    ...: result = organics.logistic(
    ...:     target = 'TargetBuy',
    ...:     inputs = ['DemAge', 'Purchase_3mon', 'Purchase_6mon'],
    ...: )
NOTE: Convergence criterion (GCONV=1E-8) satisfied.
NOTE: Convergence criterion (GCONV=1E-8) satisfied.
NOTE: Convergence criterion (GCONV=1E-8) satisfied.
```

There are three convergence messages for the three logistic models that are trained for the female customers, male customers, and customers who didn't provide gender information. You can loop through the results and generate the parameter estimations:

```
In [12]: for df in result:
    ...:     if 'ParameterEstimates' in df:
    ...:         print(result[df][['Effect','Parameter','Estimate']])
    ...:         print('')
    ...:
```

```
Parameter Estimates

                     Effect        Parameter   Estimate
DemGender
F                 Intercept        Intercept   2.181055
F                    DemAge           DemAge  -0.057016
F            purchase_3mon    purchase_3mon    0.000023
F            purchase_6mon    purchase_6mon    0.000038

Parameter Estimates

                     Effect        Parameter   Estimate
DemGender
M                 Intercept        Intercept   1.230455
M                    DemAge           DemAge  -0.056114
M            purchase_3mon    purchase_3mon  -0.000091
M            purchase_6mon    purchase_6mon    0.000065

Parameter Estimates

                     Effect        Parameter   Estimate
DemGender
U                 Intercept        Intercept   0.211336
U                    DemAge           DemAge  -0.052621
U            purchase_3mon    purchase_3mon    0.000139
U            purchase_6mon    purchase_6mon  -0.000046
```

Note that the groupby option in Python is very similar to the BY statement in the SAS language for by-group processing of repeated analytical contents. However, the BY statement requires the data set to be sorted by the variables that are specified in the BY statement. The groupby option does not require pre-sorted data. When the data set is distributed, the groupby option does not introduce additional data shuffling either.

Decision Trees

Decision trees is a type of machine learning algorithm that uses recursive partitioning to segment the input data set and to make predictions within each segment of the data. Decision tree models have been widely used for predictive modeling, data stratification, missing value imputation, outlier detection and description, variable selection, and other areas of machine learning and statistical modeling. In this section, we focus on using decision trees to build predictive models.

The following figure illustrates a simple decision tree model on data that is collected in a city park regarding whether people purchase ice cream. The response variable is binary: 1 for the people who bought ice cream and 0 for the people who didn't buy ice cream. There are three predictors in this example: Sunny and Hot?, Have Extra Money?, and Crave Ice Cream?. In this example, all of these predictors are binary, with values YES and NO. In the example, the chance is 80% that people who have extra money on a sunny and hot day will buy ice cream.

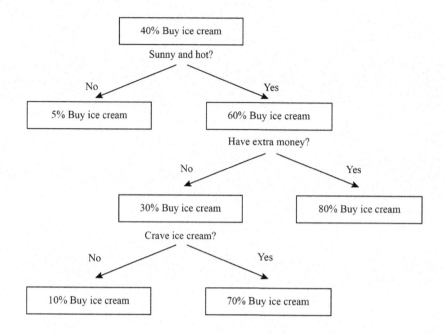

A typical decision tree model for a categorical variable contains three steps:

1. Grow a decision tree as deep as possible based on a splitting criterion and the training data.
2. Prune back some nodes on the decision tree based on an error function on the validation data.
3. For each leaf, the probability of a response outcome is estimated using the sample frequency table.

The CAS decision tree supports a variety of decision tree splitting and pruning criteria. The decision tree action set contains machine learning models that are in the tree family: decision trees, random forests, and gradient boosting. Let's first load the decisiontree action set.

```
In [1]: conn.loadactionset('decisiontree')
   ...: conn.help(actionset='decisiontree')
NOTE: Added action set 'decisiontree'.
Out[1]:
decisionTree
```

	Name	Description
		decisionTree
	Name	Description
0	dtreeTrain	Train Decision Tree
1	dtreeScore	Score A Table Using Decision Tree
2	dtreeSplit	Split Tree Nodes
3	dtreePrune	Prune Decision Tree
4	dtreeMerge	Merge Tree Nodes
5	dtreeCode	Generate score code for Decision Tree
6	forestTrain	Train Forest
7	forestScore	Score A Table Using Forest
8	forestCode	Generate score code for Forest
9	gbtreeTrain	Train Gradient Boosting Tree
10	gbtreeScore	Score A Table Using Gradient Boosting Tree

```
                          decisionTree
              Name                      Description
    11   gbtreecode       Generate score code for Gradient Boosting Trees
```

The action sets with prefix dtree are used for building a decision tree model. The dtreetrain action is used for training a decision tree. The dtreescore and dtreecode actions are designed for scoring using a decision tree and for generating as output a decision tree model, as SAS DATA step code. The other actions with prefix dtree are used in interactive decision tree modifications, where a user can manually split, prune, or merge tree nodes.

Let's get started with a simple decision tree model that contains only one response variable and one predictor.

```
In [2]: output1 = conn.CASTable('treeModel1', replace=True)
   ...: tree1 = organics.Dtreetrain()
   ...: tree1.target = 'TargetBuy'
   ...: tree1.inputs = ['DemGender']
   ...: tree1.casout = output1
   ...: tree1()
   ...:
```

```
Out[2]:
[ModelInfo]

 Decision Tree for ORGANICS

                               Descr          Value
    0           Number of Tree Nodes   5.000000e+00
    1          Max Number of Branches  2.000000e+00
    2               Number of Levels   3.000000e+00
    3               Number of Leaves   3.000000e+00
    4                 Number of Bins   2.000000e+01
    5            Minimum Size of Leaves 3.236840e+05
    6            Maximum Size of Leaves 9.233240e+05
    7            Number of Variables   1.000000e+00
    8     Confidence Level for Pruning 2.500000e-01
    9      Number of Observations Used 1.688948e+06
    10    Misclassification Error (%)  2.477163e+01

[OutputCasTables]

                 casLib          Name   Rows   Columns  \
    0   CASUSERHDFS(username)   treeModel1    5       24

                                     casTable
    0   CASTable('treeModel1', caslib='CASUS...
```

The dtreetrain action trains a decision tree model and saves it to the casout table treemodel1. The action also generates a model information table (ModelInfo) that contains basic descriptions of the trained decision tree model. Note that ModelInfo is stored at the local Python client and contains only basic information about the tree model, whereas the treemodel1 table is a CAS table that is stored on the CAS server. Let's look at what is included in the tree model output:

```
In [3]: output1.columns
```

```
Out[3]:
Index(['_Target_', '_NumTargetLevel_', '_TargetValL_',
       '_TargetVal0_', '_TargetVal1_', '_CI0_', '_CI1_', '_NodeID_',
       '_TreeLevel_', '_NodeName_', '_Parent_', '_ParentName_',
       '_NodeType_', '_Gain_', '_NumObs_', '_TargetValue_',
       '_NumChild_', '_ChildID0_', '_ChildID1_', '_PBranches_',
       '_PBNameL0_', '_PBNameL1_', '_PBName0_', '_PBName1_'],
      dtype='object')
```

The decision tree output contains one row per node to summarize the tree structure and the model fit. Let's first fetch some columns that are related to the tree structure and the splitting values.

```
In [4]: output1[['_TreeLevel_', '_NodeID_', '_Parent_', '_ParentName_',
                  '_NodeType_', '_PBName0_',
                  '_PBName1_']].sort_values('_NodeID_').head(20)
```

```
Out[4]:
Selected Rows from Table TREEMODEL1
```

	TreeLevel	_NodeID_	_Parent_	_ParentName_	_NodeType_	\
0	0.0	0.0	-1.0		1.0	
1	1.0	1.0	0.0	DemGender	1.0	
2	1.0	2.0	0.0	DemGender	3.0	
3	2.0	3.0	1.0	DemGender	3.0	
4	2.0	4.0	1.0	DemGender	3.0	

	PBName0	_PBName1_
0		
1	M	U
2	F	
3	U	
4	M	

The first column _TreeLevel_ identifies the depth of the tree nodes, where depth 0 indicates the root node. Each node has a unique node ID (_NodeID_) that is based on the order that the nodes are inserted in the decision tree. By default, the CAS decision tree model splits a node into two branches, which explains why the two nodes share the same parent (_Parent_).

The _ParentName_ column indicates which predictor is chosen to split its parent node, and the columns with prefix _PBName specifies the splitting rule, which explains how to split the node from its parent node. For example, the second row and the third row tell the first split of the decision tree to split observations with DemGender = M/U and observations DemGender = F into two nodes with _NodeID_ 1 and 2. The _NodeType_ column in this table indicates whether a node is an internal node or a terminal node (leaf).

The following figure reconstructs the decision tree structure from the preceding fetched output:

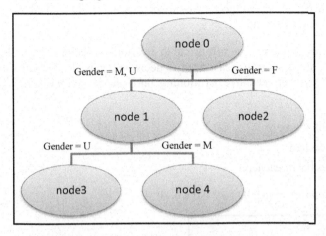

Next let's look at the distribution of the target variables and the measurement of the splits.

```
In [5]: output1[['_TreeLevel_', '_NodeID_', '_Parent_',
                  '_TargetVal0_', '_TargetVal1_', '_CI0_', '_CI1_',
                  '_Gain_', '_NumObs_']].sort_values('_NodeID_').head(20)
Out[5]:
Selected Rows from Table TREEMODEL1
```

	TreeLevel	_NodeID_	_Parent_	_TargetVal0_	_TargetVal1_	\
0	0.0	0.0	-1.0	No	Bought	
1	1.0	1.0	0.0	No	Bought	
2	1.0	2.0	0.0	No	Bought	
3	2.0	3.0	1.0	No	Bought	
4	2.0	4.0	1.0	No	Bought	

	_CI0_	_CI1_	_Gain_	_NumObs_
0	0.752284	0.247716	0.047713	1688948.0
1	0.870955	0.129045	0.012886	765624.0
2	0.653881	0.346119	0.000000	923324.0
3	0.921578	0.078422	0.000000	323684.0
4	0.833878	0.166122	0.000000	441940.0

The first row returns the overall frequency distribution of the response variable. In this case, the overall sample percentage of those who buy organic food is 24.77%. The decision tree algorithm then evaluates all possible ways to cut the entire data into two segments. Since we have only one predictor with three levels, there are only three ways to split the data into two segments:

- Gender = F versus Gender = M, U
- Gender = M versus Gender = F, U
- Gender = U versus Gender = F, M

The dtreetrain action evaluates all these three possible splits and selects the best one based on a certain criterion. The default criterion that is used by dtreetrain is information gain, which is the difference between of the entropy of the parent node and the weighted average of entropies of the child nodes. In other words, information gain tries to find a split that maximizes the difference of the target distribution between the parent node and the child nodes. The best split chosen by dtreetrain is Gender = F versus Gender = M, U with information gain 0.0477. The sample percentage of those who buy organic food and who are the two children of node 0 is 12.90% and 34.61%, respectively.

The tree model continues to evaluate the splits on the two segments and to determine whether they can be further split. The continued evaluation for more splits is the reason why a decision tree is also known as a recursive partition. The tree structure is grown using recursive partitioning, until one of the following criteria is met:

- The current partition cannot be split anymore.
- The minimum leaf size has been reached.
- The maximum depth of the tree has been reached.

The following figure shows the final decision tree model that we have built:

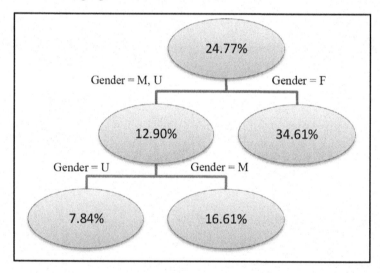

The following table lists some important parameters for training a decision tree model:

Parameter	Description	Default
maxbranch	Specifies the maximum number of children (branches) that are allowed for each level of the tree.	2
maxlevel	Specifies the maximum number of tree levels.	6
leafsize	Specifies the minimum number of observations on each node.	1
prune=True | False	Specifies whether to use a C4.5 pruning method for classification trees or minimal cost-complexity pruning for regression trees.	False
varimp=True | False	Specifies whether the variable importance information is generated. The importance value is determined by the total Gini reduction.	False
cflev	Specifies the aggressiveness of tree pruning according to the C4.5 method.	

The dtreetrain action supports the following criteria for evaluating the splits in a decision tree growing process:

Parameter	Description
crit=chaid	CHAID (Chi-square Automatic Interaction Detector) technique
crit=chisquare	Chi-square test
crit=gain	Information gain
crit=gainratio	Information gain ratio
crit=gini	Per-leaf Gini statistic

Building a decision tree model usually involves a pruning step after the tree is grown. You must enable the prune option to request dtreetrain to include an additional pruning step after the tree is grown.

```
In [6]: tree1.prune = True
   ...: tree1()
Out[6]:
[ModelInfo]

 Decision Tree for ORGANICS

                        Descr        Value
0         Number of Tree Nodes  3.000000e+00
1       Max Number of Branches  2.000000e+00
2             Number of Levels  2.000000e+00
3             Number of Leaves  2.000000e+00
4               Number of Bins  2.000000e+01
5        Minimum Size of Leaves  7.656240e+05
6        Maximum Size of Leaves  9.233240e+05
7          Number of Variables  1.000000e+00
8   Confidence Level for Pruning  2.500000e-01
9   Number of Observations Used  1.688948e+06
10  Misclassification Error (%)  2.477163e+01


[OutputCasTables]

                   casLib        Name  Rows  Columns  \
0   CASUSERHDFS(username)  treeModel1     3       24

                            casTable
0  CASTable('treeModel1', caslib='CASUS...

In [7]: output1[['_TreeLevel_', '_NodeID_', '_Parent_', '_ParentName_',
                 '_NodeType_', '_PBName0_',
                 '_PBName1_']].sort_values('_NodeID_').head(20)
Out[7]:
Selected Rows from Table TREEMODEL1

   _TreeLevel_  _NodeID_  _Parent_ _ParentName_  _NodeType_  \
0          0.0       0.0      -1.0                       1.0
1          1.0       1.0       0.0    DemGender          3.0
2          1.0       2.0       0.0    DemGender          3.0
```

```
      _PBName0_  _PBName1_
0
1              M           U
2              F
```

Compared to the code in In[2], Node 3 and Node 4 are pruned back according to the pruning criterion. The default pruning criterion is a modified C4.5 method, which estimates the error rate for validation data that is based on the classification error rate of the training data. The pruning criterion is not generated by the dtreetrain action. However, you can use the information gain output that is generated by the tree model without pruning in order to understand why this split is not significant (the information gain is 0.0129) compared to the first split (the information gain is 0.0477).

Pruning a decision tree is used to avoid model overfitting when you use the decision tree to score new data (validation data). The C4.5 method does not require validation data in order to prune a tree. If you do have holdout data, you can use the dtreeprune action to prune a given tree model.

```
data2 = conn.CASTable('your_validation_data')
output2 = conn.CASTable('pruned_tree')
data2.dtreeprune(model=output1, casout=output2)
```

Next let's add more variables to the decision tree models.

```
In [8]: varlist = ['DemGender', 'DemHomeowner', 'DemAgeGroup', 'DemCluster', 'DemReg',
                   'DemTVReg', 'DemFlag1', 'DemFlag2', 'DemFlag3', 'DemFlag4', 'DemFlag5',
                   'DemFlag6', 'DemFlag7', 'DemFlag8', 'PromClass']
   ...:
   ...: output2 = conn.CASTable('treeModel2', replace=True)
   ...:
   ...: tree2 = organics.dtreetrain
   ...: tree2.target = 'TargetBuy'
   ...: tree2.inputs = varlist
   ...: tree2.casout = output2
   ...: tree2()
Out[8]:
[ModelInfo]

Decision Tree for ORGANICS

                            Descr         Value
0            Number of Tree Nodes   4.300000e+01
1           Max Number of Branches  2.000000e+00
2                Number of Levels   6.000000e+00
3                Number of Leaves   2.200000e+01
4                 Number of Bins    2.000000e+01
5           Minimum Size of Leaves  7.600000e+01
6           Maximum Size of Leaves  5.972840e+05
7             Number of Variables   1.500000e+01
8    Confidence Level for Pruning   2.500000e-01
9    Number of Observations Used    1.688948e+06
10   Misclassification Error (%)    2.389866e+01

[OutputCasTables]

                    casLib          Name  Rows  Columns  \
0  CASUSERHDFS(username)    treeModel2    43      130

                              casTable
0  CASTable('treeModel2', caslib='CASUS...
```

The ModelInfo output in the preceding example indicates that a larger decision tree has been grown. The new tree has 43 nodes and 22 of them are terminal nodes (leaves). The tree has 6 levels and the smallest leaves have 76 observations. For data with 1.7 million observations, sometimes, we might not be interested in subsets of data with only 76 observations. You can actually control subset size by the leafsize parameter. You can set leafsize to 1000 in order to grow a smaller tree, as follows:

```
In [9]: organics.dtreetrain(
   ...:       target    = 'TargetBuy',
   ...:       inputs    = varlist,
   ...:       casout    = output2,
   ...:       leafSize  = 1000,
   ...:       maxLevel  = 4,
   ...: )
Out[9]:
[ModelInfo]
```

Decision Tree for ORGANICS

	Descr	Value
0	Number of Tree Nodes	1.500000e+01
1	Max Number of Branches	2.000000e+00
2	Number of Levels	4.000000e+00
3	Number of Leaves	8.000000e+00
4	Number of Bins	2.000000e+01
5	Minimum Size of Leaves	1.216000e+03
6	Maximum Size of Leaves	8.891240e+05
7	Number of Variables	1.500000e+01
8	Confidence Level for Pruning	2.500000e-01
9	Number of Observations Used	1.688948e+06
10	Misclassification Error (%)	2.393466e+01

[OutputCasTables]

	casLib	Name	Rows	Columns	\
0	CASUSERHDFS(username)	treeModel2	15	130	

	casTable
0	CASTable('treeModel2', caslib='CASUS...

In the previous example, the new decision tree produced only 15 nodes and 8 of them are leaves. Using this tree model to score a new observation is straightforward. You first identify the leaf node that contains this observation, and use the sample event probability of the node as the estimated event probability for that observation. The CAS decisiontree action set provides a dtreescore action for you to score a data set as well.

```
In [10]: organics.dtreescore(modelTable=conn.CASTable('treeModel2'))
Out[10]:
[ScoreInfo]
```

	Descr	Value
0	Number of Observations Read	1688948
1	Number of Observations Used	1688948
2	Misclassification Error (%)	23.934662287

The model option in dtreescore points to the tree model that we trained and stored on the CAS server, and it uses the model to score the ORGANICS CAS table. The dtreescore action in this example does not actually save the predictions to a new CAS table. You must use a casout option to save the predictions.

```
In [11]: output3 = conn.CASTable('predicted', replace=True)
   ...: organics.dtreescore(modelTable=output2, casout=output3)
   ...: output3.columns
Out[11]: Index(['_DT_PredName_', '_DT_PredP_', '_DT_PredLevel_',
'_LeafID_', '_MissIt_', '_NumNodes_', '_NodeList0_', '_NodeList1_',
'_NodeList2_', '_NodeList3_'], dtype='object')

In [12]: output3.head(10)
Out[12]:
Selected Rows from Table PREDICTED
```

	_DT_PredName_	_DT_PredP_	_DT_PredLevel_	_LeafID_	_MissIt_	\
0	No	0.840345	0.0	8.0	1.0	
1	No	0.667749	0.0	9.0	0.0	
2	No	0.840345	0.0	8.0	0.0	
3	No	0.667749	0.0	9.0	1.0	
4	No	0.667749	0.0	9.0	1.0	
5	No	0.559701	0.0	11.0	1.0	
6	No	0.667749	0.0	9.0	1.0	
7	No	0.840345	0.0	8.0	1.0	
8	No	0.667749	0.0	9.0	0.0	
9	No	0.923686	0.0	7.0	0.0	

	NumNodes	_NodeList0_	_NodeList1_	_NodeList2_	_NodeList3_
0	4.0	0.0	1.0	3.0	8.0
1	4.0	0.0	1.0	4.0	9.0
2	4.0	0.0	1.0	3.0	8.0
3	4.0	0.0	1.0	4.0	9.0
4	4.0	0.0	1.0	4.0	9.0
5	4.0	0.0	2.0	5.0	11.0
6	4.0	0.0	1.0	4.0	9.0
7	4.0	0.0	1.0	3.0	8.0
8	4.0	0.0	1.0	4.0	9.0
9	4.0	0.0	1.0	3.0	7.0

The following table summarizes the columns that are generated as output by a dtreescore action.

Output Column	Description
_DT_PredName_	The predicted value, which is the most frequent level of the leaf that the observation is assigned to.
_DT_PredP_	The predicted probability, which is equal to the sample frequency of the predicted value in the leaf that the observation is assigned to.
_DT_PredLeveL_	The index of the predicted value. If the response variable has k levels, this column takes values from $0, 1, .., k-1$
LeafID	The node ID of the leaf that the observation is assigned to.
MissIt	The indicator for misclassification.
NumNodes _NodeListK_	_NumNodes_ indicates the depth of the leaf. The list of _NodeListK_ variables stores the path from the root node to the current leaf.

Gradient Boosting, Forests, and Neural Networks

The decisiontree action set also contains the actions for building gradient boosting and random forest models. Unlike decision trees, gradient boosting and random forests are machine-learning techniques that produce predictions that are based on an ensemble of trees. Gradient boosting models are usually based on a set of weak prediction models (small decision trees or even tree stumps). By contrast, random forests are usually based on a set of full grown trees (deep trees) on subsample data. Another major difference is that gradient boosting grows decision trees sequentially and a random forest grows decision trees in parallel. For more details about tree models, refer to [1] and [2] at the end of the chapter.

Both gradient boosting and random forest models are available in the decisiontree action set through three distinct actions that cover basic steps of a machine learning pipeline: model training, scoring, and delivery (score code generation).

```
In [1]: conn.help(actionset='decisiontree')
NOTE: Added action set 'decisiontree'.
Out[1]:
decisionTree
```

```
                        decisionTree
          Name                          Description
   0   dtreeTrain    Train Decision Tree
   1   dtreeScore    Score A Table Using Decision Tree
   2   dtreeSplit    Split Tree Nodes
   3   dtreePrune    Prune Decision Tree
   4   dtreeMerge    Merge Tree Nodes
   5   dtreeCode     Generate score code for Decision Tree
   6   forestTrain   Train Forest
   7   forestScore   Score A Table Using Forest
   8   forestCode    Generate score code for Forest
   9   gbtreeTrain   Train Gradient Boosting Tree
  10   gbtreeScore   Score A Table Using Gradient Boosting Tree
  11   gbtreecode    Generate score code for Gradient Boosting Trees
```

Let's first train a simple random forest model using the Organics data set to predict the probability of buying organic food.

```
In[2]: varlist = ['DemGender', 'DemHomeowner', 'DemAgeGroup',
               'DemCluster', 'DemReg', 'DemTVReg', 'DemFlag1',
               'DemFlag2', 'DemFlag3', 'DemFlag4', 'DemFlag5',
               'DemFlag6', 'DemFlag7', 'DemFlag8', 'PromClass']
   ...:
   ...: output = conn.CASTable('forest1', replace=True)
   ...:
   ...: forest1 = organics.Foresttrain()
   ...: forest1.target = 'TargetBuy'
   ...: forest1.inputs = varlist
   ...: forest1.casout = output
   ...: forest1()

Out[2]:
[ModelInfo]

 Forest for ORGANICS

                                   Descr          Value
  0                      Number of Trees      50.000000
  1     Number of Selected Variables (M)       4.000000
```

```
2                    Random Number Seed         0.000000
3           Bootstrap Percentage (%)           63.212056
4                     Number of Bins            20.000000
5                Number of Variables            15.000000
6          Confidence Level for Pruning          0.250000
7            Max Number of Tree Nodes           57.000000
8            Min Number of Tree Nodes           19.000000
9              Max Number of Branches            2.000000
10             Min Number of Branches            2.000000
11               Max Number of Levels            6.000000
12               Min Number of Levels            6.000000
13               Max Number of Leaves           29.000000
14               Min Number of Leaves           10.000000
15              Maximum Size of Leaves      927422.000000
16              Minimum Size of Leaves           10.000000
17                  Out-of-Bag MCR (%)                 NaN


[OutputCasTables]

                    casLib      Name   Rows   Columns  \
0    CASUSERHDFS(username)    forest1   2280       132

                             casTable
0    CASTable('forest1', caslib='CASUSERH...
```

The foresttrain action returns two result tables to the client: ModelInfo and OutputCasTables. The first table contains parameters that define the forest, parameters that define each individual tree, and tree statistics such as the minimum and maximum number of branches and levels. A forest model is an ensemble of homogenous trees, with each tree growing on a different subset of the data (usually from bootstrap sampling). Therefore, the size and depth of the trees might be different from each other even though the tree parameters that you define are the same. The idea of a forest is to grow a deep tree on each subsample in order to produce "perfect" predictions for the local data (low bias but high variance) and then use the ensemble technique to reduce the overall variance.

Some key parameters that define a random forest model are listed in the following table. The foresttrain action also enables you to configure the individual trees, and the parameters are identical to those in the dtreetrain action. In general, you must grow deep trees for each bootstrap sample, and pruning is often unnecessary.

Parameter	Description
ntree	The number of trees in the forest ensemble, which is 50, by default.
m	The number of input variables to consider for splitting on a node. The variables are selected at random from the input variables. By default, forest uses the square root of the number of input variables that are used, rounded up to the nearest integer.
vote='majority'	Uses majority voting to collect the individual trees into an ensemble. This is the default ensemble for classification models.
vote='prob'	Uses the average of predicted probabilities or values to collect the individual trees into an ensemble.
seed	The seed that is used for the random number generator in bootstrapping.
bootstrap	Specifies the fraction of the data for the bootstrap sample. The default value is 0.63212055882.

Parameter	Description
oob	The Boolean value to control whether the out-of-bag error is computed when building a forest.

Random forest models are also commonly used in variable selection, which is usually determined by the variable importance of the predictors in training the forest model. The importance of a predictor to the target variable is a measure of its overall contribution to all the individual trees. In the foresttrain action, this contribution is defined as the total Gini reduction from all of the splits that use this predictor.

```
In [3]: forest1.varimp = True
   ...: result = forest1()
   ...: result['DTreeVarImpInfo']
   ...:
Out[3]:
Forest for ORGANICS
```

	Variable	Importance	Std
0	DemGender	16191.631365	7820.237986
1	DemAgeGroup	7006.819480	2827.738946
2	PromClass	2235.407366	1199.868546
3	DemTVReg	288.048039	68.934845
4	DemFlag2	249.873589	253.060732
5	DemFlag6	226.131347	309.079859
6	DemCluster	222.589229	70.478049
7	DemFlag1	162.256557	177.508653
8	DemReg	114.090856	50.533349
9	DemFlag7	40.931939	35.704581
10	DemFlag5	8.986376	23.494624
11	DemFlag4	8.583654	17.210787
12	DemFlag8	6.291225	12.721568
13	DemFlag3	5.888663	23.692049
14	DemHomeowner	0.446454	0.812748

The foresttrain action also produces an OutputCasTables result table, which contains the name of the CAS table that stores the actual forest model. The CAS table, which is stored on the CAS server, describes all the individual trees. Each row of this CAS table contains the information about a single node in an individual tree. When you have a large of number of trees, this table can be large, and therefore, is stored on the CAS server instead. In the preceding example, the forest model contains 50 trees and 2278 nodes, in total being returned to the client.

```
In [4]: result['OutputCasTables']
Out[4]:
                    casLib      Name  Rows  Columns  \
0  CASUSERHDFS(usrname)  forest1  2278      132

                            casTable
0  CASTable('forest1', caslib='CASUSERH...

                    casLib      Name  Rows  Columns  \
0  CASUSERHDFS(username)  forest1  2278      132
```

To score the training data or the holdout data using the forest model, you can use the forestscore action.

```
scored_data = conn.CASTable('scored_output', replace=True)
organics.forestscore(modelTable=conn.CASTable('forest1'), casout=scored_data)
```

Unlike the random forest model, gradient boosting grows trees sequentially, whereby each tree is grown based on the residuals from the previous tree. The following example shows how to build a gradient boosting model using the same target and predictors as in the forest model.

```
In [5]: varlist = ['DemGender', 'DemHomeowner', 'DemAgeGroup', 'DemCluster',
           'DemReg', 'DemTVReg', 'DemFlag1', 'DemFlag2', 'DemFlag3',
           'DemFlag4', 'DemFlag5', 'DemFlag6', 'DemFlag7', 'DemFlag8',
           'PromClass']
   ...:
   ...: output = conn.CASTable('gbtree1', replace=True)
   ...:
   ...: gbtree1 = organics.Gbtreetrain()
   ...: gbtree1.target = 'TargetBuy'
   ...: gbtree1.inputs = varlist
   ...: gbtree1.casout = output
   ...: gbtree1()
   ...:
   ...:
Out[5]:
[ModelInfo]

Gradient Boosting Tree for ORGANICS
```

	Descr	Value
0	Number of Trees	50.0
1	Distribution	2.0
2	Learning Rate	0.1
3	Subsampling Rate	0.5
4	Number of Selected Variables (M)	15.0
5	Number of Bins	20.0
6	Number of Variables	15.0
7	Max Number of Tree Nodes	63.0
8	Min Number of Tree Nodes	61.0
9	Max Number of Branches	2.0
10	Min Number of Branches	2.0
11	Max Number of Levels	6.0
12	Min Number of Levels	6.0
13	Max Number of Leaves	32.0
14	Min Number of Leaves	31.0
15	Maximum Size of Leaves	512468.0
16	Minimum Size of Leaves	33.0
17	Random Number Seed	0.0

```
[OutputCasTables]
```

	casLib	Name	Rows	Columns	\
0	CASUSERHDFS(username)	gbtree1	3146	119	

	casTable
0	CASTable('gbtree1', caslib='CASUSERH...

The following table lists the key parameters to grow a sequence of trees in a gradient boosting model. The gbtreetrain action also enables you configure the individual trees. These parameters are identical to those in the dtreetrain action.

Parameter	Description
ntree	The number of trees in the gradient boosting model. The default is 50.
m	The number of input variables to consider for splitting on a node. The variables are selected at random from the input variables. By default, all input variables are used.
seed	The seed for the random number generator for sampling.
subsamplerate	The fraction of the subsample data to build each tree. The default is 0.5.
distribution	The type of gradient boosting tree to build. The value 0 is used for a regression tree, and 1 is used for a binary classification tree.
lasso	The L1 norm regularization on prediction. The default is 0.
ridge	The L2 norm regularization on prediction. The default is 0.

To score the training data or the holdout data using the gradient boosting model, you can use the gbtreescore action.

```
scored_data = conn.CASTable('scored_output', replace=True)
organics.gbtreescore(modelTable=conn.CASTable('gbtree1'), casout=scored_data)
```

Neural networks are machine learning models that derive hidden features (neuron) as nonlinear functions of linear combination of the predictors, and then model the target variable as a nonlinear function of the hidden features. Such nonlinear transformations are often called *activation functions* in neural networks. The following figure illustrates a simple neural network between three predictors and a binary target that takes levels 0 and 1. In this case, there are four hidden features. Each is a nonlinear function of the linear combination of the three predictors. The probabilities of target = 1 and target = 0 are modeled as a nonlinear function of the hidden features. In neutral networks, such hidden features are called *neurons,* and it is common to have more than one layer of hidden neurons.

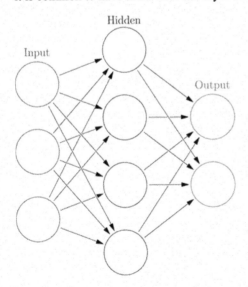

The neural network of related actions is available in the neuralnet action set. Let's load the action set and continue to use the Organics data set to build a simple neural network.

```
In [6]: conn.loadactionset('neuralnet')
   ...: conn.help(actionset='neuralnet')
   ...:
NOTE: Added action set 'neuralNet'.
NOTE: Information for action set 'neuralNet':
NOTE: neuralNet
NOTE: annTrain - Train an artificial neural network
NOTE: annScore - Score a table using an artificial neural network model
NOTE: annCode - Generate DATA step scoring code from an artificial neural
network model

In [7]: neural1 = organics.Anntrain()
   ...: neural1.target = 'TargetBuy'
   ...: neural1.inputs = ['DemAge','DemAffl','DemGender']
   ...: neural1.casout = output
   ...: neural1.hiddens = [4,2]
   ...: neural1.maxIter = 500
   ...: result = neural1()
   ...: list(result.keys())
Out[7]: ['OptIterHistory', 'ConvergenceStatus', 'ModelInfo',
'OutputCasTables']
```

In this case, we built a neural network with two layers. The first layer has four hidden neurons and the second layer has two hidden neurons. The maximum number of iterations for training the neural network is set to 500. The iteration history and convergence status of the model are reported in OptIterHistory and ConvergenceStatus result tables, respectively. The ModelInfo result table contains basic information about the neural network model:

```
In [8]: result['ModelInfo']
Out[8]:
Neural Net Model Info for ORGANICS
```

	Descr	Value
0	Model	Neural Net
1	Number of Observations Used	1498264
2	Number of Observations Read	1688948
3	Target/Response Variable	TargetBuy
4	Number of Nodes	13
5	Number of Input Nodes	5
6	Number of Output Nodes	2
7	Number of Hidden Nodes	6
8	Number of Hidden Layers	2
9	Number of Weight Parameters	30
10	Number of Bias Parameters	8
11	Architecture	MLP
12	Number of Neural Nets	1
13	Objective Value	1.7011968247

The default error function of the anntrain action is NORMAL for continuous target or ENTROPY for categorical target. The anntrain action also provides parameters for customizing the neural networks such as the error function, the activation function, and the target activation function. Some key parameters of the anntrain action are listed in the following table:

Parameter	Description
arch	Specifies the architecture of the network. arch = 'MLP': The standard multilayer perceptron network. arch ='GLIM': The neural network with no hidden layer. arch = 'DIRECT': The MLP network with additional direct links from input nodes to the target nodes.
errorfunc	Specifies the error function for training the neural network. ENTROPY is available for categorical target. GAMMA, NORMAL, and POISSON are available for continuous targets.
targetact	Specifies the target activation function that links the hidden neurons at the last layer to the target nodes. LOGISTIC and SOFMAX (default) are available for categorical targets. EXP, IDENTITY, SIN, and TANH (default) are available for continuous targets.
act	Specifies the activation function that links the input nodes to the hidden neurons at the first layer, or neurons from one layer to the next layer. Available activation functions include EXP, IDENTITY, LOGISTIC, RECTIFIER, SIN, SOFTPLUS, and TANH (default).
targetcomb	Specifies the way to combine neurons in the target activation function. Linear combination (LINEAR) is the default. Other combinations are additive (ADD) and radial (RADIAL).
comb	Specifies the way to combine neurons or read as input in the activation functions. Linear combination (LINEAR) is the default. Other combinations are Additive (ADD) and radial (RADIAL).
ntries	The number of tries for random initial values of the weight parameters.
includebias	Indicates whether to include the intercept term (usually called bias) in the combination function. This parameter is ignored if an additive combination is used. Additive combinations are Combination (comb) and Target Combination (targetComb).

Similar to the tree models in CAS, a CAS table in the server can be used for storing the neural network model. This is convenient when you build a large neural network and it avoids the I/O traffic between the Python client and the CAS server. To score a data set that uses a CAS table and that contains the neural network model, you can use the annscore action.

```
In [9]: organics.annscore(modelTable=output)
   ...:
Out[9]:
[ScoreInfo]

                        Descr         Value
   0   Number of Observations Read    1688948
   1   Number of Observations Used    1498264
   2   Misclassification Error (%)    18.448818099
```

Conclusion

In this chapter, we introduced several analytic models that are available on the CAS server for modeling categorical variables. This includes the logistic regression in the regression action set, the tree family (decision tree, random forest, gradient boosting) in the decisiontree action set, and simple neural networks in the neuralnet action set. For more information about the models, see the following references.

[1] Friedman, Jerome, Trevor Hastie, and Robert Tibshirani. 2001. *The Elements of Statistical Learning.* Vol. 1. Springer, Berlin: Springer Series in Statistics.

[2] Breiman, Leo. 2001. "Random Forests." In *Machine Learning* 45.1:5-32.

Chapter 10: Advanced Topics

There are a few topics that aren't necessary to use SWAT with CAS, but understanding them can help you in situations you may come across. We'll look at the different network interfaces used by CAS, different styles of handling CAS action responses, and other miscellaneous topics.

Binary vs. REST Interfaces

We mentioned in earlier chapters that there are two interfaces supported: binary and REST. The binary interface is a proprietary protocol supported on a limited number of platforms. This type of communication requires C extensions bundled with the SWAT installer on supported platforms. The REST interface allows SWAT to talk to the CAS server using the standard HTTP or HTTPS protocols. When using the REST interface, the SWAT client relies only on pure Python code, so it can be used on any platform that can run Python and Pandas.

We'll discuss the details of each in the following sections.

The Binary Interface

A diagram of the communication over the binary interface is shown in the figure below.

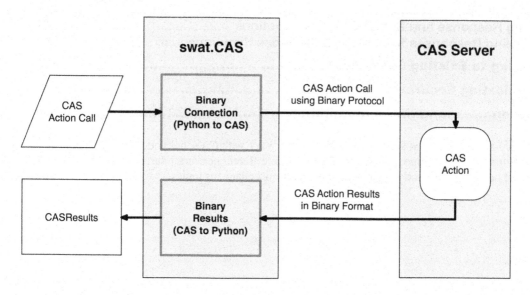

In this process, CAS action calls from the Python code are converted to a binary parameter structure that is transferred to CAS using a proprietary protocol. On the server side, the parameter structure is unpacked and the action is executed. When the action finishes, the results are returned to the client in a binary packed form. The client then converts the binary responses back to Python objects.

This form of communication is very fast and efficient, but it does require a Python C extension and supporting libraries from SAS (the SAS TK framework) to run on the client. Because of the performance aspects of this protocol, it is recommended that you use it if it is available for your platform. When you make a connection to CAS, the SWAT client will attempt to detect which type of port you are connecting to. The default is binary, but you can explicitly specify the protocol as well using the protocol parameter to the CAS object.

```
In [1]: binconn = swat.CAS(cashost, casport, protocol='cas')
```

Let's look at the REST interface now.

The REST Interface

The diagram below shows the process used in communications with CAS using the REST interface.

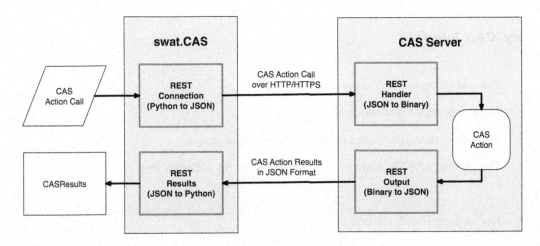

In this process, the CAS action parameters from Python are converted to JSON (JavaScript Object Notation). The JSON parameters are sent to CAS using either the HTTP or HTTPS protocol. On the server side, the JSON is converted to the binary form needed by the CAS action and the action is executed. The results, in binary form, are then converted to JSON form and sent back to the client. The client must then convert the JSON into Python objects to be returned in the CASResults object.

As you can see, there is much more overhead in using the REST interface. However, it also has the benefit of using pure Python code, so it is more portable than using the binary interface.

To explicitly specify the REST interface when making a connection, you set the protocol option to 'http' or 'https' (depending on which protocol your server is configured to use).

```
In [2]: restconn = swat.CAS(cashost, casrestport, protocol='http')
```

The Pros and Cons of Each Interface

We'll summarize the pros and cons of each interface to make it easier for you to decide which one is best for your situation.

Binary (CAS) Interface

Pros

- Fast and efficient; not as many data conversions

- More authentication methods supported

- Supports custom data loaders using data message handlers

- The required SAS TK system also includes support for SAS data formats

Cons

- Not supported on all platforms

- The download size is much larger

REST Interface

Pros

- Uses standard HTTP / HTTPS protocols

- Uses pure Python code, so it will run anywhere Python and Pandas is available

- Smaller download size

Cons

- More overhead due to conversions to and from binary formats

- Less efficient communication

- Data message handlers are not supported

Result Processing Workflows

Throughout this book, we have been calling actions using the methods on CAS connection objects and CASTable objects. This way of calling actions is the simplest but also has some limitations. It will only return the results of the action once all of the responses from the server have come back. If you want to process responses as the come back from the server, you may want to try one of the other workflows described here.

The Easy Way

The first workflow we'll talk about is the simplest one; this is the method we have been using in this book so far. The diagram below shows the process used.

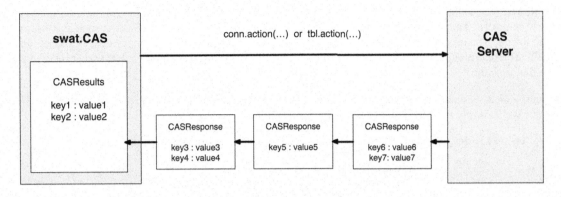

In this process, the CAS action is called on a CAS connection object or a CASTable object. The server executes the action and returns multiple responses back to the client. Each response contains one or more key / value pairs of results. The SWAT client processes each response from the server and combines them all into a single CASResults object. Once all responses have been received, the combined results are returned.

While this method is very easy and convenient, it may not be optimal if you have an action that returns a large number of responses or you have a long-running action where you want to process responses as they come back from the server. The methods of results processing in the next two sections may work better for those situations.

Using Response and Result Callback Functions

The next method of processing responses from CAS allows you to handle each response as it comes back from the server, rather than waiting until the action is complete. The diagram below shows how this workflow is handled.

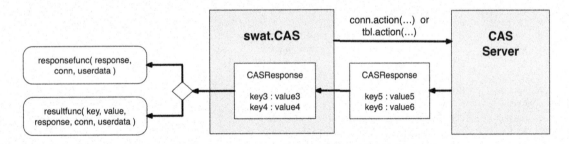

In this workflow, you still use the CAS action methods on the CAS or CASTable objects to execute the action. However, in this case, you supply either a responsefunc or resultfunc parameter that contains a callable object (typically a function).

When a responsefunc parameter is specified, the given function is called for each response from the server. The arguments to the function are the CASResponse object, the CAS connection object, and a user-specified data structure (for holding state between responses).

When a resultfunc parameter is specified, the given function is called for each key / value pair from each response. The arguments to the function are the result key, the result value, the CASResponse object, the CAS connection object, and a user-specified data structure.

Both response callbacks and result callbacks have a user-specified data object that can be used to store state between calls. This will typically be an object that gets passed by reference in Python such as a list or a dictionary. If a user-specified object is used, it should be returned by the response / result callback on each call. The return value of the response / result callback is always used as the user data object on the next call to that function.

Let's look at an example of using each of these callback types. We'll start with the result callback. In this case, we'll simply print the key and value for each result.

```
In [3]: def result_cb(key, value, response, connection, userdata):
   ...:     print('\n>>> RESULT %s\n' % key)
   ...:     print(value)
   ...:     return userdata
   ...:

In [4]: tbl.groupby('Origin').summary(resultfunc=result_cb,
   ...:                                subset=['min', 'max'])

Out[4]:
>>> RESULT ByGroupInfo

ByGroupInfo

     Origin Origin_f   _key_
0      Asia     Asia    Asia
1    Europe   Europe  Europe
2       USA      USA     USA

>>> RESULT ByGroup1.Summary

Descriptive Statistics for CARS

                Column      Min      Max
Origin
Asia              MSRP  10280.0  89765.0
Asia           Invoice   9875.0  79978.0
Asia        EngineSize      1.3      5.6
Asia         Cylinders      3.0      8.0
Asia        Horsepower     73.0    340.0
Asia          MPG_City     13.0     60.0
Asia       MPG_Highway     17.0     66.0
Asia            Weight   1850.0   5590.0
Asia         Wheelbase     89.0    140.0
Asia            Length    153.0    224.0
```

```
>>> RESULT ByGroup2.Summary

Descriptive Statistics for CARS

              Column    Min        Max
Origin
Europe           MSRP  16999.0  192465.0
Europe        Invoice  15437.0  173560.0
Europe     EngineSize      1.6       6.0
Europe      Cylinders      4.0      12.0
Europe     Horsepower    100.0     493.0
Europe       MPG_City     12.0      38.0
Europe    MPG_Highway     14.0      46.0
Europe         Weight   2524.0    5423.0
Europe      Wheelbase     93.0     123.0
Europe         Length    143.0     204.0

>>> RESULT ByGroup3.Summary

Descriptive Statistics for CARS

              Column    Min       Max
Origin
USA              MSRP  10995.0  81795.0
USA           Invoice  10319.0  74451.0
USA        EngineSize      1.6      8.3
USA         Cylinders      4.0     10.0
USA        Horsepower    103.0    500.0
USA          MPG_City     10.0     29.0
USA       MPG_Highway     12.0     37.0
USA            Weight   2348.0   7190.0
USA         Wheelbase     93.0    144.0
USA            Length    150.0    238.0
```

As you can see, the result callback is invoked for each result key. Now let's look look at response callbacks.

```
In [5]: def response_cb(response, connection, userdata):
   ...:         print('\n>>> RESPONSE')
   ...:         for k, v in response:
   ...:             print('\n>>> RESULT %s\n' % k)
   ...:             print(v)
   ...:         return userdata
   ...:

In [6]: tbl.groupby('Origin').summary(responsefunc=response_cb,
   ...:                                subset=['min', 'max'])

Out[6]:
>>> RESPONSE

>>> RESULT ByGroupInfo

ByGroupInfo

   Origin Origin_f   _key_
0    Asia     Asia    Asia
```

```
1   Europe    Europe   Europe
2     USA       USA      USA
```

```
>>> RESPONSE
```

```
>>> RESULT ByGroup1.Summary
```

Descriptive Statistics for CARS

	Column	Min	Max
Origin			
Asia	MSRP	10280.0	89765.0
Asia	Invoice	9875.0	79978.0
Asia	EngineSize	1.3	5.6
Asia	Cylinders	3.0	8.0
Asia	Horsepower	73.0	340.0
Asia	MPG_City	13.0	60.0
Asia	MPG_Highway	17.0	66.0
Asia	Weight	1850.0	5590.0
Asia	Wheelbase	89.0	140.0
Asia	Length	153.0	224.0

```
>>> RESPONSE
```

```
>>> RESULT ByGroup2.Summary
```

Descriptive Statistics for CARS

	Column	Min	Max
Origin			
Europe	MSRP	16999.0	192465.0
Europe	Invoice	15437.0	173560.0
Europe	EngineSize	1.6	6.0
Europe	Cylinders	4.0	12.0
Europe	Horsepower	100.0	493.0
Europe	MPG_City	12.0	38.0
Europe	MPG_Highway	14.0	46.0
Europe	Weight	2524.0	5423.0
Europe	Wheelbase	93.0	123.0
Europe	Length	143.0	204.0

```
>>> RESPONSE
```

```
>>> RESULT ByGroup3.Summary
```

Descriptive Statistics for CARS

	Column	Min	Max
Origin			
USA	MSRP	10995.0	81795.0
USA	Invoice	10319.0	74451.0
USA	EngineSize	1.6	8.3
USA	Cylinders	4.0	10.0
USA	Horsepower	103.0	500.0
USA	MPG_City	10.0	29.0
USA	MPG_Highway	12.0	37.0
USA	Weight	2348.0	7190.0

```
USA         Wheelbase      93.0     144.0
USA           Length      150.0     238.0

>>> RESPONSE
```

This callback is called for each response. In order to retrieve the results from each CASResponse object that is passed in, you simply iterate over it in a for loop. Each iteration over a CASResponse object returns a two-element tuple containing key and value pair of results. You'll notice that there is always an extra response at the end. This respone has no results associated with it and indicates the end of the action.

There are occasions when something happens in the server to cause the action to restart. In cases like this, the results that you have already processed may need to be thrown out. When an action sends a restart event, it means that it's going to start over and it will start sending responses from the beginning again. This event is indicated by the updateflags attribute on the response. If the set contained in the updateflags attribute contains a string 'action-restart', you will need to handle it appropriately for your callback scenario.

While using callbacks allows you to handle server responses as they come back, you can still only process the responses from a single session. To get around that limitation, we'll use another method in the next section.

Handling Responses from Multiple Sessions Simultaneously

The final method of handling responses is similar to the callback scenario except that the invocation of the action and the result processing are decoupled. This allows you to fire off multiple actions (each on a separate session) then process the results in the order that they come back. Here is a diagram of the process using multiple connection objects.

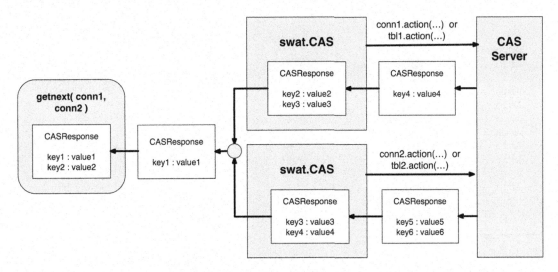

To call a CAS action without processing the results, you use the invoke method on the CAS connection object or CASTable object. This method returns immediately after calling the action and you must handle the responses yourself. To walk through the responses, you iterate over the connection object in a for loop.

Each iteration returns a CASResponse object which can then be iterated over (like when using a response callback) to get the key / value pairs of the result. Let's look at an example.

```
In [7]: conn1 = tbl1.groupby('Origin').invoke('summary',
                                               subset=['min', 'max']);
```

```
In [8]: for resp in conn1:
   ...:     print('\n>>> RESPONSE')
   ...:     for k, v in resp:
   ...:         print('\n>>> RESULT %s\n' % k)
   ...:         print(v)
   ...:
```

Out[8]:
```
>>> RESPONSE

>>> RESULT ByGroupInfo

ByGroupInfo

    Origin Origin_f    _key_
0    Asia     Asia     Asia
1  Europe   Europe   Europe
2     USA      USA      USA

>>> RESPONSE

>>> RESULT ByGroup1.Summary

Descriptive Statistics for CARS

              Column      Min      Max
Origin
Asia            MSRP  10280.0  89765.0
Asia         Invoice   9875.0  79978.0
Asia      EngineSize      1.3      5.6
Asia       Cylinders      3.0      8.0
Asia      Horsepower     73.0    340.0
Asia        MPG_City     13.0     60.0
Asia     MPG_Highway     17.0     66.0
Asia          Weight   1850.0   5590.0
Asia       Wheelbase     89.0    140.0
Asia          Length    153.0    224.0

>>> RESPONSE

>>> RESULT ByGroup2.Summary

Descriptive Statistics for CARS

              Column      Min      Max
Origin
Europe          MSRP  16999.0  192465.0
Europe       Invoice  15437.0  173560.0
Europe    EngineSize      1.6       6.0
Europe     Cylinders      4.0      12.0
Europe    Horsepower    100.0     493.0
```

```
Europe      MPG_City     12.0      38.0
Europe  MPG_Highway      14.0      46.0
Europe       Weight    2524.0    5423.0
Europe    Wheelbase      93.0     123.0
Europe       Length     143.0     204.0


>>> RESPONSE

>>> RESULT ByGroup3.Summary

Descriptive Statistics for CARS

               Column      Min       Max
Origin
USA              MSRP   10995.0   81795.0
USA           Invoice   10319.0   74451.0
USA        EngineSize       1.6       8.3
USA         Cylinders       4.0      10.0
USA        Horsepower     103.0     500.0
USA          MPG_City      10.0      29.0
USA       MPG_Highway      12.0      37.0
USA            Weight    2348.0    7190.0
USA         Wheelbase      93.0     144.0
USA            Length     150.0     238.0


>>> RESPONSE
```

The form above doesn't give us any benefit over using callbacks. However, if you want to run multiple actions across several sessions, it has a distinct advantage. You can use the getnext function of the SWAT package to process responses as they come back. The responses returned by getnext are surfaced in the order that the sessions return them. This allows you to do parallel processing without using any sort of threading or subprocesses on the client. Let's look at an example.

```python
In [9]: conn1 = tbl1.groupby('Origin').invoke('summary',
   ...:                                        subset=['min', 'max']);

In [10]: conn2 = tbl2.groupby('Origin').invoke('topk',
   ....:                                        topk=1, bottomk=1);

In [11]: for resp, conn in swat.getnext(conn1, conn2):
   ....:     print('\n>>> RESPONSE')
   ....:     for k, v in resp:
   ....:         print('\n>>> RESULT %s\n' % k)
   ....:         print(v)
   ....:
```

```
>>> RESPONSE

>>> RESULT ByGroupInfo

ByGroupInfo

    Origin Origin_f   _key_
0     Asia     Asia    Asia
1   Europe   Europe  Europe
2      USA      USA     USA
```

```
>>> RESPONSE

>>> RESULT ByGroup1.Summary

Descriptive Statistics for CARS2

          Column      Min        Max
Origin
Asia        MSRP  10280.0    89765.0
Asia     Invoice   9875.0    79978.0

>>> RESPONSE

>>> RESULT ByGroup2.Summary

Descriptive Statistics for CARS2

          Column      Min        Max
Origin
Europe      MSRP  16999.0   192465.0
Europe   Invoice  15437.0   173560.0


... output clipped ...


>>> RESPONSE

>>> RESULT ByGroup3.Topk

Top and Bottom Distinct Values for CARS2

          Column    FmtVar  Rank
Origin
USA         MSRP     81795     1
USA         MSRP     10995   145
USA      Invoice     74451     1
USA      Invoice     10319   147

>>> RESPONSE

>>> RESULT ByGroup3.TopkMisc

Miscellaneous Information on Distinct Values for CARS2

          Column    N  TruncatedTopk  TruncatedBtmk  ScoreOther
Origin
USA         MSRP  145              0              0         NaN
USA      Invoice  147              0              0         NaN

>>> RESPONSE
```

In the example above, we called the summary action and the topk action on two different sessions. The getnext function returns each CASResponse and the associated connection object at each iteration until all of the responses from all connections have been processed. In this case, the actions ran fast enough that the results still displayed in the order in which we executed them. However, for longer running actions, the output may be interleaved. You can use the returned CAS connection object to keep track of which connection the responses and results belong to.

Just as with the callback scenario, you can get an 'action-restart' event in the updateflags of the response object here as well. If necessary, your code should check this flag and act accordingly.

With these three different ways of processing results from CAS, you have options to cover the gamut from simple action calls that return all the combined results all the way up to processing results from multiple connections at once.

Connecting to Existing Sessions

While you can only run one action in a session at a time, it is possible to connect to existing sessions multiple times. This can be handy if you ran some actions while at work and want to continue your work from home when they are finished. Connecting to an existing session is fairly easy, you just need to know the session ID. While you could write down the session ID and take that with you, there is an easier way. Each Python connection is tagged with a more user-friendly name. You can see it when you display the string representation of a CAS connection object.

```
In [12]: conn
Out[12]: CAS('server-name.mycompany.com', 5570,
             'username', protocol='cas',
             name='py-session-1',
             session='c4bbd504-d4a7-134f-af62-9340b3dc8048')
```

This name is going to be much easier to remember than the full session ID. When you want to connect to that session from another location, you can use the listsessions action to display all of the current sessions in the server. This will list all of the sessions on the server created by you.

```
In [13]: conn.listsessions()
Out[13]:
[Session]

                                SessionName  \
0    py-session-1:Mon Oct 31 16:29:34 2016
1    py-session-88:Mon Oct 31 16:34:20 2016


                                UUID        State  \
0    c4bbd504-d4a7-134f-af62-9340b3dc8048  Connected
1    45b6ce2f-610f-e847-af87-78ee9a8523b9  Connected


     Authentication  Userid
0    Active Directory  username
1    Active Directory  username

+ Elapsed: 0.000429s, mem: 0.0904mb
```

We can now get the full session ID by looking for the user-friendly name in the SessionName column and copying the corresponding UUID value. Now that we have that, we can specify the UUID in the session parameter of a new connection.

```
In [14]: conn2 = swat.CAS('server-name.mycompany.com', 5570,
                    session='c4bbd504-d4a7-134f-af62-9340b3dc8048')
```

Your new connection is now connected to the specified session. Also, since the sessions are language agnostic, you can connect to existing CAS sessions created from other language interfaces such as Java or SAS.

Communicating Securely

If your server is configured to use TLS encryption either through the binary interface or using the REST interface through HTTPS, you will need to set the path to the file that contains the certificate chain to verify your connections. See SAS' documentation on the different methods for creating your certificate files for use with CAS. Configuring the client is done by setting a CAS_CLIENT_SSL_CA_LIST environment variable. The method for setting environment variables varies by platform (or even command shell on Linux). Below is the way to set the environment variable using the bash shell on Linux.

```
export CAS_CLIENT_SSL_CA_LIST='/path/to/cacerts/trustedcerts.pem'
```

With this variable set, you should now be able to connect to your CAS server securely.

Conclusion

With the information in this chapter, you should be able to make educated decisions on which interface (binary or REST) you want to use. You can take advantage of multiple different styles of response handling depending on your needs. You can also connect to existing sessions, and connect to CAS using encrypted communications. This knowledge should allow you to handle more advanced uses of CAS connections and workflows.

Appendix A: A Crash Course in Python

We expect that you have some familiarity with Python or you have at least some programming experience. We do not attempt to teach you everything about Python because there are many good books already out there for that purpose, However, we do want to briefly cover the major features that are necessary to take full advantage of the packages that are covered in this book.

IPython and Jupyter

Our first topic is which environment you would like to work in. With Python, you have many choices. You can use the standard Python interactive interpreter, which is quite nice compared to many other scripting language interpreters, but there are other choices that you might find even better.

A step up from the standard Python interpreter is the IPython interpreter. It starts from a command line just like the normal Python interpreter, but it includes some nice features that enhance interactive use. Features include tab completion of methods and attributes on objects, easy access to documentation strings, automatic display of results, and input and output history. Here is a brief demonstration of the ipython shell.

```
% ipython
Python 3.4.1 (default, Jun  3 2014, 16:31:42)
Type "copyright", "credits" or "license" for more information.

IPython 3.0.0 -- An enhanced Interactive Python.
?          -> Introduction and overview of IPython's features.
%quickref -> Quick reference.
help       -> Python's own help system.
object?    -> Details about 'object', use 'object??' for extra details.

In [1]: a = 'hello'

In [2]: b = 'world'

In [3]: a + ' ' + b
Out[3]: 'hello world'

In [4]: Out[3]
Out[4]: 'hello world'

In [5]: In[3]
Out[5]: "a + ' ' + b"

In [6]: a
Out[6]: 'hello'
```

IPython also has a web-based notebook interface called Jupyter, which was previously known as IPython notebook. This notebook includes the same behaviors as the IPython shell, but with an attractive web interface. The web interface enables Python objects to be displayed graphically inline with the code. In addition, you can document your code in the notebook as well with formatted text, equations, and so on. Notebooks can be saved in their own format for use later or for sharing with others, or they can be exported to formats such as HTML for publishing on the web. You can start the notebook interface with the command jupyter notebook, or you can start it on Windows from the Anaconda menu.

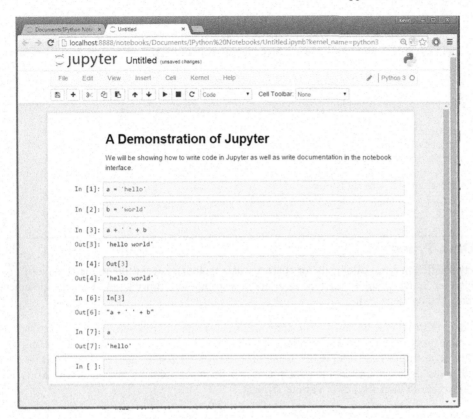

In addition to IPython and Jupyter, there are more formal integrated development environments such as Spyder, Canopy, and Wing that include better support for editing multiple Python files and debugging. As you get more experienced writing Python programs, these might be more useful. For this book, we will primarily use the IPython shell. When we get into sections where a more graphical output is beneficial, we will switch to using Jupyter.

Data Types and Collections

In any type of data science, data types become an important topic. Python has a rich data type system, which maps well to the rectangular data sets that we work with in CAS.

Numeric Data Types

The most common data types that we use are integers, floating-point numbers, and character data. Python has objects for integers (int and long (in Python 2)) and floating-point values (float).

```
In [7]: type(100)
Out[7]: int

In [8]: type(1.0)
Out[8]: float
```

When you start working with the Pandas or NumPy packages, you might encounter some alternative implementations of numeric values. They work transparently as Python numeric values, so unless you are doing something more advanced, you don't need to be concerned about them.

```
In [9]: import pandas as pd

In [10]: ser = pd.Series([100, 200])

# Pandas and Numpy use custom numeric types
In [11]: type(ser[0])
Out[11]: numpy.int64

# They still work as normal numeric values though
In [12]: ser[0] + 1000
Out[12]: 1100
```

Character Data Types

Python also has two different types of objects for character data that differ according to the version of Python used. In Python 2, the default string type is str and is a string of arbitrary bytes. The unicode object is for character data that contains text.

In Python 3, the default string type changed to unicode, and byte strings are represented using the bytes type. In either version, you can force a literal string to be represented in Unicode by preceding the string with the prefix "u". Byte strings can be forced by using the prefix "b". Each of these prefixes must be in lowercase. In either case, you can use double quotation marks or single quotation to enclose the string. The following code shows the Python 3 types of various strings.

```
In [13]: type('hello')
Out[13]: str

In [14]: type(u'hello')
Out[14]: str

In [15]: type(b' world')
Out[15]: bytes

In [16]: u'hello' + b' world'
-----------------------------------------------------------------------
TypeError                                 Traceback (most recent call last)
<ipython-input-64-0af8b45d0f72> in <module>()
----> 1 u'hello' + b' world'

TypeError: Can't convert 'bytes' object to str implicitly

In [17]: u'hello' + b' world'.decode('utf-8')
Out[17]: 'hello world'
```

Although the distinction between the two doesn't seem significant here, and both types seem to act the same, issues can arise when you include non-ASCII characters in your strings. If you put non-ASCII text in a byte string, Python has no knowledge of the encoding of those bytes. Examples of encoding are latin-1, utf-8, windows-1252, and so on. Also, your system's default encoding might cause the display of different characters than you expect when they are printed. Because of this, when you store text in variables, you should always use unicode objects. Byte strings should be used only for binary data.

Booleans

Although Python has a system to make nearly every variable act like a Boolean (for example, 1 and "hello" are true, whereas 0 and "" are false), it is best to use the explicit True and False values when possible. The use of explicit values is especially important when interacting with another system such as CAS, which might have different rules for casting values to Booleans.

Lists and Tuples

The first collection type that we look at is the list. A list is an ordered collection of any type of object. Unlike array types in many languages, Python lists can contain a mixture of object types. Another nice feature of lists is that they are mutable.

Lists can be specified explicitly using items that are enclosed in brackets. They are also zero-indexed, which means that the first index of the list is zero.

```
In [18]: items = ['a', 'b', 'c', 100]

In [19]: items
Out[19]: ['a', 'b', 'c', 100]

In [20]: items[0]
Out[20]: 'a'

In [21]: items[2]
Out[21]: 'c'
```

Another nice feature of lists is that they can be indexed using negative numbers. Negative numbers indicate indexes from the end of the list. So a -1 index returns the last item in a list, and a -3 returns the third item from the end of the list.

```
In [22]: items[-1]
Out[22]: 100

In [23]: items[-3]
Out[23]: 'b'
```

Slicing

In addition to retrieving single items, you can also retrieve *slices* of lists. Slicing is done by specifying a range of indexes.

```
In [24]: items[1:3]
Out[24]: ['b', 'c']
```

In the preceding code, we specify a slice from 1 to 3. A slice of a list includes the range of items from the initial index, up to (but not including) the last index. So this example returns a new list that includes items 1 and 2. If the first index in the slice is left empty, the slice includes everything to the beginning of the list. Accordingly, if the last index in the slice is empty, everything to the end of the list is included.

A third component of a slice can be given to specify a step size. For example, the following code returns every other item in the list starting with the first item.

```
In [25]: items[::2]
Out[25]: ['a', 'c']
```

In the following example, we get every other item in the list starting with the second item.

```
In [26]: items[1::2]
Out[26]: ['b', 100]
```

It is also possible to specify negative step sizes to step in reverse. But using negative step sizes with start and end points can get confusing. If you need to step in reverse, it might be a good idea to do that in a separate step.

Tuples

Tuples and lists behave nearly the same. The primary difference is that tuples are not mutable. Once a tuple has been created, it cannot be modified. Indexing and slicing works the same way except that slicing returns a new tuple rather than a list. Tuples are mostly used by Python internally, but you can specify them explicitly just like lists, except that you use parentheses to enclose the items.

```
In [27]: items = ('a', 'b', 'c', 100)
```

```
In [28]: items
Out[28]: ('a', 'b', 'c', 100)
```

One reason that you might need a tuple rather than a list is that lists cannot be used as a key in a dictionary or as an item of a set. Those data types are discussed in the next section.

Dictionaries and Sets

Dictionaries and sets are used to hold unordered collections of items. Dictionaries contain both a key and a value. The keys must be unique, and each one points to a stored value, which doesn't have to be unique. Sets are simply collections of unique items. You can think of them as a set of dictionary keys without associated values.

Dictionaries can be built using any of these methods: dictionary literal syntax, the dict constructor, or one key/value pair at a time. The following code demonstrates each of those methods.

```
# Dictionary literal
In [29]: pairs = {'key1': 100, 'key2': 200, 'key3': 400}
```

```
In [30]: pairs
Out[30]: {'key1': 100, 'key2': 200, 'key3': 400}
```

```
# Using the dict constructor
In [31]: pairs = dict(key1=100, key2=200, key3=400)
```

```
In [32]: pairs
Out[32]: {'key1': 100, 'key2': 200, 'key3': 400}
```

```
# Adding key / value pairs one at a time
In [33]: pairs['key4'] = 1000
```

```
In [34]: pairs['key5'] = 2000
```

```
In [35]: pairs
Out[35]: {'key1': 100, 'key2': 200, 'key3': 400, 'key4': 1000, 'key5':
2000}
```

Although we have used strings for all of the keys in these examples, you can use any immutable object as a key. Values can be any object, mutable or immutable. The only catch is that if you use the dict constructor with keywords as we did in the preceding example, your keys will always have to be valid variable names, which are converted strings.

Accessing the value of a key is just like accessing the index of a list. The difference is that you specify the key value rather than an index.

```
In [36]: pairs['key4']
Out[36]: 1000
```

In addition to accessing keys explicitly, you can get a collection of all of the keys or values of a dictionary using the keys and values methods, respectively.

```
In [37]: pairs.keys()
Out[37]: dict_keys(['key1', 'key3', 'key2', 'key5', 'key4'])
```

```
In [38]: pairs.values()
Out[38]: dict_values([100, 400, 200, 2000, 1000])
```

Depending on which version of Python you use, you might see something slightly different. Python 3 returns an iterable view of the elements, whereas Python 2 returns a list of the elements. Each version of Python has behaviors that are different from the other, but most of the time the result of the keys and values methods are used to iterate through elements in a dictionary and act consistently in that context, which we see in the next section.

Sets

As we mentioned, sets act like a set of dictionary keys without the values, including the fact that every element must be unique. In fact, the literal syntax for sets even looks like a dictionary literal without values.

```
In [39]: items = {100, 200, 400, 2000, 1000}
```

```
In [39]: items
Out[39]: {100, 200, 400, 1000, 2000}
```

You can also use the set constructor to build sets, much like you would a dictionary using the dict constructor. The set constructor takes an iterable object, usually a list, as an argument rather than multiple arguments. Or you can add items individually using the add method.

```
In [40]: items = set(['key1', 'key2', 'key3'])
```

```
In [41]: items
Out[41]: {'key1', 'key2', 'key3'}
```

```
In [42]: items.add('key4')
```

```
In [42]: items.add('key5')
```

```
In [43]: items
Out[43]: {'key1', 'key2', 'key3', 'key4', 'key5'}
```

Sets have many interesting operations that can be used to find the common elements or differences between them and other sets, but they are also used fairly often in iteration. We won't go any deeper into sets here, but we will show how they are used in a looping context in the section about flow control.

Other Types

Python's type system is very rich, so we couldn't possibly touch on all of the built-in types that Python supplies much less the types that programmers can create themselves. For more information about Python's built-in types, you can read the types Python package documentation.

Flow Control

Flow control includes conditional statements and looping. Python uses if, elif, and else statements for conditional blocks. Looping uses for or while statements.

Conditional Code

Python's conditional statements work much like conditionals in other programming languages. The if statement starts a block of code that gets executed only if the condition that is specified in the if statement evaluates to True.

```
In [44]: value = 50

In [45]: if value >= 30:
   ....:         print('value is sufficient')
   ....:
value is sufficient

In [46]: value = 20

In [47]: if value >= 30:
   ....:         print('value is sufficient')
   ....:
```

Note that in the second if block, nothing was printed because the code inside the if block did not execute. You can also add an else block to have code execute when the condition isn't true.

```
In [48]: if value >= 30:
   ....:         print('value is sufficient')
   ....: else:
   ....:         print('value is not sufficient')
   ....:
value is not sufficient
```

For cases in which you have multiple code blocks that each depend on a different condition, you use the elif statement after the initial if.

```
In [49]: value = 26

In [50]: if value >= 30:
   ....:         print('value is sufficient')
```

```
....: elif value > 25:
....:         print('getting closer')
....: elif value > 22:
....:         print('not there yet')
....: else:
....:         print('value is insufficient')
....:
getting closer
```

In any case, only the first block of code with a true condition is executed. Even if the conditions in the following elifs are true, they are ignored.

In addition to the simple conditions shown in the preceding example, compound conditions can be constructed by combining simple conditions with the and operator and the or operator. For example, to specify a condition that checks on whether a value is in the range of 20 to 30, including the endpoints, you use value >= 20 and value <=30. Such conditions can also be used in looping constructs, which we show next.

Looping

Python has two looping statements: while and for. The while loop is a lot like an if block except that the code within the block executes over and over again until the condition in the while statement is false. The for loop is used for iterating over collections or objects that support the Python iterator interface. Let's look at while loops first since they are so similar to if blocks.

While Loops

The most important thing to remember about while loops is that you need to update the variables used in the while loop's condition, or you must have another way of escaping the loop. Otherwise, you end up in an infinite loop. Here is a basic example that increments value until it reaches a specified value.

```
In [51]: value = 1

In [52]: while value < 5:
....:         print(value)
....:         value = value + 1
....:
1
2
3
4
```

Since an empty list (or a dictionary or a set) is considered to be a false value, you can use while loops to loop over elements in a list, as well.

```
In [53]: items = [100, 200, 300]

In [54]: while items:
....:         print(items.pop())
....:
300
200
100
```

In this case, we modify the list as we loop by removing the last item of the list in each iteration. To preserve the list, you can make a copy of it before using the while loop, or you can use the for loop. Let's look at that in the next section.

For Loops

Unlike for loops in most other languages, the Python for loop doesn't use a specified condition to stop the looping. It is used to loop over collections or other objects that support Python's iterator interface. The most basic use of the Python for loop is looping over a range of numbers supplied by the range function.

Depending on your Python version, the range function returns a list of integers (Python 2) or an iterable that iterates over a series of integers (Python 3). They both work the same way in the context of a for loop, though. Here is an example of this type of for loop.

```
In [55]: for i in range(5):
   ....:     print(i)
   ....:
0
1
2
3
4
```

With a single argument, the range function generates values from zero up to (but not including) the value that is specified. Just as with slicing collections, you can specify a starting value, an ending value, and a step size in the range function.

```
# Count from 2 up to 6
In [56]: list(range(2,6))
Out[56]: [2, 3, 4, 5]

# Count from 2 up to 6 with a step size of 2
In [57]: list(range(2,6,2))
Out[57]: [2, 4]
```

Although looping over numeric ranges can be useful, looping over arbitrary collections and iterators is a more common operation. To loop over all of the items in a list, you simply specify that list as the loop variable.

```
In [58]: items = [100, 200, 300]

In [58]: for i in items:
   ....:     print(i)
   ....:
100
200
300
```

Looping over dictionaries and sets works the same way. However, for dictionaries, the value that gets set at each iteration is the key name.

```
In [59]: pairs = {'key1': 100, 'key2': 200, 'key3': 300}

In [59]: for key in pairs:
   ....:     print(key)
```

```
    . . . . :
key1
key3
key2
```

To iterate over values, you specify pairs.values() as the looping variable. Another common way to loop over dictionaries is by the key/value pairs. This is done with the items method.

```
In [60]: for key, value in pairs.items():
    . . . . :        print('%s : %s' % (key, value))
    . . . . :
key1 : 100
key3 : 300
key2 : 200
```

Loop Controls

Most of the time, when looping, you continue to loop through all of the objects in the collection. However, there are times when you want to break out of a loop or you just want to skip to the next item in the loop. These are handled by the break and continue statements, respectively.

To break out of a loop completely, you use the break statement.

```
In [61]: for value in items:
    . . . . :        if value > 150:
    . . . . :            break
    . . . . :        print(value)
100
```

If you hit a condition in a loop at which you simply want to go to the next item, you use the continue statement.

```
In [62]: for value in items:
    . . . . :        if value == 200:
    . . . . :            continue
    . . . . :        print(value)
100
300
```

Looping Helper Functions

In addition to looping control statements, Python has several iterator helper functions. A couple of the most common ones are the enumerate and zip functions. The enumerate function enables you to iterate over items while also returning the index of the iteration. This prevents you from having to keep track of the iteration index yourself.

```
In [63]: for i, value in enumerate(items):
    . . . . :        print(i, value)
0 100
1 200
2 300
```

The zip function enables you to loop over multiple parallel iterators at once.

```
In [64]: labels = ['a', 'b', 'c']
```

```
In [65]: for label, value in zip(labels, items):
   ....:         print(label, value)
a 100
b 200
c 300
```

There are many intricacies of looping in Python that we won't get into here, but the information here should be sufficient to cover the cases that we use in this book.

Functions

As in many other programming languages, functions enable you to group a set of statements together in an object that you can call multiple times in your program. They commonly accept arguments in order to send in data or options to modify the behavior of the operation. Python functions (and instance methods, which we discuss later) are defined using the def statement. The def statement takes a function name and zero or more parameters that are enclosed in parentheses. The content of the function is specified in an indented block after the def statement. Let's look at a simple function with no arguments:

```
In [61]: def print_hello():
   ....:         print('hello')
   ....:

In [62]: print_hello()
hello
```

In this function, we just print the word "hello". If we want to customize the printed message, we can add a name argument to the function definition.

```
In [63]: def print_hello(name):
   ....:         print('hello %s' % name)
   ....:

In [64]: print_hello('Kevin')
hello Kevin
```

In addition to positional arguments, Python also provides keyword arguments. In the following example, we use a keyword argument to control some optional behavior within the function. The excited keyword argument specifies a default value of False and determines whether the printed message contains an exclamation point or a period.

```
In [65]: def print_hello(name, excited=False):
   ....:         if excited:
   ....:             print('hello %s!' % name)
   ....:         else:
   ....:             print('hello %s.' % name)
   ....:

In [66]: print_hello('Kevin')
hello Kevin.

In [67]: print_hello('Kevin', excited=True)
hello Kevin!
```

```
In [68]: print_hello('Kevin', True)
hello Kevin!
```

The last call to print_hello in the preceding code also demonstrates that keyword argument values can be specified as positional arguments. The order in which the keyword arguments are defined determines the order in which they must be specified in the function call. You can also specify all arguments as keywords if you want to specify them in random order.

```
In [69]: print_hello(excited=True, name='Kevin')
hello Kevin!
```

In addition to performing operations, functions can also return values using the return statement.

```
In [70]: def print_hello(name):
    ....:     return 'hello %s' % name
    ....:
```

```
In [71]: print_hello('Kevin')
Out[71]: 'hello Kevin'
```

If you don't return a value, a value of None is returned.

An interesting aspect about functions is that they are variables just like the other variable types that we previously discussed. This means that the function definitions themselves can be passed as arguments, can be stored in collections, and so on. We use this technique in other locations in the book. To demonstrate that functions are Python objects, we display the type of our function here, add it to a list, and call it from the list directly.

```
In [72]: type(print_hello)
Out[72]: function
```

```
In [73]: a = [print_hello]
```

```
In [74]: a[0]
Out[74]: <function __main__.print_hello>
```

```
In [75]: a[0]('Kevin')
Out[75]: 'hello Kevin'
```

Constructing Arguments Dynamically

When working with our function example, we specified all of the arguments (both positional and keyword) explicitly. There are times when you want to construct arguments programmatically, and then call a function using the dynamically constructed arguments. Python does this with the * and ** operators. The * operator expands a list of items into positional arguments. The ** operator expands a dictionary into a set of keyword arguments. Let's look at this example from the previous section again.

```
print_hello('Kevin', excited=True)
```

Rather than specifying the arguments explicitly, let's build a list and a dictionary that contain the arguments, and use the * and ** operators to apply them to a function.

```
In [76]: positional = ['Kevin']
```

```
In [77]: keyword = {'excited': True}
```

```
In [78]: print_hello(*positional, **keyword)
hello Kevin!
```

As with looping, there are many details that we have glossed over in this section on functions. For a more detailed description of functions, refer to any one of the many books and web pages about Python that are readily available.

Classes and Objects

Classes and objects are large topics in Python that we do not explore deeply in this book. Although we use many classes and objects in the book, defining classes is not something that is commonly required in order to use the Python interface to CAS. Class definitions in Python use the class statement and generally contain multiple method definitions created by the def statement. Here is a sample class definition for a bank account:

```
class BankAccount(object):

    def __init__(self, name, amount=0):
        self.name = name
        self.balance = amount

    def report(self):
        print('%s : $%.2f' % (self.name, self.balance))

    def deposit(self, amount):
        self.balance = self.balance + amount

    def withdraw(self, amount):
        self.balance = self.balance - amount
```

In this class, we do not inherit from another class other than Python's base object as seen in the class statement. We have several methods defined that act on the account for depositing money, withdrawing money, and so on. There is one special method in this example called __init__. This is the constructor for the class that typically initializes all of the instance variables that are stored in the self variable. As you can see in all of the method definitions, the instance object self must be specified explicitly. Specifying the instance object in Python is unlike some other programming languages that implicitly define an instance variable name for you.

Creating an instance of a BankAccount object is done by calling it as if it were a function, while supplying the arguments that are defined in the constructor. Once you have an instance stored into a variable, you can operate on it using the defined methods. Here is a quick example:

```
In [76]: ba = BankAccount('Kevin', 1000)

In [77]: ba.report()
Kevin : $1000.00

In [78]: ba.deposit(500)

In [79]: ba.report()
Kevin : $1500.00
```

```
In [80]: ba.withdraw(200)

In [81]: ba.report()
Kevin : $1300.00
```

This might be the most brief description of Python classes that you ever see. However, as we mentioned earlier, defining classes while using the Python client to CAS is uncommon. Therefore, complete knowledge about them isn't necessary.

Exceptions

Exceptions occur in programs when some event has occurred that prevents the program from going any further. Examples of such events are as simple as the division of a number by zero, a network connection failure, or a manually triggered keyboard interruption. Python defines dozens of different exception types, and package writers can add their own. To quickly demonstrate what happens when an exception occurs, you can run the following code:

```
In [82]: 100 / 0
---------------------------------------------------------------------
ZeroDivisionError                      Traceback (most recent call last)
<ipython-input-72-a187b7beb4f1> in <module>()
----> 1 100 / 0

ZeroDivisionError: division by zero
```

In this case, the ZeroDivisionError exception was raised. Python enables you to capture exceptions after they have been raised so that you can handle the issue more gracefully. This is done using the try statement and the except statement. Each contains a block of code. The try block contains the code that you run that might raise an exception. The except block contains the code that gets executed if an exception is raised. Here is the most basic form:

```
In [83]: try:
   ....:       100 / 0
   ....: except:
   ....:       print('An error occurred')
   ....:
An error occurred
```

As you can see, we prevent the continuation of the ZeroDivisionError exception and print a message instead. Although this way of capturing exceptions works, it is generally bad form to use the except statement without specifying the type of exception to be handled because it can mask problems that you do not intend to cover up. Let's specify the ZeroDivisionError exception in our example:

```
In [84]: try:
   ....:       100 / 0
   ....: except ZeroDivisionError:
   ....:       print('An error occurred')
   ....:
An error occurred
```

As you can see, this example works the same way as when you do not specify the type of exception. In addition, you can specify as many except blocks as appropriate, each with different exception types. There is also a finally block that can be used at the end of a try/except sequence. The finally block gets executed at the end of the try/except sequence regardless of the path that was taken through the sequence.

Because we introduce some custom exceptions later on in the book, it is handy to have some knowledge about how Python's exception handling works.

Context Managers

A relatively new feature of Python is the context manager. Context managers are typically used to clean up resources when they are no longer needed. However, they can also be used for other purposes such as reverting options and settings back to the state before a context was entered.

Context managers are used by the with statement. Here is a typical example that uses a file context manager to make sure that the file being read is closed as soon as execution exits the with block. Just replace myfile.txt with the name of a file that is located in your working directory.

```
In [85]: with open('myfile.txt') as f:
    ....:         print(f.closed)
    ....:
False

In [86]: f.closed
Out[86]: True
```

As you can see, while the with block is active, the closed attribute of the file is False. This means that the file is still open. However, as soon as we exit the with block, closed is set to True.

Support for context management is used in various packages that we use in this book. We use them primarily for setting options and reverting options to their previous settings.

Now that we have covered all of the general Python topics and features that you should be familiar with, let's move on to some packages used in this book.

Using the Pandas Package

The Pandas package is a data analysis library for Python. It includes data structures that are helpful for creating columnar data sets with mixed data types as well as data analysis tools and graphics utilities. Pandas uses other packages under the covers to do some of the heavy lifting. These packages include, but are not limited to, NumPy (a fast N-dimensional array processing library) and Matplotlib (a plotting and charting library).

Pandas is a large Python package with many features that have been adequately documented elsewhere. In addition, the Pandas website, pandas.pydata.org, provides extensive documentation. We provide a brief overview of its features here, but defer to other resources for more complete coverage.

In the following sections, we use the customary way of importing Pandas, shown as follows:

```
In [87]: import pandas as pd
```

Data Structures

The most basic data structure in the Pandas package is the Series. A series is an ordered collection of data of a single type. You can create a series explicitly using the Series constructor.

```
In [88]: ser = pd.Series([100, 200, 300, 1000])
```

```
In [89]: ser
Out[89]:
0      100
1      200
2      300
3     1000
dtype: int64
```

You notice that this creates a Series of type int64. Using a collection of floats (or a mixture of integers and floats) results in a Series of type float64. Character data results in a Series of type object (since it contains Python string objects). There are a large number of possible data types, including different sizes of integers and floats, Boolean, dates and times, and so on. For details about these data types, see the Pandas documentation.

The next step up from the Series object is the DataFrame. The DataFrame object is quite similar to a SAS data set in that it can contain columns of data of different types. DataFrames can be constructed in many ways, but one way is to construct a Series for each column, and then to add each column to the DataFrame. In this example, we do both operations in one step by using a dictionary as an argument to the constructor of the DataFrame. We also add the columns argument so that we can specify the order of the columns in the resulting DataFrame.

```
In [90]: df = pd.DataFrame({'name': pd.Series(['Joe', 'Chris',
    ....:                                       'Mandy']),
    ....:                    'age': pd.Series([18, 22, 19]),
    ....:                    'height': pd.Series([70., 68., 64.])},
    ....:                   columns=['name', 'age', 'height'])
```

```
In [91]: df
Out[91]:
     name  age  height
0     Joe   18      70
1   Chris   22      68
2   Mandy   19      64
```

You see that all of the data now appears as columns in the variable df. Let's look at the data types of the columns:

```
In [92]: df.dtypes
Out[92]:
name       object
age         int64
height    float64
dtype: object
```

From this code, we can see that the data types are mapped to the types that were mentioned in the discussion on Series types.

Dataframes can also have an index to help access specific rows of information. Let's convert our name column to an index. We also use the inplace=True argument to modify the DataFrame in place rather than creating a new object.

```
In [93]: df.set_index('name', inplace=True)

In [94]: df
Out[94]:
        age  height
name
Joe      18      70
Chris    22      68
Mandy    19      64
```

We can now quickly access the rows of data based on the index value.

```
In [95]: df.loc['Joe']
Out[95]:
age        18
height     70
Name: Joe, dtype: float64
```

In this case, the result is a Series object because it returns only one row. If the index value is not unique, you get another DataFrame back with the selected rows. Let's look at other ways to select data in the next section.

Data Selection

Subsetting and selecting data is done through Python's index and slicing syntax as well as several properties on the dataframe: at, iat, loc, iloc, and ix. First, let's show what the DataFrame looks like again.

```
In [96]: df
Out[96]:
        age  height
name
Joe      18      70
Chris    22      68
Mandy    19      64
```

You can access individual columns in the DataFrame using the same syntax that you use to access keys in a dictionary.

```
In [97]: df['age']
Out[97]:
name
Joe      18
Chris    22
Mandy    19
Name: age, dtype: int64
```

If you use this syntax with a slice as the key, it is used to access rows. The endpoints of the slice can be either numeric indexes of the rows to slice or values in the DataFrame's index. However, note that when you use numeric indexes, the starting point is included, but the ending point is not included. When using labels, both endpoints are included.

```
In [97]: df[1:3]
Out[97]:
       age  height
name
Chris   22      68
Mandy   19      64

In [98] : df['Chris':'Mandy']
Out[98]:
       age  height
name
Chris   22      68
Mandy   19      64
```

Python's slice step-size works in this context as well.

```
In [99]: df[::2]
Out[99]:
       age  height
name
Joe     18      70
Mandy   19      64
```

Although using the slicing syntax on the DataFrame directly is handy, it can create confusion because the value of the slice determines whether the slice refers to columns or rows. So using this form is fine for interactive use, but for actual programs, using the data selection accessors is preferred. Let's look at some examples of the data selection accessors.

The loc and iloc DataFrame Accessors

We have already seen the loc accessor, which uses the DataFrame index label to locate the rows.

```
In [100]: df.loc['Chris']
Out[100]:
age          22
height       68
Name: Chris, dtype: float64
```

The loc accessor can be combined with column names to return a subset of columns in a specified order.

```
In [101] : df.loc['Chris', ['height', 'age']]
Out[101]:
height       68
age          22
Name: Chris, dtype: float64
```

Again, if the label resolves only to a single row, you get a Series back, but if it resolves to more than one, you get a DataFrame back. You can force a DataFrame to get returned by specifying the label within a list.

```
In [102] : df.loc[['Chris'], ['height', 'age']]
Out[102]:
       height  age
name
Chris      68   22
```

The iloc accessor works the same way as loc except that it uses row and column indexes in the slices and the lists of values.

```
In [103] : df.iloc[:2, [0,1]]
Out[103]:
        age  height
name
Joe      18     70
Chris    22     68
```

The at and iat DataFrame Accessors

The at and iat accessors are much like the loc and iloc accessors except that they return a scalar value. This also means that they accept only scalar value keys as well. Just like with iloc and loc, iat uses only integer keys, and at uses only index labels and column names.

```
In [104] : df.iat[2, 1]
Out[104]: 64.0

In [105]: df.at['Chris', 'age']
Out[105]: 22
```

The ix DataFrame Accessor

The ix accessor allows for the mixing of integer and label data access. The default behavior is to look for labels, but it falls back to integer positions if needed. In most cases, ix accepts the same arguments as loc and iloc.

```
In [106] : df.ix[:2, ['height', 'age']]
Out[106]:
        height  age
name
Joe        70    18
Chris      68    22
```

Using Boolean Masks

All of the previous methods of data access required the positions and labels to be specified explicitly or through a slice. There is another way of subsetting data that uses a more dynamic method: Boolean masking. A Boolean mask is simply a Series object of Boolean type that contains the same number of items as the number of rows in the DataFrame that you apply it to. Applying a mask to a DataFrame causes a new DataFrame to be created with just the rows that correspond to True in the mask. Let's create a mask and apply it to our DataFrame.

```
In [107]: mask = pd.Series([True, True, False])

In [108]: mask
Out[108]:
0     True
1     True
2    False
dtype: bool
```

In order for the mask to work, it must have the same index labels as the DataFrame that we are applying it to. Therefore, we set the mask index labels as equal to the DataFrame index labels.

```
In [109]: mask.index = df.index
```

Now we can apply the mask to our DataFrame.

```
In [110]: df[mask]
Out[110]:
        age   height
name
Joe     18       70
Chris   22       68
```

The preceding method is the manual way of creating masks, but it demonstrates what happens behind the scenes when you use comparison operators on a DataFrame. We can generate a mask from a DataFrame by using Python comparison operators.

```
In [111]: mask = df['age'] > 20

In [112]: mask
Out[112]:
name
Joe        False
Chris      True
Mandy      False
Name: age, dtype: bool
```

In this case, we generate the mask from our DataFrame, so we don't need to set the index manually. Now we apply this mask to our DataFrame.

```
In [113]: df[mask]
Out[113]:
        age   height
name
Chris   22       68
```

If you don't need to save the mask or need to generate the mask beforehand, you can merge the mask creation and the data access into one line.

```
In [114] : df[df['age'] > 20]
Out[114]:
        age   height
name
Chris   22       68
```

If we access the column using the DataFrame attribute shortcut, we can clean up the syntax a little more.

```
In [115]: df[df.age > 20]
Out[115]:
        age   height
name
Chris   22       68
```

As we mention at the beginning of this section, Pandas is a large package, and we have just barely "scratched the surface." We haven't addressed the topics about combining DataFrames, reshaping, statistical operations, and so on. We have to leave those topics as exercises for the reader since Pandas isn't the focus of this book. In the next section, we will look at how to create graphics from the data in a DataFrame.

Creating Plots and Charts

There are many packages that were developed for Python that do plotting and charts, but there are a few that emerge as favorite tools. For static images, Matplotlib is typically the tool of choice. It handles many different types of plots and has a fine-level of detail for every part of a graph. However, it can be daunting because of its extensive repertoire. You can use Pandas DataFrame plotting features that are built on Matplotlib for quick and easy plotting.

For interactive visualization in web browsers, Bokeh is becoming the tool of choice for Python programmers. In this section, we look at some simple examples of each of these packages. We use the Jupyter interface to demonstrate graphics, so you might want to run jupyter notebook for creating output that looks like the following screenshots.

Plotting from Pandas DataFrame Methods

The Pandas DataFrame object has built-in methods for creating simple plots and charts. These methods use Matplotlib to create the plots, but the methods give you an easier API for quick plotting. We first generate some random data with the following code, and then we use the DataFrame methods to display the data.

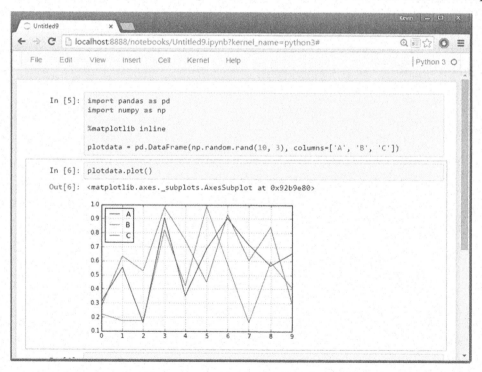

In the code in the screenshot, we used an IPython magic command called %matplotlib inline[1]. This tells Matplotlib to automatically display output in the notebook. We then generate some random data into a DataFrame and use the plot method to display the data. You can change the type of the plot by using the kind keyword parameter. It accepts values of line, bar, barh, hist, box, kde, density, area, pie, scatter, and hexbin. If you execute plotdata.plot? in the notebook, you see the Help for that method.

Here is the same data plotted as a horizontal stacked bar.

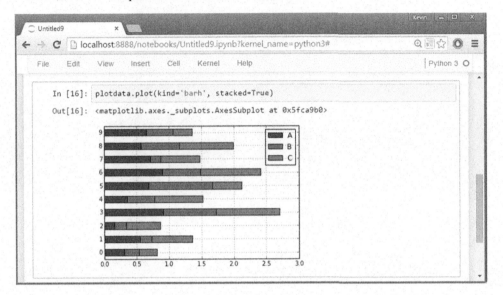

The plotting interface that is supplied by Pandas DataFrame is useful for quick plots, and it offers a fair number of customization features. However, the DataFrame methods support only static plots. For interactive environments such as Jupyter notebooks, consider Plotly and Cufflinks.

Plotting DataFrames with Plotly and Cufflinks

Plotly is another popular plotting package for Python as well as for several other languages. Although you can use the Plotly Python interface directly, it's easier to plot DataFrames with the additional package named Cufflinks. The Cufflinks package adds an iplot method to DataFrames that works much like the plot method. Note that at the time of this writing, Plotly and Cufflinks were not included in the Anaconda Python distribution, so you might need to install them separately.

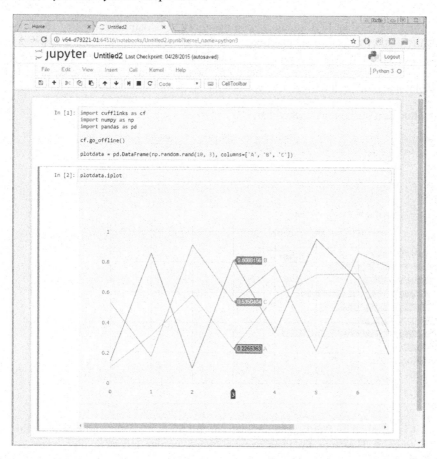

In the code in the preceding screenshot, we import Cufflinks and use the go_offline function to indicate to Plotly that the plot is not to be published to the web. We then generate some random data just as in the preceding example. In this case, we use the iplot method on the DataFrame to plot the data.

Just as with the plot method, we can change the type of the plot using the kind parameter. In the following code, you see that we changed the plot to a bar chart with stacking enabled.

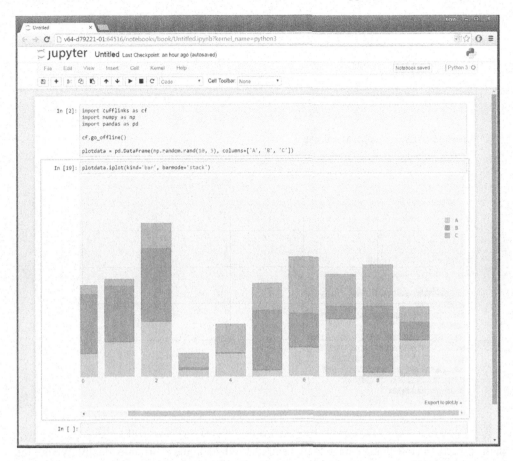

For more customized plots, Matplotlib is the preferred tool for most Python programmers. Let's look at that next.

Creating Graphics with Matplotlib

Although the Matplotlib package is powerful, it does have a bit of a learning curve. We do a simple introduction here, but going further requires some homework. Let's try to create the same stacked bar chart that we got by using the plot method of DataFrame. That way, we can see what the plot method has to do behind the scenes.

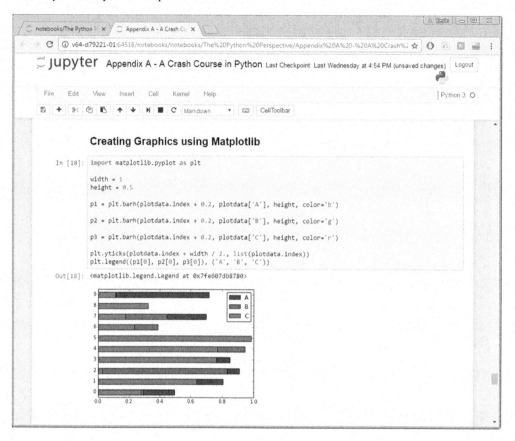

You see in the preceding code that we have to plot each set of bars in the chart individually. We use the row labels of the data on the Y axis and the value of each of the columns (A, B, C) on the X axis. In order to stack them, we must give the starting left point of each subsequent bar in the left keyword parameter. Finally, we set the color of each bar. After we complete the plotting, we adjust the ticks so that the index values are centered on the bars, and we add a legend.

Matplotlib entails more work than does the simple one-liner of the DataFrame plot method. It is easier to use the plot method unless you have specialized requirements.

If you create graphics for the web and want to use an interactive tool, consider using Bokeh. Let's take a quick look at it in the next section.

Interactive Visualization with Bokeh

Much like Plotly, Bokeh is a Python package for creating interactive visualizations in a web browser. We do a line plot and a bar chart as we did in the other examples. The line chart is fairly straightforward. You can pass a DataFrame into the Line object and display it with the show function.

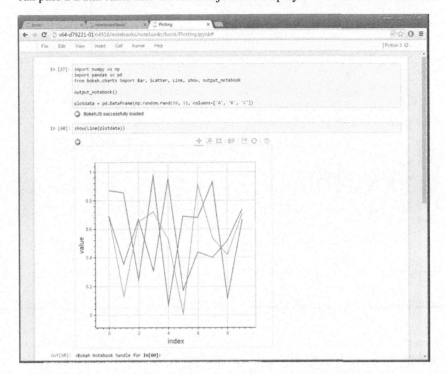

The creation of a stacked bar chart is quite challenging with the data in the form that we have. You need to restructure it so that all of the values of all columns are in a single column of a DataFrame. The column names must be a value in another column. The reason for this is that the Bokeh bar chart is primarily set up to do groupings and to compute aggregated values. So we need to structure the data so that it works in that model.

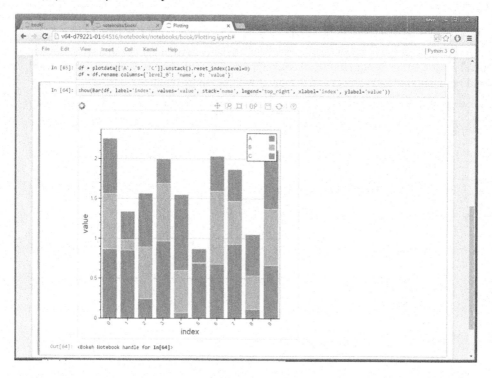

Conclusion

If you haven't used Python much in the past, this coverage might seem like a whirlwind of information. But hopefully you have a good overview of the parts of Python that are used in the rest of this book. As we mentioned previously, there are many Python resources on the web as well as many books on various areas of Python that you might explore.

---

[1] The magic commands are part of IPython. They are not included in standard Python. So they can be used only in the context of an IPython interpreter or a Jupyter notebook.

Appendix B: Troubleshooting

As with any software, especially those that are network-based, you are bound to encounter problems. We have tried to outline the most common issues here so that you can get working as soon as possible.

Software Version Issues

There are minimum versions of Python packages that are required in order to use SWAT. If you install Python from Continuum Analytics, you should not expect any problems. But if you use an existing Python installation, you might have to upgrade some of your Python packages. The SWAT installer defines minimum package version requirements, which should prevent software installation problems.

Connection Issues

Since you connect to some of your resources across a network, you might encounter problems while trying to get started. There are also dependencies on C shared libraries that can cause some issues. We'll try to cover the most common situations here.

Missing Linux Library Dependencies

If you use SWAT on Linux with the binary interface to CAS, there is one particular shared library dependency that is installed by many Linux distributions, but not all of them: libnuma.so.1. If you are missing a required shared library, you see an error like the following when creating a connection to CAS.

```
In [1]: conn = swat.CAS('server-name.mycompany.com', 5570)
tkBoot failed:  Cannot dlopen [tkmk.so] : [libnuma.so.1: cannot open
shared object file: No such file or directory]
```

In this case, the dependency can be resolved by installing the numactl package of your Linux distribution. You can also put a copy of libnuma.so.1 in a directory and set the environment variable LD_LIBRARY_PATH to point to the directory in which the package is located. It is recommended that you ask your system administrator to install it so that it can be updated with any system updates.

It is possible that there are other shared library dependencies that might not be installed by your distribution. If so, you must determine which package of your Linux distribution contains those files and install them.

Incorrect SAS Threaded Kernel Configuration

The SWAT package uses the SAS Threaded Kernel system for handling much of the heavy lifting behind-the-scenes. It consists of many shared libraries that SWAT must be able to load in order to run. Your SWAT installer should put them in the correct place. If the required shared libraries cannot be located when you attempt to create a connection, the following message is displayed:

```
In [1]: conn = swat.CAS('server-name.mycompany.com', 5570)
tkBoot failed:  Cannot Locate [tkmk] in [/usr/local/lib/swat-tk:
                                        /opt/sas/viya/SASFoundation/sasexe/:
Could not get TK handle
-------------------------------------------------------------------------

. . .

SWATError                                    Traceback (most recent call last)
<ipython-input-2-d18c0dfd66ee> in <module>()
----> 1 s = swat.CAS('my-cas', 12345)

connection.py in __init__(self, hostname, port, username, password, session,
                          locale, nworkers, name, authinfo, protocol, **kwargs)
    225                 self._sw_error = clib.SW_CASError(a2n(soptions))
    226             except SystemError:
--> 227                 raise SWATError('Could not create CAS object. Check
                                       your TK path setting.')
    228
    229         # Make the connection

SWATError: Could not create CAS object. Check your TK path setting.
```

If you know the location of your threaded kernel libraries, you can set an environment variable called TKPATH to the directory where they are installed. Note that the threaded kernel libraries should be installed for you in the SWAT package under the lib/*platform* directory.

Unable to Import _pyXXswat

If you receive an error about not being able to import _pyXXswat (where XX is the version number of your Python interpreter), it likely means that you are trying to connect to the binary interface of CAS without having the SWAT C extension installed. Here is an example of the error output:

```
In [1]: conn = swat.CAS('server-name.mycompany.com', 5570)

...

During handling of the above exception, another exception occurred:

ValueError     Traceback (most recent call last)
<ipython-input-2-cb8d2ab92685> in <module>()
----> 1 swat.CAS('my-cas', 12345)

connection.py in __init__(self, hostname, port, username, password,
                          session,
                          locale, nworkers, name, authinfo, protocol,
                          **kwargs)
```

```
    223                    self._sw_error =
                              rest.REST_CASError(a2n(soptions))
    224                else:
--> 225                    self._sw_error =
                              clib.SW_CASError(a2n(soptions))
    226            except SystemError:
    227                raise SWATError('Could not create CAS object.
                              Check your TK path setting.')

clib.py in SW_CASError(*args, **kwargs)
     84        ''' Return a CASError (importing _pyswat as needed) '''
     85        if _pyswat is None:
---> 86            _import_pyswat()
     87        return _pyswat.SW_CASError(*args, **kwargs)
     88

clib.py in _import_pyswat()
     43                raise ValueError(('Could not import import %s. This
                              is likely due to an '
     44                          'incorrect SAS TK path or an error
                              while loading the SAS TK
                              subsystem. '
---> 45                          'You can try using the REST
                              interface as an alternative.') %
                              libname)

     46
     47
```

ValueError: Could not import import _py34swat. This is likely due to an incorrect SAS TK path or an error while loading the SAS TK subsystem. You can try using the REST interface as an alternative.

Not all platforms support the binary interface to CAS. If you did not see a platform-specific installer when installing SWAT, you are limited to using the REST interface to connect to CAS. To solve the problem, change the port number of CAS to the HTTP or HTTPS port of the server.

Refused Connection

Another common issue is a refused connection. Here is an example of a typical message for this problem:

```
In [1]: conn = swat.CAS('server-name.mycompany.com', 5570)
ERROR: The TCP/IP tcpSockConnect support routine failed with error 61
(The connection was refused.).
ERROR: Failed to connect to host 'server-name.mycompany.com', port 5570.

...

During handling of the above exception, another exception occurred:

SWATError                                 Traceback (most recent call
last)
<ipython-input-3-404a7919d58a> in <module>()
----> 1 conn = swat.CAS('server-name.mycompany.com', 5570)

cas/connection.py in __init__(self, hostname, port, username,
                              password, session,
                              locale, nworkers, name, authinfo,
```

```
                               protocol, **kwargs)
      259                          raise SystemError
      260              except SystemError:
 --> 261                  raise
                           SWATError(self._sw_error.getLastErrorMessage())
      262
      263              errorcheck(
                           self._sw_connection.setZeroIndexedParameters(),
                           self._sw_connection)
```

SWATError: Could not connect to 'server-name.mycompany.com' on port 5570.

The most common reason for this problem is that you don't have a CAS server running on that host or port. Another cause might be that your network has firewall settings that prevent you from reaching that host or port.

Authentication Problems

Authentication problems can occur for several reasons, including a forgotten password or the system administrator's deliberate disablement of your account on the machine. Another explanation is that the form of authentication that you are trying to use might not be enabled on your server.

Using an Authinfo file to authenticate a user name and password might also cause problems. First, for Linux, the permissions on the Authinfo file must be set to Readable by the owner. For Windows, permissions must be set to not Readable by the Everyone group. If you have incorrect permissions on the file, the file cannot be used, for security reasons. Here is a typical error message:

```
In [1]: conn = swat.CAS('server-name.mycompany.com', 5570)
WARNING: Incorrect permissions on netrc/authinfo file.
-------------------------------------------------------------------
SystemError               Traceback (most recent call last)
connection.py in__init__(self, hostname, port, username, password,
                           session,
                           locale, nworkers, name, authinfo, protocol,
**kwargs)
    256
a2n(soptions),
--> 257
self._sw_error)
    258                   if self._sw_connection is None:

. . .

    SWATError: Could not connect to 'server-name.mycompany.com' on port 5570.
```

To solve the problem for Linux, use the chmod command to assign the correct permissions as follows:

```
chmod 0600 ~/.authinfo
```

Another issue that pertains to Authinfo files is that the name (or IP address) of the CAS server must be specified explicitly. Domain names cannot be expanded. For example, the following line in your Authinfo file will cause a problem if you use *server-name.mycompany.com* when creating the CAS connection:

```
host server-name port 5570 user username password password
```

The specification of *server-name* does not match *server-name.mycompany.com*. Exact host names must be specified in the Authinfo file and in CAS connection parameters.

Index

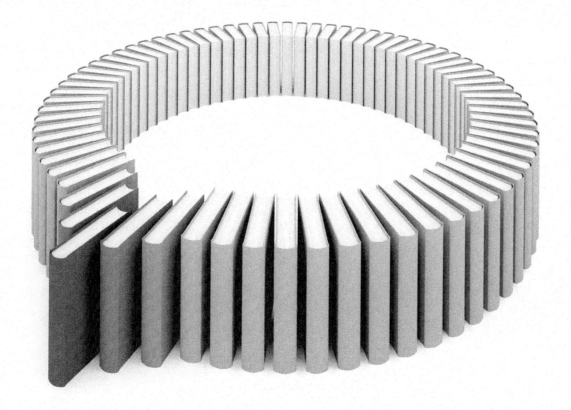

Gain Greater Insight into Your SAS® Software with SAS Books.

Discover all that you need on your journey to knowledge and empowerment.

support.sas.com/store/books
for additional books and resources.

THE POWER TO KNOW®

CPSIA information can be obtained
at www.ICGtesting.com
Printed in the USA
BVOW04s0345171117
500102BV00027B/48/P